Automatic Exchange of Information Handbook

GW00645232

Automatic Exchange of Information Handbook

John Hiddleston

Senior Manager

Azets

Bloomsbury Professional

LONDON · DUBLIN · EDINBURGH · NEW YORK · NEW DELHI · SYDNEY

BLOOMSBURY PROFESSIONAL
An imprint of Bloomsbury Publishing Plc
50 Bedford Square, London, WC1B 3DP, UK
1385 Broadway, New York, NY 10018, USA
29 Earlsfort Terrace, Dublin 2, Ireland

BLOOMSBURY and the Diana logo are trademarks of Bloomsbury Publishing Plc

British Library Cataloguing-in-Publication Data

A catalogue record for this book is available from the British Library.

ISBN:	PB:	978 1 52651 651 0
	ePDF:	978 1 52651 653 4
	ePub:	978 1 52651 652 7

Typeset by Evolution Design & Digital Ltd (Kent)

To find out more about our authors and books visit www.bloomsburyprofessional.com. Here you will find extracts, author information, details of forthcoming events and the option to sign up for our newsletters.

Preface

Welcome, and thank you for reading (or at least for picking up and browsing through) this Automatic Exchange of Information Handbook.

Precisely for the fact that you have got as far as opening this book, begun leafing through it and have read this far, I think that you are probably someone who will benefit if you carry on reading it. There is a good chance you fall into one of two broad categories (or perhaps you fall somewhere between the two). You could be someone who already knows quite a bit about the subject. This book is intended to be a research tool for someone like you. However, you could also be someone who suspects (or knows) that you do not know quite enough about FATCA, CRS or EU DAC/DAC 6. Unfortunately, you have limited time, and are not sure where to start on the complex mass of detail behind the subject. This book is meant for you too.

Automatic Exchange of Information ('AEOI') really, really matters! The OECD stated, in a 30 June 2020 press release, that 'nearly 100' countries carried out AEOI in 2019, enabling their tax authorities to obtain data on 84 million financial accounts held offshore by their residents, covering total assets of €10 trillion (or US$ 11.3 trillion). By way of comparison, in 2018, data was obtained on only 47 million financial accounts, representing €5 trillion. The comparable figures for 2017 were just 11 million financial accounts, representing €1.1 trillion – making the 2019 figure nearly €9 trillion more than 2017. The OECD concludes from this that the world is moving 'ever closer to the goal of eradicating banking secrecy for tax purposes'. That was once unthinkable to some people.

Furthermore – despite what others may say – AEOI should not be seen as a tedious or boring subject. It can get all too exciting! For example, in recent times, there was the case of Adrian Baron who was sent to prison for offences relating to FATCA.

I hope that you will find this book a useful source of reference. In particular, its aim is to comprehensively cover the UK's taxation laws, statutes and practice in relation to AEOI. It is not a book on the laws of any other country, such as US law in relation to FATCA, for example. Similarly, it is not about other aspects of UK law, such as the UK's laws on GDPR. Sometimes it was essential for the text of this book to make mention of those kinds of topics in passing, but you should certainly look elsewhere for definitive help or information about them.

Preface

Having said all of the above, I would finally like to add my thanks to Bloomsbury Professional for their support.

The law in this book is stated as at 30 September 2020.

Constructive comments and suggestions for any future editions of the handbook are welcome.

John Hiddleston
Twickenham
January 2021

Author details

John Hiddleston has held senior roles in the tax technical departments of a number of 'Top 20' accountancy firms – having been Head of Tax Technical at Vantis and, before that, National Director of Tax Technical at Horwath Clark Whitehill (now called Crowe UK).

In a career spanning several decades, John has also done an unusually wide variety of practical tax work, having worked for independent tax consultancies and, even longer ago, as in-house Tax Manager at a multinational corporate.

Contents

Contents

Contents

Table of Statutes and International Agreements

Table of Statutory Instruments and other guidance

Table of European Legislation

Table of Cases

Chapter 1

How we got here – A quick look at the recent history of Automatic Exchange

SIGNPOSTS

- For much of modern history, certain countries or jurisdictions have been famous for their 'banking secrecy'. The best known of these is Switzerland. There are others. By the 1990s, complete banking secrecy had already been undermined to a certain extent by laws such as anti-money laundering rules.

- As a result of changes that have occurred since, an article in Forbes magazine declared that by October 2018, banking secrecy had died – albeit it is open to question whether that is truly the case (see **1.1**).

- The EU had already tried to address concerns about the use of tax havens and offshore banking secrecy jurisdictions to hide the proceeds of tax evasion. The EU Savings Directive was introduced in 2005 in an effort to deal with this (see **1.2**).

- However, it was the introduction of the US Foreign Account Tax Compliance Act ('FATCA') and, later on, the Organisation for International Co-operation and Development ('OECD') Common Reporting Standard ('CRS') that really changed things a lot.

- In around 2008, the US Senate interviewed executives from certain Swiss and other banks. A subcommittee of the Senate published a report saying that 'tax abuse' was causing an estimated US\$ 100 billion of taxes to be lost to the US government each year. In 2010, the US Congress introduced FATCA. Conceptually, FATCA had certain similarities with the EU Savings Directive (see **1.3**).

- The introduction of FATCA and other Automatic Exchange laws and treaties, as well as other initiatives that were intended to promote cross-border co-operation in tax matters and the promotion of taxation 'fairness' were assisted by a mood among the public and therefore much of the media, which was against tax planning, tax avoidance and tax evasion. Much of this seemed to have arisen from the damage to public finances caused by the great financial crisis of around 2008 onwards (the collapse of Lehman Brothers and the Troubled Asset Relief Program ('TARP') in the US, and similar events in other countries) and resulting austerity programmes (see **1.8**).

- In around 2013, the UK introduced the 'UK FATCA' or the Crown Dependencies and Overseas Territories ('CDOT') regime, which was conceptually along similar sorts of lines to the US FATCA, but which only applied to CDOTs. The UK FATCA/ CDOT became redundant a few years later when the OECD CRS was introduced (see **1.6**).

- The OECD developed CRS which was a regime for the Automatic Exchange of Financial Account Information. This was along similar lines to FATCA, except that CRS involved exchange between jurisdictions which had agreed to participate. This was in contrast with FATCA which in all cases involved exchange between the US and a second jurisdiction that had signed a FATCA agreement with the US (see **1.4**).

- The OECD also drew up and published a list of 'BEPS Actions' (base erosion and profit shifting), each of which was intended to promote cross-border co-operation in relation to taxation matters and fairness, between different jurisdictions (see list at **1.5**).

- The EU Directive on Administrative Cooperation 2011/16/EU ('EU DAC') is designed to bring about co-operation in taxation matters between EU Member States. Despite Brexit, EU DAC continues to apply to the UK, at least until the end of the Brexit transition period (see **Chapter 2**).

- EU DAC has applied to EU Member States, and therefore for the time being to the UK, CRS as well as certain other regimes that are intended to comply with the BEPS Actions (see **1.7**).

IS 'BANKING SECRECY' DEAD? WHO OR WHAT KILLED IT?

Introduction

1.1

Focus

The US Congress introduced FATCA, following a period when there had been high-profile reviews of, and interviews with, members of Swiss and other non-US banks in 'banking secrecy jurisdictions'.

In common with members of the public in certain other wealthy countries, the US public was concerned about losses of tax arising from tax evasion. There was a perception that this was facilitated to an extent by banking secrecy jurisdictions.

Because of its enormous economy and power, the US was able to persuade (or perhaps to compel?) many of the other countries of the world to sign up to FATCA by entering into 'FATCA agreements'. See **Appendix I** for a list a countries that have entered into such agreements with the US.

FATCA involves withholding tax being deducted from payments by non-US financial institutions which are not compliant with the Act. Those that are compliant with FATCA must exchange (or provide to the US tax authorities) financial account information relating to US residents and citizens, but because these financial institutions are compliant, these financial institutions do not have to deduct withholding tax from payments to US residents and citizens.

FATCA has considerably reduced (some say it has killed) banking secrecy. However, FATCA, was not the first attempt internationally to deal with cross-border tax compliance issues. See, for example, the EU Savings Directive, which pre-dated FATCA and was along somewhat similar lines.

An October 2019 article in Forbes magazine declared that 'banking secrecy has died'. Indeed, the article stated that banking secrecy had died 12 months earlier than that – in around October 2018. In particular, this gradual erosion of secrecy occurred when the Swiss tax agency, the Federal Tax Administration ('FTA'), officially started exchanging bank account data with tax authorities in other countries for the first time.

According to the US Treasury's website, Switzerland's FATCA agreement with the US came into force on 30 June 2014 (see **1.3**).

According to the OECD's website, Switzerland committed to its first exchange of financial account information under the OECD CRS during 2018 (see **1.4**).

If FATCA and OECD CRS reporting regimes, truly represented the end of banking secrecy, then so far as Switzerland is concerned the timing of the end of banking secrecy referred to in the Forbes article sounds about right. See **Appendix I** and **Appendix II**.

That said, since Switzerland signed up to FATCA a few years before committing to its first exchange under CRS, one must assume that Swiss banking secrecy effectively died rather earlier for US residents and citizens than for residents of other OECD member countries.

On the one hand, there have been anti-money laundering laws for many years. The anti-money laundering laws will presumably have precluded total 'banking secrecy' – assuming that those laws were properly observed.

On the other hand, although Switzerland is a jurisdiction which used to be famous for its banking secrecy, there are other jurisdictions which have still not signed up to FATCA and CRS. Hence those other jurisdictions have not signed up to exchanging bank account data with tax authorities in other countries.

Could it be that banking secrecy is still possible in some of those countries?

In truth, to what extent the introduction of FATCA and CRS regimes do indeed represent the end of banking secrecy, no doubt depends on who you are, and your particular circumstances. It also depends to a considerable extent, on what we mean by 'banking secrecy'.

More than 100 countries have entered into FATCA agreements with the US – again, see **Appendix I**. A similar number have committed to their first exchange under CRS.

There are then a further few dozen countries who, whilst they have not committed to a first exchange, they are nevertheless signatories of the OECD's Multilateral Convention on Mutual Administrative Assistance in Tax Matters.

The latter is intended to work against taxation 'non-compliance' and to promote international tax co-operation and 'fairness'. Again, see **Appendix II**.

There will therefore be countries in the world that have not entered into these various international taxation co-operation and fairness initiatives and agreements, and which do not exchange information with the tax authorities of other countries under CRS. Perhaps one might tend to assume that for residents of such countries, banking secrecy could still be possible?

It is probably true to say, that the chances of true banking secrecy being able to apply to someone who is resident in the UK are greatly reduced following the implementation in the UK of FATCA and CRS; something which has happened in the past few years.

However, it is still open to question whether banking secrecy can truly be said to have died.

Probably it is not so much that banking secrecy has died. It is more a case that banking secrecy has gradually, over quite a few years, become more difficult to achieve (assuming one wanted to achieve it) – at least for those of us who live in most of Western Europe, North America, Australasia and the wealthier countries of the Pacific Rim, Asia and elsewhere.

If you went to live somewhere else – in a country that had not signed up to a FATCA agreement with the US, and had not committed to exchanging financial account information under the OECD CRS – perhaps you could access banking secrecy of some sort.

This Chapter briefly describes some of the key changes to international tax law over the past few years, that have helped to bring banking secrecy to its present greatly reduced state (even if, in reality, banking secrecy isn't quite dead).

As this is book is primarily aimed at UK professional practitioners and others, analysis is mainly from a UK perspective.

WERE THERE INTERNATIONAL ANTI-EVASION MEASURES BEFORE FATCA?

EU Savings Directive

1.2

Focus

FATCA, despite its enormous implications and impact, was neither unique nor the first of its kind.

The EU Savings Directive 2003/48/EC ('EUSD') was an earlier attempt by the EU to counter cross border tax evasion by means of co-operation among EU Member States. It has since been superseded by EU DAC, as amended.

In an article published on 22 June 2005 and entitled 'Europe is No Longer a Tax Haven', the Telegraph stated:

'Under this new European Union Savings Tax Directive, financial institutions in all EU Member States, plus a number of neighbouring territories, will be required to either disclose information about your investments to the relevant tax authority – or charge a punitive withholding tax.

'In other words, if you are resident in the UK, but have a savings account elsewhere in the EU, the bank will automatically inform the Inland Revenue how much interest you earned last year.'

The Telegraph's description makes EUSD sound pretty similar to the US FATCA, which came into being a few years later.

EUSD aimed to counter cross border tax evasion by requiring EU Member States to automatically disclose information on savings income paid in circumstances where the recipient of the interest was resident outside the Member State in which the paying institution was situated.

The rules mainly affected banks, registrars, custodians and other financial institutions that made interest payments to individuals in prescribed territories and was also relevant to those who held or administered money debts on behalf of others and those who advised paying agents.

The Directive was implemented in the UK through regulations with effect from 1 January 2005 and was repealed on 10 November 2015.

So far as UK legislation and regulations are concerned, the last reporting year under EUSD was therefore the UK tax year ending 5 April 2016. See HMRC's International Exchange of Information Manual IEIM400570.

It was replaced by the new EU DAC from 1 January 2016 (see **1.7**).

What is the US FATCA?

1.3

Focus

FATCA was enacted by the US Congress in 2010 in order to target non-compliance by US taxpayers using foreign accounts.

FATCA requires foreign financial institutions ('FFIs') to report to the Internal Revenue Service ('IRS') information about financial accounts held by US taxpayers, or by foreign entities in which US taxpayers hold a substantial ownership interest. FFIs are encouraged to either directly register with the IRS to comply with FATCA regulations (and FFI agreement, if applicable) or comply with FATCA intergovernmental agreements ('IGAs') treated as in effect in their jurisdictions.

The US legislation allows for a 30% withholding tax to be applied to the US source income of any non-US financial institution that fails to comply with this requirement.

Provided UK financial institutions comply with the requirements of the UK's 'FATCA agreement', they will not be subject to the 30% withholding tax on US source income that is provided for in the US' FATCA legislation (see **2.4**).

In a paper published in 2008, the US Senate Permanent Subcommittee on Investigations stated: 'Each year the United States loses an estimated US$ 100 billion due to offshore tax abuses.' The paper considered certain issues which had arisen relating to one bank in Liechtenstein and another in Switzerland. See 'Staff Report on Tax Haven Banks and US Tax Compliance', published 17 July 2008.

A few years later, FATCA was introduced.

One can argue that FATCA was not the first ever attempt to introduce the Automatic Exchange of Information ('AEOI'). See, for example, at **1.2** regarding EUSD.

However, FATCA was certainly of critical importance in the history of AEOI. That said, the OECD's CRS (see **1.4**) and BEPS (see **1.5**) initiatives have been of critical importance too.

By 27 May 2020, the US Treasury Department website listed 113 jurisdictions of which 105 had signed IGAs in relation to FATCA (one of these being the UK), while the remaining eight jurisdictions (including China) are listed as having entered into 'agreement in substance'. See https://home.treasury.gov/about/offices/tax-policy/foreign-account-tax-compliance-act; see also https://www.gov.uk/government/publications/uk-us-automatic-exchange-of-information-agreement/uk-us-automatic-exchange-of-information-agreement.

However, FATCA is not without its critics. On 5 July 2018, the European Parliament passed a motion on 'The adverse effects of the US Foreign Account Tax Compliance Act on EU citizens'. This included a statement that the European Parliament:

> 'Regrets the inherent lack of reciprocity of IGAs signed by Member States, especially in terms of the scope of information to be exchanged, which is broader for Member States than it is for the US; calls on all Member States to collectively suspend the application of their IGAs (or the sharing of all information other than that in respect of accounts held in the EU by US citizens resident in the US) until such time as the US agrees to a multilateral approach to the automatic exchange of information (AEOI), by either repealing FATCA and joining CRS or renegotiating FATCA on an EUwide basis and with identical reciprocal sharing obligations on both sides of the Atlantic'.

See also **20.7** regarding possible legal challenges to AEOI, including FATCA.

Although the US is a signatory, it has not (so far) committed to exchange information under the OECD's CRS. See **Appendix II** for a list of countries which have committed to do so.

See also OECD's and the Council of Europe's Convention on Mutual Administrative Assistance in Tax Matters ('the Convention').

See too HMRC's International Exchange of Information Manual IEIM400040.

What is the OECD Common Reporting Standard ('CRS')?

1.4

Focus

The OECD developed CRS, which broadly is along similar lines to the US FATCA, in that it involves the exchange of financial account information of a financial institution based in one jurisdiction concerning usually the tax residents of another jurisdiction. In the case of CRS, the two jurisdictions will each be jurisdictions that have agreed to exchange financial account information under CRS.

This is slightly different from the US FATCA where in all cases, one of the two jurisdictions that is a party to the exchange is the US. Thus far, the US has not agreed to exchange information under CRS.

> The first countries began to exchange information under CRS in around 2017, which was a few years after the US FATCA was first introduced. See **Appendix II** for a list of countries that have committed to making exchanges of information under CRS.

Until 2014, the parties to most treaties for sharing assets, incomes and tax information internationally had shared it upon request.

In a declaration adopted on 6 May 2014, 49 countries (including the US) plus the EU, welcomed a 'common reporting standard', formally referred to as the Standard for Automatic Exchange of Financial Account Information: an agreement to share information on residents' assets and incomes automatically in conformation with the standard. Endorsing countries included all 34 OECD countries, as well as Argentina, Brazil, China, Colombia, Costa Rica, India, Indonesia, Latvia, Lithuania, Malaysia, Saudi Arabia, Singapore, and South Africa. See Annex 6 of 'Standard for Automatic Exchange of Financial Account Information in Tax Matters' published by the OECD on 21 July 2014.

There are some significant differences between FATCA and CRS. Key differences are that FATCA incorporates specific features of the US tax system, such as tax residency in the US including citizenship and FATCA, whereas CRS does not incorporate these features.

CRS is imposed in the European Union via EU DAC; as a result, it is the Directive which governs the obligations imposed on reporting financial institutions in the UK, which arises from the UK's membership until recently of the EU. This means that for UK reporting purposes, it is the application of EU DAC that takes precedence over CRS. See HMRC's International Exchange of Information Manual IEIM400015. See also **Chapter 2** regarding the impact of Brexit on the UK's AEOI regime.

CRS contains a number of options that are open to participating jurisdictions to apply if they choose. The EU Member States came to agreement on which of those should be incorporated into EU DAC and therefore applicable across the EU.

Preamble (13) of EU Directive 2014/107/EU, amending EU DAC states:

> 'In implementing this Directive, Member States should use the Commentaries on the Model Competent Authority Agreement and Common Reporting Standard, developed by the OECD, as a source of illustration or interpretation and in order to ensure consistency in application across Member States. Union action in this area should continue to take particular account of future developments at OECD level.'

See the 'Standard for Automatic Exchange of Financial Account Information in Tax Matters', 2nd edition, published by the OECD. CRS is at IIB and the Commentaries are at III.

By 27 May 2020, the OECD listed 108 jurisdictions which it said had committed to a first exchange under CRS during 2020 or an earlier year. The US is not currently among the jurisdictions that are committed to CRS. See **Appendix II**.

See HMRC's International Exchange of Information Manuals IEIM400015, IEIM400060, IEIM 400090 and IEIM 400100.

What is OECD BEPS?

1.5

Focus

CRS is not the only work that the OECD has been doing in relation to cross-border co-operation and 'fairness' in relation to international tax matters. For example, there is also the BEPS initiative.

The OECD published a series of papers making up its Final Report on 5 October 2015. These papers set out a 15-point action plan for areas identified by the BEPS project as needing to be addressed.

BEPS results from tax planning deliberately set up to exploit gaps and inconsistencies in tax rules of different countries and jurisdictions.

On 7 June 2017, 68 countries and jurisdictions, including the UK, signed a Multilateral Instrument ('MLI') in order to implement the treaty-based recommendations of the BEPS process. In effect this is BEPS Action Point 15 (see below).

It was expected that further countries would sign in due course. As at 22 July 2020, the OECD list 94 signatory jurisdictions (see https://www.oecd.org/tax/treaties/beps-mli-signatories-and-parties.pdf).

The OECD 15 BEPS Action Points are as follows:

(1)   Address the tax challenges of the digital economy.

(2)   Neutralise the effects of hybrid mismatch arrangements.

(3)   Strengthen controlled foreign companies rules.

(4)   Limit base erosion via interest deductions and other financial payments.

(5)   Counter harmful tax practices more effectively, taking into account transparency and substance.

(6)   Prevent treaty abuse.

(7)   Prevent the artificial avoidance of permanent establishment status.

(8–10)   Assure that transfer pricing outcomes related to intangibles are in line with value creation.

(11) Establish methodologies to collect and analyse data on BEPS and the actions to address it.

(12) Require taxpayers to disclose their aggressive tax planning arrangements. In effect, EU DAC 6 2018/822/EU may be seen as an attempt to put this 'Action 12' into effect – see 13.3 and elsewhere in this book regarding EU DAC 6.

(13) Re-examine transfer pricing documentation.

14) Make dispute resolution mechanisms more effective.

(15) Develop a multilateral instrument.

See OECD BEPS Actions at https://www.oecd.org/tax/beps/beps-actions/.

WHAT WAS THE UK FATCA, AND WHY DON'T WE NEED IT ANYMORE?

The Crown dependencies and overseas territories

1.6

Focus

It is at least arguable that, having seen the US successfully imposing FATCA on much of the rest of the world, the UK decided to impose the 'UK FATCA' on the Crown dependencies.

The Crown dependencies include Jersey, Guernsey and the Isle of Man (together the Crown dependencies). The overseas territories include Anguilla, Bermuda, the British Virgin Islands, the Cayman Islands, Gibraltar, Montserrat and the Turks and Caicos Islands (together the overseas territories).

Following the FATCA model (and therefore referred to by some as the 'UK FATCA'), in Budget 2013 the UK Chancellor of the Exchequer announced enhanced automatic exchange of information agreements with the Crown dependencies.

The IGAs that the UK then entered into with the Crown dependencies (and Gibraltar) were fully reciprocal and therefore required domestic legislation in both the UK and the Crown dependencies to implement the agreements.

In effect, the CDOT or UK FATCA became redundant when the UK – through its then membership of the EU – became subject to the OECD CRS exchange of financial account information (via EU DAC).

For the UK, regulations implementing these IGAs, the International Tax Compliance (Crown Dependencies and Gibraltar) Regulations 2014, SI 2014/520, came into force on 31 March 2014. The Regulations were subsequently amended by the International Tax Compliance (Crown Dependencies and Gibraltar) (Amendment) Regulations 2015, SI 2015/873.

The package of measures negotiated with the overseas territories closely followed those negotiated with the Crown dependencies. However, the IGAs entered into between the UK and the overseas territories (other than Gibraltar) were non-reciprocal, meaning that UK financial institutions did not have to provide data on financial accounts held by residents of those overseas territories. Consequently, IGAs with the overseas territories (other than Gibraltar) did not need to be implemented by way of domestic UK legislation.

The UK FATCA was originally intended to operate from 2014 onwards with no specific end date envisaged. However, following the full implementation of CRS – a multilateral automatic exchange of information regime developed by the OECD – the UK FATCA has become obsolete.

As regards the timetable and what had to be reported under the CDOT or the UK FATCA, see HMRC's International Exchange of Information Manual IEIM400540.

As regards the transition from the CDOT or the UK FATCA to CRS in the case of Crown dependencies and overseas territories, see HMRC's International Exchange of Information Manual IEIM400550 and IEIM400555.

See HMRC's International Exchange of Information Manual IEIM400020 and IEIM400060.

EU DIRECTIVE ON ADMINISTRATIVE COOPERATION

1.7

Focus

The participation in the OECD CRS by EU Member States (including the UK until Brexit) is via EU DAC. EU DAC mostly imports CRS principles into Annex I of the Directive.

Hence, the UK itself did not directly sign up for CRS. Instead, the EU signed up for CRS. EU DAC applied CRS rules to the UK.

See **Chapter 2** regarding the post-Brexit UK's relationship with EU DAC (and via EU DAC with the OECD CRS).

In addition, EU DAC also imposed:

(1)   the EU DAC 6 regime on the UK – see **Chapter 13** onwards;

(2)   the exchange of cross-border tax rulings regime – see **19.1**;

---

(3)   country-by-country reporting on the UK – see **19.2**.

Of these, points (1) and (2) are in line with BEPS Actions 5 and 12; point (3) relates to BEPS Action 12. See **1.5**.

HAVE FATCA AND CRS KILLED BANKING SECRECY?

1.8   Whether FATCA and CRS can be said to have killed off banking secrecy or not, when both regimes first came on the scene, starting from when FATCA was created, both the Act and CRS, and AEOI, were ideas whose time had come.

There is less scope for banking secrecy than there used to be – although this is hard to measure and therefore to prove. More information is undoubtedly now exchanged between the tax authorities of different countries of the world, including information exchanged in many cases by low-tax jurisdictions, which some people would call 'tax havens'.

FATCA and CRS, although not perfect, would each seem to have achieved much of what they were intended to achieve.

Even if banking secrecy isn't quite dead, it does appear, probably, to be a shadow of its former self.

Chapter 2

The UK and Automatic Exchange today, including the impact of Brexit

SIGNPOSTS

- In the past the UK has been an enthusiastic participant in various international cross-border initiatives aimed at preventing international tax evasion and tax avoidance. To that end, the UK has a FATCA agreement with the US and – and, via the UK's former membership of the EU – is a participant in the OECD's Common Reporting Standard ('CRS') and other BEPS-related OECD programmes (see **1.5** regarding BEPS). It is unclear precisely how and in what form the UK will continue to participate in those arrangements since the UK has ceased to be a Member State following the Brexit referendum of 2016. However, the publication in December 2020 of the EU-UK Trade and Cooperation Agreement and the passing into UK law of the European Union (Future Relationship) Act 2020, have begun to clarify many things that were previously uncertain.

- Other arrangements which the UK entered into independently of the EU will continue in their pre-Brexit form (such as FATCA) (see **2.1**).

- The UK has an intergovernmental agreement ('IGA') with the US implementing FATCA – a 'FATCA agreement'. As a result of this, provided that UK financial institutions comply with the requirements of FATCA, they will not be subject to the 30% withholding tax on US source income that is provided for in the US FATCA legislation (see **2.2** and **2.4**).

- The UK has regulations implementing various of its exchange of information obligations – including those under FATCA and the CRS. The regulations are made under powers granted in the Finance Act 2013, s 222 (see **2.3**).

- **Chapters 1** to **12** of this book are mostly about the obligations of UK financial institutions under FATCA (and also the CRS). However, it is important to note that US financial institutions can have obligations under FATCA too (see **2.5**).

- The UK was one of the first jurisdictions that committed to exchange information under the OECD CRS (see **2.6**).

- In addition to CRS, the EU DAC 6 Mandatory Disclosure regime (see **Chapter 13** onwards) as well as the Exchange of Cross-Border Tax Rulings and Country-by-Country Reporting regimes (see **Chapter 19**) have been applied to the UK by virtue of the EU Directive on Administrative Cooperation 2011/16/EU ('EU DAC'), Annex I. These regimes continued to apply to the UK during the transitional period following the UK's 'Brexit' or departure from the EU after 31 January 2020 (see **2.7**, **2.8** and **2.9**). They continue to apply to the UK following the end of the transitional period, albeit with certain changes, particularly in relation to UK reporting under EU DAC 6.

THE UK AND INTERNATIONAL ANTI-EVASION MEASURES

Overview, including the impact of Brexit

2.1

Focus

Until the 'Brexit Referendum' of 23 June 2016, members of the UK government frequently made plain that the UK considered itself an enthusiasm proponent of international cooperation to prevent tax evasion and tax avoidance.

There is no particular reason to think that the UK's underlying thinking in relation to cross-border tax evasion and tax avoidance has changed.

However, many of the UK's international arrangements had previously been made in collaboration with its then fellow EU Member States. The OECD CRS, for example, was applied to the UK by EU DAC.

At the time of writing, the UK and the EU are still in talks to discuss aspects of the arrangements that will apply between them after 31 December 2020. That will then help to determine which of the UK's past international arrangements that were put in place at EU level will continue, and in what form.

Towards the end of December 2020, the EU-UK Trade and Cooperation Agreement was provisionally agreed by the negotiating parties on 24 December 2020 and published in the Official Journal of the European Union on 31 December 2020. Amongst other things, it says:

'A Party shall not weaken or reduce the level of protection provided for in its legislation at the end of the transition period below the level provided for by the standards and rules which have been agreed in the OECD at the end of the transition period, in relation to (a) the exchange of information … concerning … potential cross-border tax planning arrangements'. The reference to OECD rules on exchange of information on cross-border arrangements is a reference to the OECD's model Mandatory Disclosure Rules ('MDR'). Therefore, under the terms of the free trade agreement, the UK must not reduce the level of protection in its legislation below the level of protection afforded by the OECD's MDR. Consequently, the UK will, for example, be continuing to apply those aspects of EU DAC 6 that are also contained in the OECD MDR.

However, certain things will continue, presumably unchanged. For example, it is important to note that the UK's intergovernmental agreement ('IGA') with the US – the 'FATCA agreement' – is an arrangement directly between the UK and the US. In other words, it is not via the UK's former membership of the EU.

Furthermore, the UK is a member of the OECD – see, for example, the 'United Kingdom and the OECD' section of the OECD website ('OECD.org'). Again, the UK has not been a member of the OECD via its former membership of the EU.

Following the G20 meeting in Lima, Peru in October 2015, the then Chancellor of the Exchequer, George Osborne, was quoted as saying:

'The UK has led the campaign to change the international tax system … We've already demonstrated our commitment to tackling BEPS and we will take new steps to introduce these new international laws into our domestic tax laws. My view is simple – the UK will have the most competitive and lowest business taxes in the world, but these taxes must be paid.'

See 'UK leads international efforts to clampdown on tax avoidance', published on the www.gov.uk website on 9 October 2015.

There is no particular reason to think that, in principle, the UK's frequently stated enthusiasm for international cooperation to combat cross-border tax evasion and tax avoidance has fundamentally changed as a result of Brexit.

However, at the time of writing, the UK's relationship with the rest of the world is a work in progress, the UK having left the EU at 11 p.m. GMT on 31 January 2020, with certain aspects of the EU-UK relationship still under discussion, even following the publication of the EU-UK Trade and Cooperation Agreement in December 2020.

Between 31 January 2020 and the end of the transition period on 31 December 2020, the UK continued to be a party to most such arrangements (including the

CRS via EU DAC) because the UK's withdrawal agreement with the EU said that for most purposes of EU law, during the transitional period, the phrase 'Member State' should continue to be read as including the UK. See **2.8** and **2.9**.

See **Chapters 1 to 12** regarding FATCA and CRS. See **Chapter 13** onwards, regarding EU Directive 2018/822/EU amending EU DAC ('EU DAC 6'). See **Chapter 19** regarding other forms of international exchange arising from EU DAC.

The UK and FATCA, CRS and EU DAC
2.2

Focus

The UK has a current IGA with the US in relation to FATCA and is one of 49 jurisdictions which committed to a first exchange of information under the OECD CRS during 2017. The UK was a party to EU DAC as an EU Member State until Brexit. See **2.1**; see also **2.8** and **2.9**.

All references in EU law to Member States are treated as including the UK during the Brexit transitional period. See **2.8** and **2.9**.

As regards FATCA, see **Appendix I** and see also https://home.treasury.gov/about/offices/tax-policy/foreign-account-tax-compliance-act.

As regards the OECD CRS, see **Appendix II** and see also https://www.oecd.org/tax/automatic-exchange/crs-implementation-and-assistance/crs-by-jurisdiction/#d.en.345489.

UK laws and regulations applying FATCA, CRS and EU DAC
2.3

Focus

The Finance Act 2013, s 222 was enacted to empower the Treasury to make regulations to give effect to FATCA agreement and any other agreement between the UK and any other country in similar terms. According to s 222(2) regulations made may:

- make provision (including provision imposing penalties) about contravention of, or non-compliance with, the regulations; and

- make provision about appeals in relation to the imposition of any penalty.

Regulations were made in exercise of the powers in s 222 which give effect to the UK's participation in FATCA, the CRS and EU DAC.

As regards the UK's Regulations in relation to FATCA and CRS, see the International Tax Compliance Regulations 2015, SI 2015/878.

As regards EU DAC 6 (see **Chapter 13** onwards), see the International Tax Enforcement (Disclosable Arrangements) Regulations 2020, SI 2020/25.

See **Chapter 20** regarding the UK's legal framework for international exchange of information.

The UK and FATCA

2.4

Focus

The UK is one of 108 jurisdictions listed by the US Treasury Department as having signed an IGA with the US in relation to FATCA (by 27 May 2020) – also known as 'FATCA agreement'. See **Appendix I**; see also **1.3**.

As a result of this, provided that UK financial institutions ('FIs') comply with the requirements of FATCA they will not be subject to the 30% withholding tax on US source income that is provided for in the US FATCA legislation (see **1.3**).

There have been significant changes to the FATCA agreement since it was first signed in September 2012. Where appropriate these changes are reflected in the current UK Regulations that came into force on 15 April 2015, namely the International Tax Compliance Regulations 2015, SI 2015/878. See HMRC's International Exchange of Information Manual IEIM400040.

In October 2014, HMRC launched an online service for UK FIs to register and report FATCA financial information on behalf of their US customers in accordance with UK/US agreement. Registration with HMRC's FATCA service requires a global intermediary identification number ('GIIN') which can be obtained via registration with the US IRS. Once registration has been completed, a FATCA ID and a HMRC registration identification number for each FI registered is issued. Both these reference numbers are needed to submit a return and once registered and enrolled to use the HMRC FATCA service the registrant has to wait approximately 24 hours to file a report. The first returns were due by 31 May 2015.

'Financial institution' means a custodial institution, a depository institution, an investment entity, or a specified insurance company. Each of these terms is also defined in the FATCA agreement. See **4.9**.

See HMRC's International Exchange of Information Manual IEIM400040.

See also **1.3**; the FATCA agreement; the International Tax Compliance Regulations 2015, reg 1(5A). See too https://www.gov.uk/government/

publications/uk-us-automatic-exchange-of-information-agreement/uk-us-automatic-exchange-of-information-agreement.

What is reportable by a reporting US financial institution to the UK authorities under FATCA?

2.5

Focus

The first dozen or so chapters of this book are mostly about the obligations that UK FIs (as defined for these purposes) have under FATCA (as well as under CRS).

It is also the case that US FIs can have obligations under FATCA (see below). However, see below regarding what some see as a lack of reciprocity in the US FATCA agreements with international partner jurisdictions.

Under the FATCA agreement, a reporting US FI is to report the following, to be passed to the UK authorities, in respect of each UK reportable account:

(1)   the name, address, and date of birth of any person that is a resident of the UK and is an account holder of the account;

(2)   the account number (or the functional equivalent in the absence of an account number);

(3)   the name and identifying number of the reporting US FI;

(4)   the gross amount of interest paid on a depository account;

(5)   the gross amount of US source dividends paid or credited to the account; and

(6)   the gross amount of other US source income paid or credited to the account, to the extent subject to reporting under chapter 3 or 61 of subtitle A of the US Internal Revenue Code.

However, see 'Are Problems Looming for FATCA and the 'Reciprocal' IGA?' by Laurie Hatten Boyd, J.D., LL.M., Seattle published 1 June 2016 (at https://www.thetaxadviser.com/issues/2016/jun/problems-looming-for-fatca-and-reciprocal-iga.html):

'A vital component of [their particular FATCA agreement] for many countries is the ability to, once approved, enter into an agreement that calls for reciprocity of information exchange … no legislative action has been taken on these expanded reporting proposals, and it is unknown what impact, if any, continued inaction will have on the future of FATCA IGAs.'

See also **1.3** regarding a 2018 statement of the European Parliament regretting a perceived 'inherent lack of reciprocity' in relation to the US FATCA agreements.

See Agreement between the Government of the UK and the Government of the US to improve international tax compliance and to implement FATCA (the 'FATCA agreement'). See **1.3** and **2.4**.

The UK and CRS

2.6

Focus

The UK is one of 108 jurisdictions listed by the OECD as having committed to a first exchange under CRS by 2020 or earlier (by 27 May 2020). Indeed, it is one of 49 which committed to a first exchange in around 2017. See **1.4**, and also **Appendix II**.

The first CRS reporting by UK reporting FIs will therefore have been in respect of calendar year 2016, with reporting due by 31 May 2017.

The Finance (No 2) Act 2015, s 50 gave the Treasury the power to impose obligations on certain categories of persons to write to their clients to notify them of the developments and advising them to come forward if they have undisclosed tax liabilities. The legislation that crystallised that obligation, the International Tax Compliance (Client Notification) Regulations 2016, SI 2016/899, came into force on 30 September 2016.

This affected many organisations offering financial or legal services, including tax services.

Around this time significant changes to HMRC powers and sanctions around tax evasion and tax avoidance, particularly anything offshore, were introduced. Exchange of information under the OECD CRS was also due to commence imminently.

The obligations apply to 'specified financial institutions' ('SFI') and 'specified relevant persons' ('SRP'). These had until 31 August 2017 to comply with these requirements.

It was necessary for each organisation to:

- determine whether the provisions applied to it;
- if so, determine their 'specified clients' to whom a notification has to be made; and
- decide how to send the notification and the full wording of the covering letter/email.

Failure to comply with the requirements could result in a penalty of £3,000. No penalty would apply if an SFI or SRP had a 'reasonable excuse' for non-compliance. The penalty had to be notified by HMRC within 12 months from 1 September 2017.

See the International Tax Compliance (Client Notification) Regulations 2016 which amended the International Tax Compliance Regulations 2015, in particular inserting regs 12A to 12F. See also the Finance (No 2) Act 2015, s 50 which amended the Finance Act 2013, s 222 giving powers for these Regulations to be introduced.

EU DAC, CRS and certain other exchange of information regimes

2.7

> **Focus**
>
> The participation in the OECD CRS of EU Member States (including the UK until Brexit) is (or has been in the case of the UK) via EU DAC. EU DAC mostly imports CRS principles into Annex I to the Directive.
>
> See elsewhere in this Chapter regarding the post-Brexit UK's relationship with EU DAC (and via EU DAC with the OECD CRS) (see **1.7**).
>
> EU DAC also deals with other exchange of information regimes, mostly in an effort to comply with certain of the BEPS Action Points (see **1.5**).
>
> For example, EU DAC now includes EU DAC 6 Mandatory Disclosure Regime (see **Chapter 13**).
>
> The EU DAC also includes an Exchange of Cross-Border Tax Rulings regime and a Country-by-Country Reporting regime (see **Chapter 19**).

Brexit and the UK's participation in EU DAC

2.8

> **Focus**
>
> The participation of EU Member States in OECD CRS is through EU DAC. Annex I of EU DAC applies the CRS regime.
>
> EU DAC also applies certain other Exchange of Information regimes, including the EU DAC 6 Mandatory Disclosure regime (see **Chapter 13** onwards) and Exchange of Cross-Border Tax Rulings and Country-by-Country Reporting regimes (see **Chapter 19**).

The UK remained a party to these arrangements during the transition period that began when the UK left the EU on 31 January 2020 and ended on 31 December 2020. See below.

Towards the end of December 2020, the EU-UK Trade and Cooperation Agreement was provisionally agreed by the negotiating parties on 24 December 2020 and published in the Official Journal of the European Union on 31 December 2020. This document sets out the terms which are to apply to many aspects of the UK's relationship with the EU after the transition period ended on 31 December 2020.

In light of the EU-UK Trade and Cooperation Agreement, the UK has adapted certain of its domestic rules so that its participation in the various regimes covered by EU DAC mostly continues after 31 December 2020. A major exception is that all of the EU DAC 6 hallmarks, except for those under category D, will no longer apply for the purposes of UK reporting. See **Chapters 13** and **17**.

EU DAC says that Member States will cooperate in relation to the subject matter of that Directive. See, for example, EU DAC at Art 1(1).

EU DAC 6 too envisages reporting between Member States. See for example new Art 8ab of EU DAC, as inserted by EU DAC 6, Art 1(2).

Following the UK's withdrawal from the EU, this raised the question of whether the UK was a 'Member State' for these purposes during the Brexit transition period. The Brexit transition period commenced when the UK left the EU on 31 January 2020 and was scheduled to end on 31 December 2020. It appears that it was still a Member State until the transition period ended. See, for example, the Agreement on the withdrawal of the United Kingdom of Great Britain and Northern Ireland from the European Union and the European Atomic Energy Community ('the Brexit Withdrawal Agreement') at Art 127 which said that Union law would continue to apply to the UK during the Brexit transitional period. Article 127 went onto say that except where otherwise agreed all references in Union law to Member States would be treated as including the UK during the transitional period. In accordance with Art 126, the transition period ended on 31 December 2020. See also the European Union (Withdrawal Agreement) Act 2020.

The Preamble to the Brexit Agreement stated:

'Considering that it is in the interest of both the Union and the United Kingdom to determine a transition or implementation period during which – notwithstanding all consequences of the United Kingdom's withdrawal from the Union … – Union law, including all international agreements, should be applicable to and in the United Kingdom, and, as a general rule, with the same effect as regards the Member States, in order to avoid disruption in the period during which the agreement(s) on the future relationship will be negotiated'.

Accordingly, the European Union (Withdrawal) Act 2018, s 1A(3)(f)(ii) amended the definition of 'Member' in the expression 'Member State' in Sch 1 to the European Communities Act 1972 (as it had effect during the transition period), so that it continued to include the UK during the transition period, following the UK's departure from the EU. The Interpretation Act 1978, s 5 and Sch 1 applied that definition across the statute book during the transition period, including to the International Tax Enforcement (Disclosable Arrangements) Regulations 2020, SI 2020/25 (also known as the 'DAC 6 Regulations').

The 'Political Declaration' at Part II(XIV)(77) says:

> 'The Parties should in particular maintain a robust and comprehensive framework for competition and state aid control that prevents undue distortion of trade and competition; commit to the principles of good governance in the area of taxation and to the curbing of harmful tax practices; and maintain environmental, social and employment standards at the current high levels provided by the existing common standards.'

This seemed, at the least, to keep open the likelihood of the UK's continued participation in the CRS and other reporting regimes applied by EU DAC, after Brexit. See Political Declaration setting out the framework for the future relationship between the European Union and the United Kingdom, 19 October 2019 (the 'Political Declaration').

In the event, the EU-UK Trade and Cooperation Agreement, following negotiations between the UK and the EU, was provisionally agreed by the negotiating parties on 24 December 2020 and published in the Official Journal of the European Union on 31 December 2020. This document sets out the terms which are to apply to many aspects of the UK's relationship with the EU after the transition period ended on 31 December 2020.

In light of the EU-UK Trade and Cooperation Agreement, the UK has adapted certain of its domestic rules so that its participation in the various regimes covered by EU DAC mostly continue after 31 December 2020. A major exception is that all of the EU DAC 6 Hallmarks, except for those under Category D, will no longer apply for the purposes of UK reporting. See **Chapters 13** and **17**.

See also the European Union (Future Relationship) Act 2020.

2.9   For these purposes, the overseas territories and dependencies of the UK and EU Member States are considered to be separate jurisdictions and arrangements involving those jurisdictions should be analysed accordingly for EU DAC 6 reporting purposes.

HM Treasury was given powers, in the Finance Act 2019, s 84, to make the UK's Regulations implementing EU DAC 6. Section 84 gave the powers to make the Regulations on condition (in subsections (8) and (9)) that the Chancellor of the Exchequer first laid a report before the House of Commons on how those powers would be used in a variety of circumstances relating to the UK's withdrawal from the EU.

In the event, a paper was published on 8 January 2020 by HM Treasury, entitled 'A report on "International Tax Enforcement: Disclosable Arrangements": A report on how the power in Finance Act 2019, which enables regulations to implement Council Directive (EU) 2018/822, will be used in different EU Exit scenarios' (available at https://www.gov.uk/government/publications/international-tax-enforcement-disclosable-arrangements--2).

Accordingly, the powers in s 84 were duly exercised and the Regulations were made.

It is also the case that s 84 states (at subsection (1)) that it is 'for the purpose of securing compliance with an obligation of the government of the United Kingdom under an international tax provision' and makes regulations accordingly.

The legislation then defines 'international tax provision' (at subsection (3)) to cover both EU DAC 6 and also 'any arrangements specified in an Order in Council made under section 173 of FA 2006 (international tax enforcement arrangements)'.

This would seem at least to make it conceivable that the Regulations could remain in place, even if the UK proves no longer to be within the remit of EU DAC 6 after the end of the Brexit transitional period.

In relation to this, the 8 January 2020 HM Treasury paper that is referred to above stated (at 2.3 on page 4) that, if the UK had left the EU with no withdrawal agreement and without having agreed a framework for its future relationship with the EU:

> 'The UK's commitment to tax transparency will not be weakened as a result of leaving the EU. The Government will continue to work with international partners to tackle offshore tax avoidance and evasion.'

The Regulations that were made in relation to the UK's participation in EU DAC 6 took the form of the International Tax Enforcement (Disclosable Arrangements) Regulations 2020, which were made on 9 January 2020 and came into force on 1 July 2020.

Hence EU DAC, including EU DAC 6, continued to apply to the UK, at least until 31 December 2020.

After 31 December 2020, the UK will continue to apply EU DAC 6 in a modified form. This is intended to continue the UK's participation in those aspects of EU DAC 6 that are also contained in the OECD MDR. In particular, only the DAC 6 hallmarks under category D will now apply for the purposes of UK reporting. This is in light of the EU-UK Trade and Cooperation Agreement of December 2020 and the European Union (Future Relationship) Act 2020. See **Chapters 13** and **17**.

See HMRC's International Exchange of Information Manual IEIM630030.

Chapter 3

An overview of FATCA and CRS

SIGNPOSTS

- In 2010, the US Congress enacted a US Federal law called the Foreign Account Tax Compliance Act ('FATCA'). This was intended to combat offshore non-compliance by US taxpayers. FATCA allows for a 30% withholding tax to be applied to the US source income of any non-US financial institution that fails to comply with the requirements of FATCA. Complying with FATCA (therefore not being subject to the 30% withholding tax) requires either that foreign financial institutions register with the US tax authorities and then exchange information with them about their US account-holders or – where their domestic government has entered into an intergovernmental agreements ('IGAs') or 'FATCA agreement' – that registration and exchange of information are carried out through that country's own tax authorities (see **3.1**).

- In February 2012, the governments of the US, France, Germany, Italy, Spain and the UK made a joint statement of their wish to intensify their co-operation in combatting international tax evasion. They therefore agreed to explore a common approach to FATCA implementation through domestic reporting and reciprocal automatic exchange. Since then, some people have questioned whether there is sufficient reciprocity in the US FATCA agreements with other countries (see **3.2**).

- The UK entered into a FATCA agreement with the US in 2012 and the UK Parliament enacted powers in the Finance Act 2013 to enable HM Treasury to make regulations in relation to FATCA (see **3.3**).

- The OECD then published its Common Reporting Standard ('CRS'), which was similar to FATCA, except that exchange under CRS would be between participating jurisdictions (instead of between the US and each of its 'partner jurisdictions' as under FATCA). CRS was applied to the UK by an EU Directive, since at that time the UK was an EU Member State. The UK's first due diligence under CRS needed to be completed by 31 December 2017, with the first reporting required by 31 May 2018 (see **3.4**).

FATCA

Overview of FATCA

3.1

Focus

FATCA is a US federal law requiring non-US foreign financial institutions ('FFIs') to search their records for customers with indicia of a connection to the US, and to report the assets and identities of such persons to the US authorities. FATCA applies to US residents and also to US citizens and green card holders residing outside the US

FATCA was enacted by the US Congress in 2010 in order to target non-compliance by US taxpayers using foreign accounts.

The US legislation allows for a 30% withholding tax to be applied to the US source income of any non-US financial institution that fails to comply with the requirements of FATCA.

According to the US Treasury Department, FATCA requires FFIs to report to the IRS information about financial accounts held by US taxpayers, or by foreign entities in which US taxpayers hold a substantial ownership interest. FFIs are encouraged to either directly register with the IRS to comply with FATCA regulations (and FFI agreement, if applicable) or comply with FATCA IGAs treated as in effect in their jurisdictions.

The UK, for example, has entered into an IGA (the UK/US FATCA agreement). Accordingly, provided UK financial institutions comply with the requirements of the UK's 'FATCA agreement' they will not be subject to the 30% withholding tax on US source income that is provided for in the USA's FATCA legislation. See **2.4**.

See the US Treasury Department website at https://home.treasury.gov/about/offices/tax-policy/foreign-account-tax-compliance-act.

The February 2012 joint statement regarding FATCA

3.2

Focus

In February 2012, the governments of the US, France, Germany, Italy, Spain and the UK made a joint statement of their wish to intensify their co-operation in combatting international tax evasion.

They said that FATCA raised a number of issues, including that FFIs in some jurisdictions might be unable to comply because of local legal restrictions. An intergovernmental approach could simplify and reduce the local burden from complying as well as addressing these legal impediments to complying.

They said that the US was willing to reciprocate in collecting and exchanging on an automatic basis information on accounts held in US financial institutions by residents of France, Germany, Italy, Spain and the UK.

They therefore agreed to explore a common approach to FATCA implementation through domestic reporting and reciprocal automatic exchange.

As regards concerns that some people have about the principle of 'reciprocity' under FATCA agreement between the UK and the USA (as well as under the US FATCA agreements of other countries), see **2.5**.

Each 'partner country' would enact legislation whereby FFIs would be required to carry out FATCA due diligence and to report FATCA information to the partner country's authorities, who would then transfer it to the US on an automatic basis.

In consideration of this the US would:

- eliminate the obligation of FFIs in partner countries to enter into a separate FFI agreement with the IRS, provided the FFI either registered with the IRS or is exempt from doing so under the partner country agreement or IRS guidance;

- allow FFIs established in the partner country to comply with their FATCA reporting obligations by reporting information to the partner country authorities, instead of to the IRS;

- eliminate US withholding under FATCA on payments to FFIs established in the partner country; and

- commit to reciprocity with respect to collecting and reporting information to the partner countries on the US accounts of residents of the partner countries.

See 'Joint Statement regarding an Intergovernmental Approach to Improving International Tax Compliance and Implementing FATCA', which was published by HM Treasury on 8 February 2012.

See **Appendix I** for a list of countries with an FATCA agreement with the USA.

The UK and FATCA

3.3

Focus

The UK and US entered into an IGA to implement FATCA on 12 September 2012. This was called the 'Agreement between the Government of the UK and the Government of the USA to improve international tax compliance and to implement FATCA'.

This agreement was later amended by the 'Exchange of Notes Amending the Agreement to implement FATCA' in June 2013.

The Finance Act 2013, s 222 was enacted to empower the Treasury to make regulations which give effect to FATCA agreement and any other agreement between the UK and any other country in similar terms.

In October 2014, HMRC launched an online service for UK financial institutions ('FIs') to register and report FATCA financial information on behalf of their US customers in accordance with UK/US agreement. The first returns were due by 31 May 2015.

According to s 222(2) regulations made may:

(a) authorise HMRC to require persons specified ('relevant financial entities') to provide HMRC with information of specified descriptions;

(b) require that information to be provided at such times and in such form and manner as may be specified;

(c) impose obligations on relevant financial entities (including obligations to obtain from specified persons details of their place of residence for tax purposes and (per the Finance (No 2) Act 2015, s 50 amendment) client notification obligations);

(d) (per the Finance (No 2) Act 2015, s. 50 amendment) impose client notification obligations;

(e) make provision (including provision imposing penalties) about contravention of, or non-compliance with, the regulations; and

(f) make provision about appeals in relation to the imposition of any penalty.

The International Tax Compliance Regulations 2015, SI 2015/878, were made in exercise of the powers in s 222 as referred to above.

These Regulations were operative from 15 April 2015. HMRC also published directions concerning the form and manner by which an electronic return must be made by FIs under SI 2015/878, effective for returns made on or after 1 July 2015.

The directions are available at www.gov.uk/government/uploads/system/ uploads/attachment_data/file/486804/Directions_signed_and_dated_by_two_ Commissioners.pdf.

OECD CRS

Overview of the Common Reporting Standard

3.4

Focus

The Common Reporting Standard ('CRS') is an information standard for the Automatic Exchange of Information ('AEOI') regarding financial accounts on a global level, between tax authorities, which the OECD developed in 2014.

Its purpose is to combat tax evasion. The idea was based on the US FATCA implementation agreements and its legal basis is the Convention on Mutual Administrative Assistance in Tax Matters.

Broadly, under CRS, reporting FIs of one participant jurisdiction exchange information about their account holders who are tax residents of another participating jurisdiction, with the latter's tax authorities.

The participation in the OECD CRS of EU Member States (including the UK until Brexit) is via the EU Directive on Administrative Cooperation 2011/16/EU ('EU DAC'). EU DAC imports CRS principles into the Directive (mostly in Annex I).

The UK committed (through the EU) to a first exchange of information under CRS in respect of 2017. In effect, the first due diligence under CRS had to be completed by 31 December 2017 (see **Chapter 9** onwards). The first report under CRS would then have been required by 31 May 2018 (see **Chapter 12**).

See **Chapter 2** regarding the post-Brexit UK's relationship with EU DAC (and via EU DAC with the OECD CRS). See **1.7**.

See **Appendix II** for a list of OECD CRS participant countries.

Chapter 4

What is a reporting financial institution under FATCA/CRS? Why is it important?

SIGNPOSTS

- Typically, under FATCA/CRS, a firm, business or other entity first needs to decide whether it is a 'reporting financial institution'. See this Chapter regarding the meaning of reporting financial institution ('RFI').

- If the entity concludes that it is an RFI, it probably needs next, to carry out the due diligence procedures that are stipulated under FATCA and CRS in relation to its financial accounts (see **Chapter 5** regarding the meaning of 'financial account').

- The results of the RFI's due diligence exercise should then enable it to decide whether and what it needs to report under FATCA and CRS. It should then do that within the appropriate timeframe for doing so (see **Chapter 12**).

- An account holder of an RFI could well find that the RFI sends them a form to fill in, asking for information that the RFI needs as part of its due diligence under FATCA and/or CRS/EU DAC. In the case of an entity, this is likely to include asking the entity to state what type of entity it is for the purposes of FATCA or CRS/EU DAC – for example, is it a financial institution, Active non-financial entity ('NFE') or non-financial foreign entity ('NFFE') or passive NFE or NFFE? Accordingly, even entities that do not consider themselves to be a financial institution may need to assess carefully what kind of entity they are and will be impacted by FATCA and/or CRS/EU DAC at least to the extent of having to consider carefully what answers to provide in reply to such due diligence forms (see **4.1**, **4.2** and **4.3**).

- When considering whether an entity is an RFI, it will first need to decide whether it meets the definition of a 'financial institution' (see **4.5**, **4.6** and **4.7**).

- The definition of financial institution under FATCA and CRS/EU DAC is wide. Hence it can encompass entities which one might not normally think of as a financial institution, including firms of solicitors, trusts, charities and others (see **Chapter 6**).

- If the entity is a financial institution, it is likely to be a UK RFI if it is resident (or has a UK representative or branch located) in the UK, provided that it is not a non-RFI. See **4.9**, **4.10** and **4.11** regarding the meaning of RFI; see **4.12** regarding the meaning of UK representative.

- Under CRS/EU DAC, the list of entities that are a non-RFI consists broadly of certain kinds of government entities, retirement funds and trusts (see **4.13**).

- Under FATCA, the list of entities that are a non-RFI consists of entities that are considered either exempt beneficial owners or deemed-compliant financial institutions. These are listed in **4.14**, **4.15** and **4.16**.

- Throughout this Chapter, where reference is made to 'CRS/EU DAC', this is in relation to the CRS rules as they apply to the UK through the EU/EU DAC. See **Chapter 2** regarding the impact of Brexit on this.

WHY MUST ENTITIES DECIDE IF THEY ARE A FINANCIAL INSTITUTION FOR FATCA AND CRS/EU DAC?

4.1   The broad thrust of the Automatic Exchange of Information ('AEOI') under FATCA, CRS/EU DAC is a requirement for UK financial institutions (or in some cases their UK representative) to undertake due diligence on their account holders and to make reports to HMRC where required.

The various UK regulations for AEOI impose obligations on UK financial institutions.

A UK financial institution is any financial institution resident in the UK (excluding any of its branches that are located outside the UK), as well as any branch of a non-resident financial institution located in the UK.

If the financial institution is resident for tax purposes in the UK, then HMRC will regard the financial institution as within the scope of the UK agreement.

See HMRC's International Exchange of Information Manual IEIM400620; see also the same article from IEIM regarding the meaning for this purpose of 'resident for tax purposes in the UK'.

Why is that important?

4.2

Focus

For any individual or any entity (any 'person') who is affected by FATCA and/or CRS/EU DAC, it will usually be critically important to decide on that person's status under FATCA/CRS – in particular, is the person a financial institution as defined for those purposes? If the person is not, what is it then?

Under FATCA and CRS/EU DAC, financial institutions are required to report accounts that are subject to reporting, which is to say reportable accounts.

Reportable accounts are accounts held by persons or passive NFEs (or NFFEs) with controlling persons resident in an AEOI partner country (also in the case of FATCA controlling persons who are US citizens). See, for example, CRS at Section VIII, and EU DAC at Annex I, Section VIII; see the FATCA agreement at Annex I(VI)(B). See **9.10** regarding controlling persons.

A reportable account is an account held by one or more reportable persons or by a passive NFE (see **11.15**) with one or more controlling persons (see **9.10**) that is a reportable person. See **9.8** and **9.9** and HMRC's International Exchange of Information Manual regarding the meaning of 'reportable person'.

There are two principal ways in which one may find oneself affected by this, as follows:

(1) Categorisation

An entity or an individual may receive forms from someone such as its bank and/or investment manager requesting that it 'categorise' itself for the purposes of FATCA, CRS and EU DAC. Banks, investment managers do this as part of the due diligence that they are required to carry out for AEOI purposes. See **Chapters 9** and **11**.

The FATCA and CRS/EU DAC regimes divide all entities into two broad categories – 'financial institutions' and 'non-financial entities'.

There are also a number of sub-categories. Typically, these include NFEs.

NFEs are then categorised either as an active NFE or a passive NFE. See this Chapter regarding the meanings of these terms.

---

(2)   Reports to HMRC

An entity that is a UK financial institution (or a UK representative of one) will need to consider whether it must carry out due diligence and report accordingly. See **4.9** onwards regarding who has an obligation to report under FATCA and/or CRS/EU DAC.

See **Chapters 13** to **17** regarding reporting and other implications of the Mandatory Disclosure regime under EU Directive 2018/822/EU ('EU DAC 6'). See this Chapter regarding certain other forms of exchange under EU DAC.

Hence an entity that concludes that it is a financial institution could well find that it must get heavily involved in applying FATCA and/or CRS/EU DAC. Note that, even then, it will still need to work out whether it is an RFI (see the remainder of this Chapter).

An entity that concludes it is not a financial institution, but which holds accounts with financial institutions, could well find that it still has to self-categorise for the purposes of forms received from those financial institutions. Such an entity will therefore need to decide what kind of entity it is, for the purposes of FATCA and/or CRS/EU DAC, for example, whether an active NFE or NFFE or a passive NFE or NFFE.

An individual cannot be a financial institution or an NFE or NFFE. However, even an individual should ensure that they fill in, with appropriate due care, any categorisation form received from any financial institution with which they are an account holder.

See the remainder of this Chapter as regards the meaning of 'financial institution'.

See **Chapter 11** regarding the definitions of other entities under FATCA and CRS/EU DAC, including active and passive NFEs and NFFEs.

FILLING IN FATCA/CRS 'CATEGORISATION' FORMS RECEIVED FROM FINANCIAL INSTITUTIONS

4.3

Focus

Tips for entities completing FATCA and CRS/EU DAC forms sent to them by financial institutions of whom they are a financial account holder include:

- reading the form carefully. Often the form itself will contain notes for completion and an explanation of any defined terms used. Consider these carefully and where necessary ask the institution who provided the form for an explanation;

- noting carefully any deadline for completion specified in the form including, in some cases, any action threatened by the financial institution in the event of failure to meet the deadline;

- checking which version of AEOI the form requires the entity to categorise under (in other words, whether under FATCA, CRS or EU DAC) as each has its own slightly different definitions and rules;

- considering carefully any declaration(s) that the form requests; and

- if unsure, consulting a professional adviser.

WHO MUST CARRY OUT DUE DILIGENCE AND POTENTIALLY REPORT UNDER FATCA, CRS/EU DAC?

4.4

Focus

Under FATCA, CRS/EU DAC, an RFI must make a return each calendar year in relation to each reportable account that is maintained by the institution at any time during the calendar year in question.

In order to be an RFI, an entity first of all needs to be a financial institution. See **4.5**, **4.6** and **4.7** regarding the meaning of 'financial institution' under FATCA and CRS/EU DAC.

If an entity is indeed a financial institution, it then needs to decide whether it is a 'reporting financial institution'. See **4.9**, **4.10** and **4.1**.

For calendar years 2015 and 2016 only, RFIs had additional reporting obligations under FATCA only, in respect of payments to non-participating financial institutions.

An entity that is non-compliant with FATCA may find itself classified as a non-participating financial institution, which is a concept that exists in FATCA, but not in CRS or EU DAC. For this to happen, there needs to be significant non-compliance (see **8.5** to **8.6**).

An RFI may use a service provider to undertake its reporting obligations, but in such cases those obligations continue to be the obligations of the RFI.

HMRC provide, as an example of a financial institution using a service provider in respect of its due diligence obligations, a situation where an independent financial adviser ('IFA') has the customer relationship for introducing business to a financial institution, such as a broker selling cash value insurance contracts.

An IFA is often best placed to obtain the self-certification needed to carry out the due diligence process on the new account. However, the obligation under

FATCA and/or CRS/EU DAC rules to carry out due diligence, such as obtaining suitable self-certification, remains an obligation of the financial institution, rather than an obligation of the service provider (ie in this case an IFA). See HMRC's International Exchange of Information Manual IEIM402600.

See **4.9** to **4.11** for the meaning of 'reporting financial institution'.

If an RFI is not resident in the UK, the obligations of the institution under the UK's FATCA and CRS/EU DAC Regulations are to be treated as if they were also the obligations of any UK representative of the institution. See **4.12** for the meaning of 'UK representative'.

See the International Tax Compliance Regulations 2015, SI 2015/878, regs 6, 9, 11 and 12.

THE TERM 'FINANCIAL INSTITUTION' UNDER FATCA AND CRS/EU DAC

4.5

Focus

The term 'financial institution' is widely defined under FATCA and CRS/EU DAC.

As a result, a wide range of types of entity may fall within the definitions – some of which one might not normally think of as being a financial institution.

See **Chapter 6** regarding the way in which this definition may or may not apply to various kinds of entity, including banks and other financial institutions and entities, professional firms, trusts and charities.

See **4.6** regarding the meaning of financial institution under FATCA. See **4.7** regarding the meaning of financial institution under CRS/EU DAC.

What is a financial institution under FATCA?

4.6

Focus

Under FATCA, the term 'financial institution' means:

- a custodial institution;
- a depository institution;
- an investment entity; or
- a specified insurance company.

Each of these is itself defined as follows in the FATCA agreement.

'*Custodial institution*' means any entity that holds, as a substantial portion of its business, financial assets for the account of others. An entity holds financial assets for the account of others as a substantial portion of its business if the entity's gross income attributable to the holding of financial assets and related financial services equals or exceeds 20 percent of the entity's gross income during the shorter of:

(i)   the three-year period that ends on December 31 (or the final day of a non-calendar year accounting period) prior to the year in which the determination is being made; or

(ii)   the period during which the entity has been in existence.

'*Depository institution*' means any entity that accepts deposits in the ordinary course of a banking or similar business.

'*Investment entity*' means any entity that conducts as a business (or is managed by an entity that conducts as a business) one or more of the following activities or operations for or on behalf of a customer:

(1)   trading in money market instruments (cheques, bills, certificates of deposit, derivatives, etc); foreign exchange; exchange, interest rate and index instruments; transferable securities; or commodity futures trading;

(2)   individual and collective portfolio management; or

(3)   otherwise investing, administering, or managing funds or money on behalf of other persons.

'*Specified insurance company*' means any entity that is an insurance company (or the holding company of an insurance company) that issues, or is obligated to make payments with respect to, a cash value insurance contract or an annuity contract.

See the agreement reached between the Government of the United Kingdom of Great Britain and Northern Ireland and the Government of the United States of America to improve international tax compliance and to implement FATCA, signed on 12 September 2012 ('the FATCA agreement'). See in particular the definitions in Art 1.

What is a financial institution under CRS/EU DAC?

4.7

Focus

Under CRS/EU DAC, the term 'financial institution' means:

-     a custodial institution;
-     a depository institution;
-     an investment entity; or
-     a specified insurance company.

4.7   *What is a reporting financial institution under FATCA/CRS?*

Each of these is itself defined as follows in CRS/EU DAC.

'*Custodial institution*' and '*depository institution*' are defined the same as in FATCA (see **4.6** above).

'*Investment entity*' means any entity that conducts as a business (or is managed by an entity that conducts as a business) one or more of the following activities or operations for or on behalf of a customer:

(1)   trading in money market instruments (cheques, bills, certificates of deposit, derivatives, etc); foreign exchange; exchange, interest rate and index instruments; transferable securities; or commodity futures trading;

(2)   individual and collective portfolio management;

(3)   otherwise investing, administering, or managing funds or money on behalf of other persons; or

(4)   the gross income of which is primarily attributable to investing, reinvesting, or trading in financial assets, if the entity is managed by another entity that is a depository institution, a custodial institution, a specified insurance company, or an investment entity described in any of (1) to (3) above.

An entity is treated as primarily conducting as a business one or more of the activities described in (1) to (3) above, or an entity's gross income is primarily attributable to investing, reinvesting, or trading in financial assets for the purposes of (4) above, if the entity's gross income attributable to the relevant activities equals or exceeds 50% of the entity's gross income during the shorter of:

(i)   the three-year period ending on 31 December of the year preceding the year in which the determination is made; or

(ii)   the period during which the entity has been in existence.

See **Example 4.1** below for an example of how this applies in the case of a corporate trustee associated with a firm of solicitors.

For these purposes, the term 'investment entity' also specifically excludes certain kinds of 'active NFE'. See EU DAC or the CRS as appropriate, for further details.

'*Specified insurance company*' is defined the same as in FATCA (see **4.6** above).

Under both EU DAC and CRS, the term 'NFE' means any entity that is not a financial institution.

EU DAC and CRS each list the categories of entities that are non-RFIs for their respective purposes.

EU DAC and CRS each list the categories of entities that are active NFEs for their respective purposes.

As regards EU DAC, see Annex I, Section VIII.

As regards CRS, see Standard for Automatic Exchange of Financial Account Information in Tax Matters, published by the OECD. See particularly CRS at Section VIII.

Example 4.1 – company investing and trading in financial assets

Francis carries on a business providing advice to clients on their investments in financial assets.

One of his clients is a company, XYZ Ltd that has earned more than 50% of its gross income in the last three years from investing, reinvesting and trading in financial assets. Ben primarily conducts investment-related activities on behalf of clients.

Francis is not an investment entity, so is not a financial institution, because he is an individual.

XYZ Ltd, however, is an investment entity, and is therefore a financial institution, because it primarily invests, reinvests and trades in financial assets as a business.

Example 4.2 – entities investing in property

An investment company (VWX Ltd), the gross income of which is primarily attributable to investing, reinvesting, or trading in real property is not an investment entity (irrespective of whether it is professionally managed) because real property is not a financial asset.

If, instead, another investment company (PQR Ltd) holds an interest in another entity that directly holds real property, the interest held by PQR Ltd is a financial asset, and the gross income from that interest must be taken into account to determine whether PQR Ltd will meet the definition of investment entity, and therefore of financial institution.

FATCA AND FINANCIAL INSTITUTIONS: HOLDING COMPANIES AND TREASURY CENTRES – A SPECIAL RULE

4.8

Focus

The previous definition of a UK financial institution included relevant holding companies and treasury companies.

> HMRC say that it is content for an entity that has already registered as a 'lead financial institution' to choose to use the extended definition of financial institution included in the US Treasury Regulations, should they wish to do so.

HMRC say that the US Treasury Regulations have as a final category of financial institution 'an entity that is a holding company or a treasury company'.

Nevertheless, it is the relevant agreement such as that between the UK and US to implement FATCA that determines the meaning of 'foreign financial institution' ('FFI').

However, because the previous definition of a UK financial institution included relevant holding companies and treasury companies, some holding company members of financial groups would have registered with the IRS as the lead financial institution of an expanded affiliated froup ('EAG') for FATCA purposes.

HMRC say they understand that reversing the registration and re-registering an entire group with new global intermediary identification numbers would be onerous.

If an entity registered as a lead financial institution also comes within the definition of a UK financial institution then they will continue to be defined and treated as a UK financial institution – this may be the case, for example, for treasury companies where they also come within the definition of an investment entity.

Where that is not the case, HMRC is content for an entity that has already registered as a 'lead financial institution' to choose to use the extended definition of financial institution included in the US Treasury Regulations, should they wish to do so.

See HMRC's International Exchange of Information Manual IEIM400630.

WHAT IS A REPORTING FINANCIAL INSTITUTION UNDER CRS/EU DAC?

4.9

> **Focus**
>
> If an entity concludes that it is a 'financial institution' for the purposes of FATCA and/or CRS/EU DAC, it must then decide whether it is therefore a 'reporting financial institution'; if it is, it will then need to carry out due diligence in respect of its financial accounts (see **Chapter 5** regarding the meaning of that term). In light of that due diligence, it may then need to report to HMRC under FATCA and/or CRS.

Broadly for CRS/EU DAC, an RFI is:

- a financial institution (or a branch of a financial institution);

- that is resident (or located) in a jurisdiction that is a CRS 'participating jurisdiction' (excluding any branch that is not located in a participating jurisdiction);

- but that is not a non-RFI.

If an RFI is not resident in the UK, the obligations of the institution under the UK's FATCA and CRS/EU DAC Regulations are to be treated as if they were also the obligations of any UK representative of the institution. See **4.12** for the meaning of 'UK representative'.

Note that because of the UK's past history as an EU Member State, CRS is applied to the UK by EU DAC. EU DAC uses the phrase Member State instead of the phrase 'participating jurisdiction'.

'Reporting financial institution' is defined, for the purposes of CRS/EU DAC, in Section VIII(A)(1) of CRS and Section VIII(A)(1) of Annex I of EU DAC.

See **4.11** regarding the definition of 'reporting financial institution' for the purposes of FATCA.

For the purposes of CRS/EU DAC, the International Tax Compliance Regulations 2015, SI 2015/878, adopt the following definitions of 'reporting financial institution' (see reg 24).

In EU DAC, the term 'reporting financial institution' means any Member State financial institution that is not a non-RFI:

'"Member State financial institution" means: (i) any financial institution that is resident in a Member State, but excludes any branch of that financial institution that is located outside that Member State; and (ii) any branch of a financial institution that is not resident in a Member State, if that branch is located in that Member State.'

As regards the phrase 'Member State', all references in EU law to Member States is treated as including the UK during the Brexit transition period. See **2.8** and **2.9**.

'Non-reporting financial institution' means any financial institution which is:

(a) a governmental entity, international organisation or central bank, other than with respect to a payment that is derived from an obligation held in connection with a commercial financial activity of a type engaged in by a specified insurance company, custodial institution, or depository institution;

(b)   a broad participation retirement fund, a narrow participation retirement fund, a pension fund of a governmental entity, international organisation or central bank, or a qualified credit card issuer;

(c)   any other entity that presents a low risk of being used to evade tax, has substantially similar characteristics to any of the entities described in (a) and (b), and is included in the list of non-RFIs provided to the EU Commission by the UK, provided that the status of such entity as a non-RFI does not frustrate the purposes of EU DAC;

(d)   an exempt collective investment vehicle; or

(e)   a trust to the extent that the trustee of the trust is an RFI and reports all information required to be reported pursuant to EU DAC with respect to all reportable accounts of the trust.

Regarding (c) above, the UK has not defined in domestic law or provided to the EU Commission as a list any financial institutions excluded by reference to sub-paragraph B(1)(c) of Section VIII of CRS or of Annex I of EU DAC (low-risk non-RFIs). See HMRC's International Exchange of Information Manual IEIM400925.

Key terms are defined further in EU DAC, including 'governmental entity', 'international organisation', 'central bank', 'specified insurance company', 'custodial institution', 'depository institution', 'broad participation retirement fund', 'narrow participation retirement fund' and 'exempt collective investment vehicle'. See EU DAC.

See EU DAC, Annex I, Section VIII(A)(1) onwards. See **4.7** regarding the meaning of 'financial institution' under EU DAC. See also HMRC's International Exchange of Information Manual IEIM400920 onwards.

Regarding the equivalents under CRS, see **4.6**; and under FATCA, see **4.11**.

4.10   In the OECD CRS, 'Reporting financial institution' means any participating jurisdiction financial institution that is not a non-RFI.

'Participating jurisdiction financial institution' means:

(i)   any financial institution that is resident in a participating jurisdiction, but excludes any branch of that financial institution that is located outside such participating jurisdiction; and

(ii)   any branch of a financial institution that is not resident in a participating jurisdiction, if that branch is located in such participating jurisdiction.

'Participating jurisdiction' means a jurisdiction (i) with which an agreement is in place pursuant to which it will provide the information specified in CRS, and (ii) which is identified in the OECD's published list of participating jurisdictions. See **Appendix II** regarding these jurisdictions.

See CRS, Section VIII(A)(1) onwards.

See **4.7** regarding the meaning of 'financial institution' under the CRS. See also HMRC's International Exchange of Information Manual IEIM400920 onwards.

Regarding the equivalents under EU DAC, see **4.9**; and under FATCA, see **4.11**.

WHAT IS A REPORTING FINANCIAL INSTITUTION UNDER FATCA?

4.11

Focus

For the purposes of FATCA:

'Reporting financial institution' means a reporting UK financial institution or a reporting US financial institution, as the context requires.

'Reporting United Kingdom financial institution' means any UK financial institution that is not a non-reporting UK financial institution. See **4.10**.

'United Kingdom financial institution' means (i) any financial institution resident in the UK, but excluding any branches of such financial institution that are located outside the UK, and (ii) any branch of a financial institution not resident in the UK, if such branch is located in the UK.

If an RFI is not resident in the UK, the obligations of the institution under the UK's FATCA and CRS/DAC Regulations are to be treated as if they were also the obligations of any UK representative of the institution. See **4.12** for the meaning of 'UK representative'.

See also HMRC's International Exchange of Information Manual IEIM400920 onwards.

See below regarding the meaning of reporting US financial institution.

The term 'reporting US financial institution' means:

(i) any financial institution that is resident in the US, but excluding any branches of such financial institution that are located outside the US, and

(ii) any branch of a financial institution not resident in the US, if such branch is located in the US, provided that the financial institution or branch has control, receipt, or custody of income with respect to which information is required to be exchanged (ie reported to the UK authorities) under the FATCA agreement.

4.12 *What is a reporting financial institution under FATCA/CRS?*

See the FATCA agreement', in particular the definitions in Art 1.

Regarding the meaning of investment entity, see also **Examples 4.1** and **4.2** in this Chapter. See **4.7** regarding the meaning of investment entity under CRS and EU DAC.

See also **4.6** regarding the meaning of 'financial institution' under FATCA.

'Reporting financial institution' is defined, for the purposes of FATCA, in Art 1(1)(n) of the FATCA agreement.

Regarding the equivalents under EU DAC, see **4.7** and **4.9**; and under CRS, see **4.7** and **4.10**.

UK REPRESENTATIVE

4.12

Focus

If an RFI is not resident in the UK, the obligations of the institution under the UK's FATCA and CRS/DAC Regulations are to be treated as if they were also the obligations of any UK representative of the institution.

UK representative can include such things as a UK permanent establishment, as well as a branch or agency in the UK through which a non-resident carries on a trade.

'UK representative' is a term which applies under FATCA, CRS/EU DAC. It is defined in the International Tax Compliance Regulations 2015, SI 2015/878, reg 11 and has the same meaning as it has in:

(a)   the Corporation Tax Act 2010 ('CTA 2010'), Part 22, Chapter 6 in relation to an RFI that is within the charge to corporation tax, and

(b)   the Income Tax 2007 ('ITA 2007'), Part 14, Chapter 2C in relation to any other RFI.

Hence for corporation tax purposes a permanent establishment in the UK through which a non-resident company carries on a trade is the UK representative of the company in relation to the chargeable profits attributable to that establishment. It continues to be the company's UK representative in relation to those profits even after ceasing to be a permanent establishment carrying on the company's trade. It is treated as a separate person from the non-resident company. See CTA 2010, s 969(3), (4).

Hence too, for income tax purposes a branch or agency in the UK through which a non-resident carries on a trade is the UK representative of the non-resident in relation to the chargeable profits attributable to that branch or agency. This section applies if a non-UK resident carries on (alone or in partnership) any trade, profession or vocation through a branch or agency in the UK. See ITA 2007, s 835E.

In certain circumstances, the following persons are exempt from treatment as a UK representative:

- agents (see ITA 2007, s 835G);

- brokers (see ITA 2007, s 835H);

- investment managers (see ITA 2007, s 835I).

As well as applying for income tax purposes, the above exemptions in ss 835G, 835H and 835I also apply for corporation tax – see the Taxation (International and Other Provisions) Act 2010 ('TIOPA 2010'), ss 370 and 506.

WHAT IS A NON-REPORTING UK FINANCIAL INSTITUTION UNDER CRS/EU DAC?

4.13

Focus

In CRS, 'reporting financial institution' means any participating jurisdiction financial institution that is not a non-RFI.

'Non-reporting financial institution' means any financial institution which is:

(a) a governmental entity, international organisation or central bank, other than with respect to a payment that is derived from an obligation held in connection with a commercial financial activity of a type engaged in by a specified insurance company, custodial institution, or depository institution;

(b) a broad participation retirement fund, a narrow participation retirement fund, a pension fund of a governmental entity, international organisation or central bank, or a qualified credit card issuer;

(c) any other entity that presents a low risk of being used to evade tax, has substantially similar characteristics to any of the entities described in (a) and (b), and is defined in domestic law as a non-RFI, provided that the status of such entity as a non-RFI does not frustrate the purposes of CRS (see below);

(d) an exempt collective investment vehicle; or

(e) a trust to the extent that the trustee of the trust is an RFI and reports all information required to be reported pursuant to the CRS with respect to all reportable accounts of the trust.

Regarding (c) above, the UK has not defined in domestic law any financial institutions excluded by reference to sub-paragraph B(1)(c) of Section VIII of CRS or of Annex I, Section VIII of EU DAC (low-risk non-RFIs). See HMRC's International Exchange of Information Manual IEIM400925.

Key terms are defined further in the CRS, including 'governmental entity', 'international organisation', 'central bank', 'specified insurance company', 'custodial institution', 'depository institution', 'broad participation retirement fund', 'narrow participation retirement fund' and 'exempt collective investment vehicle'.

WHAT IS A NON-REPORTING UK FINANCIAL INSTITUTION UNDER FATCA?

4.14

Focus

Under the FATCA agreement, 'reporting United Kingdom financial institution' means any UK financial institution that is not a non-reporting UK financial institution. See **4.9**.

Under the FATCA agreement (see particularly Annex II), the following are within the meaning of a non-reporting UK financial institution':

- exempt beneficial owners;

- deemed-compliant financial institutions; or

- an excepted FFI under relevant US Treasury Regulations.

The persons that are considered exempt beneficial owners under FATCA are listed in **4.15**; deemed-compliant financial institutions under FATCA are listed in **4.16**.

4.15   See **4.14** regarding the significance of the term 'exempt beneficial owner'.

The FATCA agreement defines 'exempt beneficial owners' as follows:

(1)   UK governmental organisations

- The devolved administrations as per:

  – the Northern Ireland Act 1998 (updated by the Northern Ireland (St Andrews Agreement) Acts 2006 and 2007, and the Northern Ireland Act 2009);

  – the Scotland Act 1998;

  – the Government of Wales Act 2006;

- Local government authorities as per:
  - – s 33 of the Local Government Act 2003;
  - – the Local Government Act (NI) 1972 (as amended by the Local Government (Miscellaneous Provisions) Act (NI) 2010 and the Local Government Finance Act (NI) 2011);
  - – the Local Government etc. (Scotland) Act 1994;
  - – the Local Government (Wales) Act 1994.

(2) The Bank of England and any of its wholly owned subsidiaries.

(3) Any UK office of:

- the International Monetary Fund;
- the World Bank;
- the International Bank for Reconstruction and Development;
- the International Finance Corporation;
- the International Finance Corporation Order 1955, SI 1955/1954;
- the International Development Association;
- the Asian Development Bank;
- the African Development Bank;
- the European Community;
- the European Coal and Steel Community;
- the European Atomic Energy Community;
- the European Investment Bank;
- the European Bank for Reconstruction and Development;
- the OECD Support Fund;
- the Inter-American Development Bank.

(4) Any pension scheme or other retirement arrangement established in the UK and described in Art 3 (General Definitions) of the UK/USA Double Taxation Convention, including pension funds or pension schemes covered by IRS Announcement 2005-30, 2005-1 C.B. 988, on the Mutual Agreement on UK Pension Agreements.

4.16 See **4.14** regarding the significance of the term 'deemed-compliant financial institution'.

Under the FATCA agreement, 'deemed-compliant financial institutions' are as follows:

4.16 *What is a reporting financial institution under FATCA/CRS?*

(1)   Non-profit organisations:

- any entity registered as a charity with the Charity Commission of England and Wales;

- any entity registered with HMRC for charitable tax purposes;

- any entity registered as a charity with the Office of the Scottish Charity Regulator;

- any Community Amateur Sports Club if registered as such with HMRC.

(2)   Financial institutions with a local client base:

    (a)   Any financial institution, including any of the following entities that meets 'the requirements' as listed below:

        (i)   Credit Unions that are a body corporate registered under the Industrial and Provident Societies Act 1965 as a credit union in accordance with:

- the Credit Unions Act 1979; or

- the Credit Unions (Northern Ireland) Order 1985, SI 1985/1205 (NI 12); or

- the Industrial and Provident Societies Act (Northern Ireland) 1969;

        (ii)   Industrial and Provident Societies registered or deemed to be registered under the Industrial and Provident Societies Act 1965;

        (iii)   Friendly Societies within the meaning of the Friendly Societies Act 1992;

        (iv)   Building Societies incorporated or deemed to be incorporated under the Building Societies Act 1986;

        (v)   Mutual Societies as defined in the Building Societies (Funding) and Mutual Societies (Transfers) Act 2007;

        (vi)   investment trust companies where approved under s 1158 of CTA 2010 and meets the requirements of the Investment Trust (Approved Company) (Tax) Regulations 2011, SI 2011/2999;

        (vii)   venture capital trusts where approved by HMRC under ITA 2007, Chapter 3.

In order to meet the 'requirements' referred to at (2) above, a financial institution must:

(a)   be licensed and regulated under the laws of the UK;

(b)   have no fixed place of business outside the UK;

(c)   not solicit account holders outside the UK. For this purpose, a financial institution shall not be considered to have solicited account holders outside of the UK merely because it operates a website, provided that the website does not specifically indicate that the financial institution provides accounts or services to non-residents or otherwise target or solicit US customers;

(d)   be required under the tax laws of the UK to perform either information reporting or withholding of tax with respect to accounts held by residents of the UK;

(e)   provide at least 98 percent of its accounts to residents of the UK or a Member State of the EU;

(f)   have implemented policies and procedures to monitor whether (beginning on 1 January 2014) it provides or provided any account held by:

    (i)   any specified US person who is not a resident of the UK (including a US person that was a resident of the UK when the account was opened but subsequently ceases or ceased to be a resident of the UK);

    (ii)   a non-participating financial institution; or

    (iii)   any passive NFFE with controlling persons who are US citizens or residents;

See **9.8** and **9.9** as well as FATCA agreement, Art 1(8)(gg) regarding the meaning of specified US person.

Regarding (ii) above, an entity that is non-compliant with FATCA may find itself classified as a non-participating financial institution, which is a concept that exists in FATCA, but not in CRS or EU DAC. For this to happen, there needs to be significant non-compliance (see **8.5** to **8.6**);

(g)   report under FATCA any accounts that it identifies under the procedure in (f) as if it were a reporting UK financial institution;

(h)   review the accounts that it maintains or maintained in accordance with the procedures described in the FATCA agreement applicable to pre-existing accounts to identify any US reportable accounts or accounts held by a non-participating financial institution (see the above comments at (f) regarding non-participating financial institutions). It must close any such accounts or report them under FATCA as if it were reporting UK financial institution (a pre-existing account is an account which the financial institution maintained as of 31 December 2013); and

(i)   must incorporate or organise each related entity of the financial institution in the UK and must also meet the requirements that are set out above.

See **11.4** and **11.5** regarding the meaning of related entity for the purposes of the FATCA agreement.

Chapter 5

What is a financial account? Why is that important?

<table>
<tr><td>

SIGNPOSTS

- Typically, under FATCA/CRS, a firm, business or other entity first needs to decide whether it is a 'reporting financial institution'. See **Chapter 4** regarding the meaning of reporting financial institution ('RFI').

- If the entity concludes that it is an RFI, it probably needs next, to carry out the due diligence procedures that are stipulated under FATCA and CRS in relation to its financial accounts. See **Chapter 9** regarding due diligence. See this Chapter regarding the meaning of 'financial account'.

- For the purposes of FATCA and CRS/EU DAC, 'financial account' is an account maintained by a 'financial institution'. There are five categories of financial account (see **5.1** to **5.6**).

- Certain 'exempt products' are specifically not reportable (see **5.7** and **5.8**).

- Throughout this Chapter, where reference is made to 'CRS/EU DAC', this is in relation to the CRS rules as they apply to the UK through the EU/EU DAC. See **Chapter 2** regarding the impact of Brexit on this.

</td></tr>
</table>

WHAT IS A FINANCIAL ACCOUNT FOR THE PURPOSES OF FATCA AND CRS/EU DAC?

5.1

<table>
<tr><td>

Focus

Only accounts that fall within any of the five categories of financial account defined by FATCA and CRS/EU DAC need to be reviewed using the due diligence procedures described in **Chapters 9**, **10** and **11**, and therefore, potentially, to be reported.

</td></tr>
</table>

A 'financial account' is an account maintained by a 'financial institution', as the latter term is defined for the purposes of FATCA and CRS/EU DAC (see **Chapter 4**).

The five categories of financial account are:

- depository accounts;
- custodial accounts;
- equity and debt interests in investment entities;
- cash value insurance contracts; and
- annuity contracts.

'Financial account' specifically does not include any account that is an excluded account as defined for the purposes of FATCA and CRS. An excluded account is specifically not reportable for the purposes of CRS/EU DAC. See **5.7** and **5.8**.

See the FATCA agreement, Art 1(1). See CRS, Section VIII(C). See EU DAC, Annex I, Section VIII(C).

DEPOSITORY ACCOUNT

5.2

Focus

'Depository account' includes any commercial, checking, savings, time, or thrift account, or an account that is evidenced by a certificate of deposit, thrift certificate, investment certificate, certificate of indebtedness, or other similar instrument maintained by a financial institution in the ordinary course of a banking or similar business.

A depository account also includes an amount held by an insurance company pursuant to a guaranteed investment contract or similar agreement to pay or credit interest thereon.

See the FATCA agreement, Art 1(1)(t). See CRS, Section VIII(C)(2). See EU DAC, Annex I, Section VIII(C)(2).

CUSTODIAL ACCOUNT

5.3

Focus

'Custodial account' means an account (other than an insurance contract or annuity contract) that holds one or more financial assets for the benefit of another person.

See the FATCA agreement, Art 1(1)(u). See CRS, Section VIII(C)(3). See EU DAC, Annex I, Section VIII(C)(3).

EQUITY INTEREST
5.4

Focus

'Equity Interest' means:

(a) in the case of an investment entity, any equity or debt interest in the financial institution.

In CRS and EU DAC, notwithstanding the foregoing, the term 'financial account' does not include any equity or debt interest in an entity that is an investment entity solely because it:

(i) renders investment advice to, and acts on behalf of; or

(ii) manages portfolios for, and acts on behalf of, a customer for the purpose of investing, managing, or administering Financial Assets deposited in the name of the customer with a financial institution other than such entity.

In FATCA, interests that are regularly traded on an established securities market specifically do not fall within the term 'financial account';

(b) in the case of a financial institution that is not an investment entity, any equity or debt interest in the financial institution, if the class of interests was established with a purpose of avoiding reporting in accordance with FATCA, CRS or EU DAC;

(c) any cash value insurance contract and any annuity contract issued or maintained by a financial institution, other than a non-investment-linked, non-transferable immediate life annuity that is issued to an individual and monetises a pension or disability benefit provided under an account that is an excluded account;

(d) in the case of a partnership that is a financial institution, either a capital or profits interest in the partnership;

(e) in the case of a trust that is a financial institution, an equity interest held by any person treated as a settlor or beneficiary of all or a portion of the trust, or any other natural person exercising ultimate effective control over the trust.

A reportable person will be treated as being a beneficiary of a trust if such reportable person has the right to receive directly or indirectly (for example, through a nominee) a mandatory distribution or may receive, directly or indirectly, a discretionary distribution from the trust. See **9.8** and **9.9** regarding the meaning of 'reportable person'.

5.5 *What is a financial account? Why is that important?*

See the FATCA agreement, Art 1(1)(v). See CRS, Section VIII(C)(4). See EU DAC, Annex I, Section VIII(C)(4).

CASH VALUE INSURANCE CONTRACT

5.5

> **Focus**
>
> 'Cash value insurance contract' means an insurance contract (other than an indemnity reinsurance contract between two insurance companies) that has a cash value.

'Insurance contract' means a contract (other than an annuity contract) under which the issuer agrees to pay an amount upon the occurrence of a specified contingency involving mortality, morbidity, accident, liability, or property risk.

'Cash value' means the greater of:

(i)   the amount that the policyholder is entitled to receive upon surrender or termination of the contract (determined without reduction for any surrender charge or policy loan); and

(ii)   the amount the policyholder can borrow under or with regard to the contract.

For the purposes of FATCA, CRS and EU DAC, 'cash value' does not include an amount payable under an insurance contract as:

(i)   a personal injury or sickness benefit or other benefit providing indemnification of an economic loss incurred upon the occurrence of the event insured against;

(ii)   a refund to the policyholder of a previously paid premium under an insurance contract (other than under a life insurance contract) due to policy cancellation or termination, decrease in risk exposure during the effective period of the insurance contract, or arising from a redetermination of the premium due to correction of posting or other similar error;

(iii)   a policyholder dividend based upon the underwriting experience of the contract or group involved;

In addition, for the purposes only of CRS and the DAC, 'cash value' also does not include an amount payable under an insurance contract:

(iv)   solely by reason of the death of an individual insured under a life insurance contract; or

(v)   as a return of an advance premium or premium deposit for an Insurance Contract for which the premium is payable at least annually if the amount of the advance premium or premium deposit does not exceed the next annual premium that will be payable under the contract.

See the FATCA agreement, Art 1(1)(w), (y) and (z). See CRS, Section VIII(C) (5), (7) and (8). See EU DAC, Annex I, Section VIII(C)(5), (7) and (8).

ANNUITY CONTRACT

5.6

Focus

'Annuity contract' means a contract under which the issuer agrees to make payments for a period of time determined in whole or in part by reference to the life expectancy of one or more individuals. The term also includes a contract that is considered to be an annuity contract in accordance with the law, regulation, or practice of the jurisdiction in which the contract was issued, and under which the issuer agrees to make payments for a term of years.

See the FATCA agreement, Art 1(1)(x). See CRS, Section VIII(C)(6). See EU DAC, Annex I, Section VIII(C)(6).

ARE THERE ANY FINANCIAL ACCOUNTS THAT ARE EXCLUDED FROM FATCA?

5.7   Certain 'exempt products' are specifically not reportable under the FATCA agreement only. These are listed in the FATCA agreement between the US and the UK.

Under FATCA, 'exempt products' are as follows.

(1)   Certain retirement accounts or products:

- pension schemes registered with HMRC under the Finance Act 2004 ('FA 2004'), Part 4 and pension arrangements where the annual contributions are limited to £50,000 and funds contributed cannot be accessed before the age of 55 except in circumstances of serious ill health;

- those that are UK-registered pension arrangements (including authorised payments) as set out in FA 2004.

(2)   Certain other tax-favoured accounts or products:

- individual savings accounts ('ISAs');

- junior ISAs;

- child trust funds;

- premium bonds – where issued by UK National Savings and Investments ('NS&I');

- children's bonus bonds – where issued by NS&I;

- fixed interest savings certificates – where issued by NS&I;

- index-linked savings certificates – where issued by NS&I;

- tax exempt savings plans – where issued by a Friendly Society;

- save-as-you-earn ('SAYE') share option schemes – approved by HMRC under the Income Tax (Earnings and Pensions) Act 2003 ('ITEPA 2003'), Sch 3;

- share incentive plans – approved by HMRC under ITEPA 2003, Sch 2;

- company share option plans ('CSOP') – approved by HMRC under ITEPA 2003, Sch 4.

In addition, an escrow account is an account held by a third party on behalf of the beneficial owner of the money in the account. Such accounts are excluded accounts where they are established in certain specified circumstances. See HMRC's International Exchange of Information Manual IEIM401860 and IEIM401870.

See Annex II of the agreement reached between the Government of the United Kingdom of Great Britain and Northern Ireland and the Government of the United States of America to improve international tax compliance and to implement FATCA, signed on 12 September 2012 ('the FATCA agreement').

See also HMRC's International Exchange of Information Manual IEIM400920 onwards.

ARE THERE ANY FINANCIAL ACCOUNTS THAT ARE EXCLUDED FROM CRS/EU DAC?

5.8 Certain 'exempt products' are specifically not reportable under CRS/ EU DAC only. These are as follows.

Certain retirement accounts or products:

(1) pension schemes registered with HMRC under Part 4 of FA 2004;

(2) non-registered pension arrangements where the annual contributions are limited to £50,000 and funds contributed cannot be accessed before the age of 55 except in circumstances of serious ill health;

(3) immediate needs annuities within ITTOIA 2005, s 725;

Certain tax-favoured accounts and products:

(4)   an account within the meaning of the Individual Savings Account Regulations 1998, SI 1998/1870, relevantly amended by SIs 2002/1974, 2007/2119, 2008/704, 2009/1994, 2010/2957, 2011/782 and 2011/1780;

(5)   a child trust fund within the meaning of the Child Trust Funds Act 2004;

(6)   premium bonds issued by NS&I;

(7)   children's bonds issued by NS&I;

(8)   fixed interest savings certificates issued by NS&I;

(9)   index-linked savings certificates issued by NS&I;

(10) tax exempt savings plans issued by a friendly society within the meaning of the Friendly Societies Act 1992;

(11) a share incentive plan approved by HMRC under Sch 2 to ITEPA 2003;

(12) a SAYE option scheme approved by HMRC under Sch 3 to ITEPA 2003;

(13) a CSOP scheme approved by HMRC under Sch 4 to ITEPA 2003.

In addition, an escrow account is an account held by a third party on behalf of the beneficial owner of the money in the account. Such accounts are excluded accounts where they are established in certain specified circumstances. See HMRC's International Exchange of Information Manual IEIM401860 and IEIM401870.

In addition, escrow accounts are excluded accounts in certain specified circumstances (see commentary at **5.7** above).

See the International Tax Compliance Regulations 2015, SI 2015/878, Sch 2.

Chapter 6

How are different kinds of entities and persons affected by FATCA/CRS?

SIGNPOSTS

- Typically, under FATCA/CRS, a firm, business or other entity first needs to decide whether it is a 'reporting financial institution'. See **Chapter 4** regarding the meaning of a reporting financial institution ('RFI').

- Many entities, such as many banks and other financial services providers, that might commonly be thought of as a 'financial institution' as that term is used in common parlance, may be both a financial institution and in particular an RFI as those terms are defined for the purposes of FATCA and CRS. However, some such entities may not (see **6.1**).

- By way of an example, some collective investment schemes ('CISs') are non-reporting financial institution, but some are not. Furthermore, the definitions applicable to CISs differ under FATCA as compared with CRS. Hence, for example, some CISs could be an RFI under one of these regimes but not under the other regime (see **6.2**).

- Furthermore, the definition of a financial institution is broad enough that it can sometimes include entities or persons that might not be thought of as a financial institution as that term is used in common parlance. Hence a professional firm, such as a firm of solicitors or accountants could in some cases fall within the definition of a financial institution under FATCA and CRS, while other such firms may not. Where such firms fall within the FATCA/CRS definition of a financial institution, it will often be because they operate a trust company (see **6.3**).

- A family or other trust can sometimes fall within the definition of an RFI. A trust could also be impacted in other ways such as, for example, if it is a passive non-financial entity (see **6.4** and **6.5**).

- Where a trust does have to report, it is likely that it will then be necessary to identify the financial accounts and the account

---

holders for the purposes of FATCA and CRS. This is also likely to be the case where a charitable trust is reportable under FATCA and CRS (see **6.5** and **6.6**).

- Under the FATCA agreement with the US all charities are excluded from reporting under the exemption for non-profit organisations. However, for CRS and the EU Directive on Administrative Cooperation 2011/16/EU ('EU DAC'), a charity, or other not-for-profit association, may fall within the definition of an investment entity where it is managed by a financial institution and more than 50% of its income comes from investing in financial assets (see **6.6**).

- Throughout this Chapter, where reference is made either to 'CRS/ EU DAC' or 'CRS as applied by EU DAC', this is in relation to the CRS rules as they apply to the UK through the EU/EU DAC. See **Chapter 2** regarding the impact of Brexit on this.

BANKS AND OTHER FINANCIAL SERVICES PROVIDERS

6.1

Focus

It might initially seem obvious that many banks and other financial services providers will probably be within the scope of FATCA and CRS. However, each entity will need to consider carefully whether and how it is affected.

Many entities, such as many banks and other financial services providers, that might commonly be thought of as a 'financial institution', may be both a financial institution and in particular an RFI as those terms are defined for the purposes of FATCA and CRS. However, some such entities may not.

In broad terms, FATCA/CRS (as applied by EU DAC) require 'financial institutions' to carry out due diligence and to report information to the authorities about the holders of their 'financial accounts'. The potential for banks and other financial services providers to fall within the definition of 'financial institution', and therefore of 'reporting financial institution' for these purposes is obvious – although not a given in view of various exceptions that can apply. See the rest of this book generally for further details.

Certain entities that are part of the world of finance may not be RFIs as that term is defined for the purposes of FATCA/CRS. See, for example, **6.2** regarding CISs, of which some are, and some are not RFIs, under FATCA/CRS.

In broad terms, EU Directive 2018/822/EU amending EU DAC ('EU DAC 6') is similar except that the requirement to carry out due diligence and to report information falls either on 'intermediaries' or 'taxpayers', instead of on financial institutions. See those parts of this publication (ie **Chapter 13** onwards) that deal with EU DAC 6 for further details.

Moreover, a 'bank' or a 'financial services provider' can cover an extremely wide range of commercial entities, providing a correspondingly wide range of services. Accordingly, members of such entities may wish to look carefully at **6.3** dealing with professional firms and business services providers too. Readers will find much there that could also be relevant to certain business streams of a bank or a firm of financial services providers.

As regards a bank or financial services provider that operates a trust company, see **6.3**.

COLLECTIVE INVESTMENT VEHICLES

6.2

Focus

Certain collective investment vehicles ('CIVs') are non-reporting financial institutions ('NRFIs') for FATCA and CRS purposes.

The definitions vary as between FATCA/CRS (as applied by EU DAC). Investment entities will therefore need to consider each of these regimes separately in order to decide whether they fall within the definitions for each, or not.

Under the FATCA agreement, the CIV must be regulated as such under UK law. If all of the interests in the CIV are held by or through one or more financial institutions (see HMRC's International Exchange of Information Manual IEIM400600) that are not NRFIs (see HMRC's International Exchange of Information Manual IEIM402360) then the CIV will be an NRFI.

The term used in HMRC Manuals for treating a CIV as an NRFI under CRS is an exempt collective investment vehicle. The CIV must be an investment entity that is regulated in the UK as a CIV. It will then qualify to be a NRFI if all the interests in the CIV are held by or through individuals or entities that are not reportable persons except where that person is a passive non-financial entity ('NFE') (see **11.15**) with controlling persons (see **9.10**) who are reportable persons. See **9.8** and **9.9** and HMRC's International Exchange of Information Manual IEIM402010 regarding the meaning of 'reportable person'.

Under CRS there are special rules if a CIV has issued shares in bearer form such that the beneficial owners of the shares cannot be identified. These are set out in and HMRC's International Exchange of Information Manual IEIM400980.

PROFESSIONAL FIRMS AND BUSINESS SERVICES PROVIDERS (INCLUDING SOLICITORS AND ACCOUNTANTS)

6.3

Focus

The definition of financial institution under FATCA/CRS (as applied by EU DAC) is broad and could therefore include some legal and accountancy firms and other business services providers, as well as some of their clients. See **4.7**.

The most likely routes by which a professional firm will fall within the FATCA/CRS definitions of a financial institution are either if it is an investment entity or if it is a custodial institution. See below.

As regards FATCA/CRS (as applied by EU DAC) there are two major issues for solicitors, accountants and other firms of professional advisers:

(1)   Assessing whether the firm (or any part of the firm) constitutes a financial institution under FATCA/CRS (as applied by EU DAC) – if so, the firm (or relevant part of the firm) must:

- conduct due diligence on new and existing clients and make reports to HMRC in relation to any qualifying US clients; and

- (if a financial institution under FATCA) register with the IRS.

(2)   Subject to the firm's terms of engagement with the particular clients, assessing whether any client entities fall within the definition of financial institution for FATCA/CRS (as applied by EU DAC).

A professional firm is most likely to be caught by the definition of financial institution if it owns a separate:

- trust company that acts as trustee for clients of the firm; or

- an investment management arm.

See **6.4** and **6.5** regarding trusts and trust companies.

If the firm or a part of the firm is a financial institution, it must:

(1)   appoint a 'responsible officer';

(2)   carry out suitable due diligence in accordance with the rules of FATCA/CRS;

(3)   (if the firm is a financial institution under FATCA) register with the IRS in the US;

(4)   report as necessary to HMRC.

If no part of the firm meets the definition of a financial institution for any of FATCA/CRS, the firm will not have to:

- register with the IRS in the US;

- report on clients to HMRC under FATCA/CRS.

However, the firm should consider whether any of its clients fall within the definition of a financial institution and, subject to the firm's terms of engagement with those clients, provide advice and assistance to those clients accordingly.

EU DAC 6 is also a potential issue for professional firms. In the case of solicitors, accountants or other firms of professional advisers, the firm could be an intermediary. See **14.3** to **14.5** regarding the definition of an intermediary for these purposes.

Example 6.1 – Corporate trustee of a family trust

A firm of solicitors has a trust department.

A corporate trustee acts as a trustee for one of the law firm's trust clients. The corporate trustee has done this ever since the firm came into existence, on 1 January 2016.

All of the trust's income derives from investing, reinvesting or trading in financial assets.

The corporate trustee does not itself charge fees. However, the law firm has charged the following fees for the corporate trustee's services of managing assets.

Calendar year	Fee (excluding VAT)
2016	£3,000
2017	£3,050
2018	£3,100
2019	£3,150

Even though the corporate trustee does not charge fees, it is an investment entity and therefore a financial institution for the purposes of Automatic Exchange of Information ('AEOI').

The trust is therefore also a financial institution because it is managed by a financial institution.

For FATCA, an investment entity is an entity that conducts as a business (or is managed by an entity that conducts as a business) one or more of the activities listed in **4.9**. The test is met in this case.

In order to be an investment entity for CRS (as applied by EU DAC), at least 50% of the corporate trustee's income must derive from investment

---

activities (see **4.15**). For the purposes of applying this test, in effect the law firm's fees for the services of the corporate trustee are attributed to the corporate trustee.

The 'at least 50%' test must be applied to the shorter of:

(i)   the three-year period ending on 31 December of the year preceding the year in which the determination is made; or

(ii)   the period during which the entity (ie the corporate trustee) has been in existence.

The 'at least 50%' test is therefore met for calendar year 2019, because at least 50% of income attributed to the corporate trustee for 2016, 2017 and 2018 derived from investment activities.

The 'at least 50%' test is also met for calendar years 2016, 2017 and 2018 because for those years it was necessary to examine the period during which the corporate trustee had been in existence.

Example 6.2 – nominee company

Derek and Simon are two chartered accountants, who practise through a limited liability partnership ('LLP').

They are also directors of a company which they set up to act as nominee for certain of their clients in relation to residential properties that they own.

The nominee company does not itself charge fees. However, the LLP has charged the following fees to its clients for the nominee company's services.

Calendar year	Fee (excluding VAT)
2016	£1,110
2017	£1,500
2018	£940
2019	£1,300

In order to be a custodial institution for FATCA/CRS (as applied by EU DAC), at least 20% of the nominee company's gross income needs to be attributable to holding financial assets and providing related financial services in the shorter of:

•   its last three accounting periods; or

•   the period since it commenced business.

In this case, the nominee company is *not* a custodial institution, so is not a financial institution, because it holds residential property on behalf of the LLP's clients, *not* financial assets.

See HMRC's International Exchange of Information Manual IEIM400650.

See also the meaning of 'custodial institution' in **4.6** (for FATCA) and **4.7** (for CRS/EU DAC).

Focus

The actions a firm of professional advisers should now consider taking include:

- ensuring fee earners and other key personnel are aware of the FATCA/CRS rules (and potential penalties and other costs of non-compliance – see **Chapter 8**);

- circulating EU DAC 6 hallmarks to key personnel for them to identify cases of theirs that could be reportable (again ensuring that they are aware of the rules and also the penalties and other costs of non-compliance – see **Chapter 13**);

- reviewing new client take-on procedures to ensure that where possible FATCA/CRS (also EU DAC 6) issues are identified at that stage;

- reviewing standard engagement letters to ensure FATCA/CRS (as well as EU DAC 6) is appropriately catered for;

- considering whether particular business streams or departments are at particular risk and whether specific training and guidance should be provided.

TRUSTS

6.4

Focus

See **4.1** to **4.3** regarding the possibility that a trust or its trustees may need to 'categorise' in reply to a form from their bank or other financial institution with whom they have a financial account.

Most family trusts are not classed as a 'financial institution' for FATCA/CRS purposes. However, the definition of 'financial institution' under

> FATCA/CRS is very broad and some trusts will be categorised as a 'financial institution'. Where this is the case, the trust may itself be under an obligation to make reports to HMRC.
>
> Whether a trust has reporting obligations under FATCA/CRS (including EU DAC 6) will depend on how it sits within the criteria described elsewhere in this book. The same applies to the parties to that trust – such as say its trustees.
>
> The most likely route by which a family trust will be an RFI for FATCA/CRS purposes, is therefore where the trust is managed by a trust company. This is likely to include situations where a trust company is a trustee of the trust. Solicitors, accountants and other firms of professional advisers may often operate a trust company for their clients (see **6.3**). Banks and financial services providers may also operate a trust company for their customers and clients (see **6.8**).

Therefore, in relation to FATCA/CRS and EU DAC (except for EU DAC 6), see key definitions such as 'reporting financial institution' discussed at **4.9** and 'UK representative' at **4.13**. See also the International Tax Compliance Regulations 2015, SI 2015/878, reg 24 regarding the application of those definitions in the UK's main FATCA/CRS regulations.

In relation to EU DAC 6, see also the discussion of the terms 'UK intermediary' and 'UK relevant taxpayer' at **14.3** to **14.5**. See also the International Tax Enforcement (Disclosable Arrangements) Regulations 2020, SI 2020/25 (also known as the 'DAC 6 Regulations'), reg 2 regarding the application of those definitions.

In general, in order for a trust to have reporting obligations under FATCA/CRS and/or EU DAC (except for EU DAC 6), it will probably need to fall within the definitions of 'financial institution' for the purposes of each of those FATCA/CRS regimes. See **1.2** regarding the term 'financial institution' under FATCA, and see **4.15** regarding the definition of that term under CRS and EU DAC.

If the trust is to be a financial institution for FATCA/CRS purposes, it will probably need to fall within the definition of 'investment entity' – again see **1.2** regarding FATCA and **4.15** regarding CRS and EU DAC. However, see below regarding the possibility that a trust may meet the requirements for being a custodial institution.

See **12.5** to **12.8** regarding the possible impact on what needs to be reported under FATCA/CRS if an entity either is or is not a custodial institution with financial accounts that are custodial accounts.

For the purposes of FATCA/CRS and EU DAC, 'investment entity' means any entity that conducts as a business (or is managed by an entity that conducts as a business) certain specified activities or operations for or on behalf of a customer.

It seems arguable that in most cases a trust will not be conducting a 'business'. It is plausible that in most cases a trust will not have 'customers'. Note, however, that for CRS and EU DAC, a financial institution also includes certain kinds of active NFE.

The most likely route by which a family trust will be an RFI for FATCA/CRS purposes, is therefore where the trust is managed by a trust company. This is likely to include situations where a trust company is a trustee of the trust. Solicitors, accountants and other firms of professional advisers may often operate a trust company for their clients (see **6.3**). Banks and financial services providers may also operate a trust company for their customers and clients (see **6.8**).

Note, however, that in those circumstances, the trust may often prove to be a 'trustee documented trust' – which is to say, a trust that is a financial institution where the trustee of the trust is itself an RFI and reports all the information required in respect of the reportable accounts of the trust.

In those circumstances, such a trustee documented trust is an NRFI, because the information which it would otherwise have needed to report, must instead be reported by the RFI that is its trustee.

When registering a trustee documented trust on the HMRC portal, the trustee is the RFI, not the trust. See HMRC's International Exchange of Information Manual IEIM400990.

For FATCA reporting in the case of a trustee documented trust, the global intermediary identification number used will be that of the trustee, acting in its capacity as trustee.

HMRC say that where a trust meets one of the definitions for being a financial institution (see HMRC's International Exchange of Information Manual IEIM400600), it is most likely to be an investment entity but that it may, alternatively, meet the requirements for being a custodial institution. HMRC cite the example of an employee benefit trust ('EBT') which continues to hold financial assets, such as shares, for an employee after they have been granted – in that situation, the EBT may be a custodial institution.

See above comments about the possible impact on what needs to be reported under FATCA/CRS if an entity either is or is not a custodial institution.

However, HMRC also cite other circumstances where an EBT would not be a custodial institution. See HMRC's International Exchange of Information Manual IEIM400700.

6.5

Focus

A trust that is an RFI must identify and report on its financial account holders. In the case of a trust, financial accounts are defined by FATCA/CRS and EU DAC as 'a debt or equity interest' in the trust.

> Debt interest is not defined in CRS, EU DAC or FATCA, so what is considered a debt interest will be determined under the local law of the implementing jurisdiction, for example, the UK.
>
> For CRS, EU DAC and also for FATCA, the equity interests in a trust are deemed to be held by any person treated as a settlor or beneficiary of all or a portion of the trust, or any other natural person exercising ultimate effective control over the trust (this will include the trustee as an equity interest holder).
>
> See below regarding differences between trusts that are an RFI and trusts that are a passive NFE.

In the case of a trust, controlling person means for the purposes of CRS and EU DAC the settlor, the trustees, the protector (if any), the beneficiaries or class of beneficiaries, and any other natural person exercising ultimate effective control over the trust, and in the case of a legal arrangement other than a trust, such term means persons in equivalent or similar positions.'

The OECD commentary on CRS deems the settlor, the trustee, the protectors (if any) and the beneficiaries to be controlling persons, regardless of whether they actually control the trust as a controlling person.

As a result, discretionary beneficiaries of a trust that is a passive NFE, who have not yet received any distributions from the trust or the foundation, are controlling persons so must be reported under CRS and EU DAC by an RFI that has an obligation to report.

However, STEP have said in relation to this: 'In order to make the reporting of discretionary beneficiaries sensible and manageable, it would seem sensible that a discretionary beneficiary should only be treated as a controlling person where the discretionary beneficiary concerned is eligible to receive a distribution in the year concerned.' See, for example, STEP Guidance Note, 'CRS and trusts' by John Riches TEP, Chair, STEP Public Policy Committee, 8 March 2017 at 4.2.

By contrast trusts/foundations which qualify as an investment entity (and therefore themselves qualify as an RFI) only need to report discretionary beneficiaries for the purposes of CRS and EU DAC (except for EU DAC 6) in the years when the beneficiary actually receives distributions. In this situation a discretionary beneficiary who has not yet received an actual distribution is not yet a reportable person for the purposes of CRS and EU DAC.

For the purposes of CRS and EU DAC (but not FATCA), a trust is not itself required to report to the extent that the trustee of the trust is an RFI and reports all information required to be reported pursuant to FATCA/CRS with respect to all reportable accounts of the trust.

It would seem to follow that in this latter situation too, for the purposes of CRS and EU DAC (but not FATCA) a discretionary beneficiary who had not yet received an actual distribution would not need to be reported by the trustee because that beneficiary would not have been a reportable person if the trust itself had had the obligation to report.

However, the same STEP Guidance Note, referred to above, says at 4.1: 'if discretionary beneficiary receives a distribution in a particular year but not in subsequent years, the absence of a distribution should not be treated in effect as an account closure "as long as the beneficiary is not permanently excluded from receiving future distributions from the trust"'.

On the face of things, this could, for example, mean that the discretionary beneficiary would have to be reported as an account holder, unless an election were made each year to exclude the account from reporting on the basis that it is a dormant account.

See the OECD Commentary on Section VIII of CRS, margin nos. 69 and 70. See EU DAC, Annex I, Section VIII. See also the FATCA agreement.

See **Example 4.1** in relation to a trust managed by a corporate trustee.

Example 6.3 – Individual trustee of a family trust

Jeremy manages the assets of a family trust.

All of the trust's income derives from investing, reinvesting or trading in financial assets.

The trust deed provides for Jeremy to be paid a small amount each year, for his time and efforts in relation to managing the trust. In recent years Jeremy has been paid by the trust, as follows.

Calendar year	Fee (excluding VAT)
2016	£450
2017	£480
2018	£510
2019	£540

Jeremy is not a financial institution because, as an individual, he cannot be a financial institution.

The trust itself is an investment entity as it is not primarily conducting as a business one or more of the relevant activities or operations for or on behalf of a customer, and although its gross income is primarily attributable to investing, reinvesting, or trading in financial assets, it is not an entity that is managed by a financial institution. Accordingly, the trust is not itself a financial institution.

CHARITIES

6.6

Focus

HMRC have undertaken to 'support' and to 'work with' charities in relation to their FATCA/CRS obligations. However, they also warn: 'we will not rule out the imposition of penalties where charities have failed to engage with the requirements.' See HMRC's International Exchange of Information Manual IEIM404980.

See also **6.9** regarding FATCA/CRS reporting by charities.

Under the FATCA agreement with the US all charities are excluded from reporting under the exemption for non-profit organisations. See HMRC's International Exchange of Information Manual IEIM400790.

However, for CRS and EU DAC, a charity, or other not-for-profit association, may fall within the definition of an investment entity where it is managed by a financial institution and more than 50% of its income comes from investing in financial assets. See **4.9** regarding the meaning of 'investment entity' under FATCA and **4.15** regarding its meaning under CRS and EU DAC.

An entity is not regarded as managed by a financial institution if that financial institution does not have discretionary authority to manage the entity's assets either in whole or in part.

An entity may be managed by a mix of other entities and individuals. If one of the entities involved in the management of the entity is a financial institution within the meaning of the agreements, then the entity meets the requirements for being managed by a financial institution.

See also **4.1** regarding the possibility that an entity may need to 'categorise' in reply to a form from their bank or other financial institution with whom they have a financial account.

Most charities are not classed as a 'financial institution' for FATCA/CRS purposes. However, the definition of 'financial institution' under FATCA/CRS is very broad and some charities – particularly endowed charities and those that receive a large proportion of their income from investments – will be categorised as a 'financial institution'. Where this is the case, the charity may itself be under an obligation to make reports to HMRC.

Whether a charity has reporting obligations under FATCA/CRS (including EU DAC 6) will depend on how it sits within the criteria described elsewhere in this book.

Therefore, in relation to FATCA/CRS/EU DAC, see key definitions such as 'reporting financial institution' discussed at **4.9** and 'UK representative' at **4.12**. See also the International Tax Compliance Regulations 2015, SI 2015/878, reg 24 regarding the application of those definitions in the UK's main FATCA/CRS regulations.

In general, a charity may be regarded as an investment entity (a type of financial institution) if it is managed by a financial institution and its gross income is primarily attributable to investing, reinvesting, or trading in financial assets.

A charity must meet both of these criteria to be deemed a financial institution.

In relation to EU DAC 6, see also the discussion of the terms 'UK intermediary' and 'UK relevant taxpayer' at **14.3** to **14.5**. See also the DAC 6 Regulations, reg 2 regarding the application of those definitions.

In the case of a charitable trust, see also **6.3** regarding FATCA/CRS and trusts.

Under the FATCA agreement (but not under either CRS or EU DAC) the following non-profit organisations are classified as a 'non-reporting UK financial institution'. Hence the following entities do not need to report under FATCA:

- any entity registered as a charity with the Charity Commission of England and Wales;

- any entity registered with HMRC for charitable tax purposes;

- any entity registered as a charity with the Office of the Scottish Charity Regulator;

- any community amateur sports club ('CASC') if registered as such with HMRC.

See **4.14**. See Agreement between the Government of the UK and the Government of the US to improve international tax compliance and to implement FATCA (the 'FATCA agreement'), Annex II.

This is one of the key areas in which FATCA and the CRS differ: the rules implementing FATCA in the UK contain an exemption meaning that UK charities do not have reporting requirements under FATCA. However, the CRS does not contain such an exemption; all charities who fall into the 'financial institution' category should consider whether they are required to make reports.

In practice, all UK charities that are not financial institutions and that are registered with one of the UK charities commissions or registered with HMRC as a charity and all non-charitable CASCs registered with HMRC, will be within the definition of an active NFE and so will not be required to identify controlling persons.

Focus

A charitable trust will be a trust for the purposes of the FATCA/CRS regimes.

A charitable company or charitable incorporated organisation that holds property in trust (eg as permanent endowment) separately from its corporate assets may therefore have a reporting obligation in respect of the assets held in trust that is separate from its reporting obligation in respect of its corporate assets.

A settlor of a trust has an equity interest in the trust for FATCA/CRS purposes. In most cases a donor to a charity is not treated as a settlor. Conditional donations, where the donor specifies the use of the donation, may result in the donor being treated as a settlor.

For charitable trusts most equity interests will be the grants made to beneficiaries. See also **4.15** regarding 'indirect beneficiaries'.

Loans made to a charity or other debts are likely to be financial accounts for FATCA/CRS. However, debts owed by a charity to trade creditors that do not relate to the lending of money are not included. See HMRC's International Exchange of Information Manual IEIM404750.

Charities that are set up as unincorporated associations may also be financial institutions. See HMRC's International Exchange of Information Manual IEIM404770.

A charity may obtain a self-certification from the account holder to establish its status, or instead may use:

- Information in its possession; or
- Information that is publicly available (such as information published by an authorised government body or standardised industry coding system) based upon which it can reasonably determine that the account holder is an active NFE or a financial institution.

For charities that are account holders a financial institution may use the public registers maintained by the Charities Commission for England and Wales, the Charities Commission for Northern Ireland and the Office of the Scottish Charity Register to establish that a charity is an active NFE.

See HMRC's International Exchange of Information Manual IEIM404700 onwards.

6.7

Example 6.4 – charity with a little investment income

Most of one particular charity's income is from public donations. However, it has some investments, and the income from these is around 2% of its overall income.

The charity is not a financial institution and has no FATCA/CRS reporting obligations because less than half of its income is derived from investing in financial assets.

If asked to self-certify its status (eg by a bank, say), the charity should indicate that it is an active NFE.

Example 6.5 – charity with significant investment income

Most of a second charity's income is from a mix of public donations and investing in financial assets. The financial assets are managed by a financial institution. Income from the financial assets makes up more than half of the charity's overall income.

If asked to self-certify its status (eg by a bank, say), the charity should indicate that it is a financial institution.

Example 6.6 – charity with a specific investment strategy

A third charity has more than 50% gross income from investing in financial assets. The charity has an investment strategy, in accordance with which, its financial assets are invested externally by a financial institution.

The external financial institution, however, decides on a day-to-day basis which particular stocks and industries to invest into.

Despite the investment strategy, the financial institution has the discretion over investment decisions within those parameters. Hence, the charity is a financial institution as its financial assets are managed by a financial institution.

Example 6.7 – charity which retains discretion over its investments

A fourth charity also has more than 50% gross income from investing in financial assets.

The charity makes the decisions on which shares or unit trusts to invest into, albeit the charity takes advice from a financial adviser to help in making decisions.

The charity is not a financial institution. It has not given discretionary management of its financial assets to a financial institution.

> **Example 6.8 – charity with common deposit and common investment funds**
>
> Yet another charity receives all of its income from a mix of investing in a common deposit fund and investing in a common investment fund.
>
> HMRC consider that investments in a common deposit funds are akin to cash deposits and the income from these is not from investing in financial assets.
>
> HMRC also consider that investments in common investment funds are similar to shares in a unit trust, investing in a common investment fund is akin to buying shares in a company, it does not lead to passing discretionary management of funds to a manager.
>
> The charity is not a financial institution. It has not given to a financial institution, discretionary management of financial assets from which it derives more than 50% of its income.

See also the examples in HMRC's International Exchange of Information Manual IEIM404725.

6.8   HMRC say whether the income from social investments or other assets held by a charity is income from financial assets, will be determined by the legal form of the investment.

If the investment takes the form of a loan or a shareholding it will generally be treated as a financial asset and any income derived from the investment will be income from financial assets.

Interest received on a cash deposit is not income from a financial asset.

Where a charity has a trading subsidiary which pays up profits to the charity under gift aid, HMRC consider that this element of the charity's income is not income from financial assets.

Where a charity receives rental income from a property, if that property is held directly by the charity the income is not from financial assets.

Where the real property is held via a subsidiary entity, then the situation will be as above for distributions from trading entities.

Sometimes a charity may make a grant to one organisation or an individual that are for the benefit of another organisation or individual. That other organisation or individual is an 'indirect beneficiary'.

In relation to FATCA/CRS in these situations, the charity should consider the facts of the particular grant in question when deciding whom it should report as the account holder. The charity should also record the steps it took to reach that decision.

Example 6.9 – charitable funding of university research

A charity makes a grant to a university to fund the work of individuals engaged by the grantee to carry out research. The university is the beneficiary of the grant, and so the account holder for FATCA/CRS purposes.

However, in this case, the individuals who are to carry out the research then move to another organisation taking the research with them, and the grant follows. The second organisation is now the account holder.

The charity made another award to another individual carrying out research, and she had the discretion over its use. In that situation, that individual is the account holder.

Example 6.10 – priest administering charitable grants

A charity provides a grant to provide assistance to needy individuals, which is to be administered by a local priest. The priest has no discretion over how the grant monies are used. The needy individuals are therefore the account holders.

A second charity provides a second grant to the same priest, for a similar purpose. However, with this grant, the priest has discretion over which individuals benefit and how. With this grant, the priest is therefore the account holder.

See HMRC's International Exchange of Information Manual IEIM404730 and IEIM404755.

See also **6.9** regarding FATCA/CRS reporting by charities.

Reporting by charities

6.9

Focus

Where two or more charities are treated by their regulator as a single charity for registration and reporting purposes, each charity retains its identity as a separate entity for CRS purposes. However, it is possible for the charities to appoint one of their number as a service provider to file a single report covering all the linked charities. See International Exchange of Information Manual IEIM402600 and IEIM404960.

See also **6.6** regarding charities in relation to FATCA/CRS generally.

Chapter 7

FATCA/CRS – Advising, assisting, looking after and dealing with clients

---

SIGNPOSTS

- Many organisations will wish to review the impact of Automatic Exchange of Information ('AEOI') and other issues that are dealt with in this book, as regards the impact on their clients (see this Chapter as a whole).

- The UK's FATCA/CRS Regulations specify that certain kinds of 'financial institution', as well as other persons, must notify clients and others in certain circumstances (see **7.1** to **7.8**).

- In particular, reporting financial institutions ('RFIs') must notify individual reportable persons that information is to be reported about them. This follows the first year in which the individual's account is a reportable account (see **7.1** and **7.2**).

- Secondly, certain kinds of organisation, likely to include financial institutions and professional advisers, had an obligation to certain information in relation to 'specified clients' by no later than 31 August 2017 (see **7.3** to **7.5**).

- Specifically, that obligation fell on 'specified financial institutions' and specified relevant persons (see **7.6** to **7.8**).

- Many organisations will also need to review their terms of engagement with their clients or customers. Organisations may also decide to provide staff with additional training in relation to AEOI issues, where that is needed (see **7.9** and **7.10**).

- Many organisations will need to review their client on-boarding procedures to ensure that these enable them, as RFIs, to carry out their due diligence and reporting obligations under FATCA and/ or CRS (see **7.11**).

- To ensure good 'client care' is achieved, many organisations will wish to review whether and how to provide clients with enough information about what they are doing (see **7.12**).

- It also critically important for client-facing organisations (and their staff) to be aware that providing clients with the wrong kind of help in relation to AEOI can have severe consequences. In exceptional cases it can even lead to a criminal conviction (see **7.13**).

STATUTORY CLIENT NOTIFICATION LETTERS

7.1

Focus

The UK's FATCA/CRS Regulations, namely the International Tax Compliance Regulations 2015, SI 2015/878, include a requirement in reg 10 that RFIs must notify individual reportable persons that information is to be reported in relation to them. This must follow the first year in which the account held by the individual is a reportable account (see **7.2**).

In addition, there were more detailed requirements for specified financial institutions and specified reportable persons in relation to the year ended 30 September 2016. See the International Tax Compliance Regulations 2015, reg 12D (see **7.3**).

Notification following the first year of a reportable account

7.2   An RFI must notify each reportable person that information relating to that person will be reported to HMRC and may be transferred to the government of another territory in accordance with a relevant agreement.

The RFI must make the notification by 31 January in the calendar year following the first year in which the account held by the individual is a reportable account.

See the International Tax Compliance Regulations 2015, reg 10.

Notification in respect of the year ended 30 September 2016

7.3   On 30 September 2016, the International Tax Compliance (Client Notification) Regulations 2016, SI 2016/899 came into force. These Regulations inserted regs 12A to 12F into the International Tax Compliance Regulations 2015, which required certain financial institutions and professional advisers to contact their UK tax resident clients who had overseas income and assets, to:

- notify them about information HMRC would be receiving about offshore accounts, structures, trusts and investments under automatic exchange of financial information agreements with overseas jurisdictions;

- remind them of their tax obligations;

- highlight how they could make a disclosure; and

- warn them about the increasing penalties and possible criminal prosecution if they failed to declare offshore assets.

These requirements were to be met by financial institutions/professional advisers.

Those affected

7.4 The 2015 Regulations applied to 'specified financial institutions' and 'specified relevant persons' (see reg 12D). See **7.6** to **7.7**.

Note that tax agents and advisers, solicitors and financial advisers could all be classed as specified relevant persons. See SI 2015/878, regs 12A(2), (4), (5).

If a person was both a specified financial institution and a specified relevant person, it was the rules for specified financial institutions that applied (see SI 2015/878, reg 12A(6)).

The notification letters had to be sent to relevant clients on or before 31 August 2017.

The Regulations also included a one-off non-compliance penalty.

If a person failed to identify and send the notification letter to relevant clients, the Regulations provided that a one-off penalty of £3,000 could be charged. Any penalty must be assessed within 12 months of the date on which the failure first came to the attention of an HMRC officer or, in any event, within six years.

Specified clients

7.5 Under the rules in regs 12A to 12F, 'specified financial institutions' ('SFI') and 'specified relevant persons' ('SRP') needed to identify and send a notification to their specified clients by no later than 31 August 2017.

The definition of 'specified client' was different depending on whether the organisation or person was an SFI or an SRP. It was also different depending on which 'approach' that SFI or SRP chose to adopt.

All of these definitions of 'specified client' had the following in common.

- the SFI or SRP reasonably believed that the individual was resident in the UK for income tax purposes for the tax year 2015–16 or would be so resident for the tax year 2016–17; and

- the individual is an account holder with the SFI or client of the SRP on 30 September 2016.

See the International Tax Compliance Regulations 2015, reg 12A.

See **7.6** regarding specified financial institutions and **7.7** regarding specified relevant persons.

Specified financial institutions

7.6   A person was a specified financial institution ('SFI') if it was a financial institution under the EU Directive on Administrative Cooperation 2011/16/EU ('EU DAC') or CRS, unless the financial institution was:

(a)   a non-RFI under EU DAC or CRS; or

(b)   a financial institution that, if it was a non-financial entity ('NFE'), would be an active NFE under EU DAC or CRS.

See the International Tax Compliance Regulations 2015, reg 12A.

Specified relevant persons

7.7   A person was a specified relevant person ('SRP') if:

(1)   it was a relevant person under the Finance (No 2) Act 2015, s 50(5), that is a tax adviser (as defined in the Finance Act 2014, s 272(5)) or any other person who in the course of business provided advice to another person about that person's financial or legal affairs, or provided other financial or legal services to another person; and

(2)   in the year to 30 September 2016, the person:

    (a)   provided 'offshore advice or services' (see below), in the course of business, which was not solely the preparation and delivery of the client's tax return as required under the Taxes Management Act 1970, s 8; or

    (b)   referred an individual to a connected person, for example, a subsidiary, outside the UK for the provision of advice or services related to the individual's personal tax affairs.

'Offshore advice or services' means advice or services relating to, in general terms, offshore sources of self-employment, employment, savings and investment income, together with assets and income within the charge to capital gains tax. Specifically, this is any of the following that are situated in, or arise from, the US, or a participating jurisdiction, having agreed to adopt CRS, and is one of the signatories that is listed in Sch 1 to the International Tax Compliance Regulations 2015:

- a financial account;

- a source of relevant foreign income;

- a source of employment income; or

- an asset.

The above are further defined in the Regulations (see **7.8**) .

There are two main exceptions to SRP status:

(1)   if the offshore advice and services (or referral) are only provided to the person's own employees and officers (including the partners of a partnership), or to those of a connected person, the person is not an SRP;

(2)   offshore advice or services are excluded if those services only comprised completing and submitting a tax return. So, an agent who did not provide any advice will not have been an SRP and will not have needed to make any notifications.

See the International Tax Compliance Regulations 2015, reg 12A.

7.8   Key definitions for the purposes of reg 12A include the following. See **7.7**.

As regards 'financial account', reg 24 applies the definitions in the FATCA agreement, CRS and EU DAC, as applicable. See **Chapter 5** regarding FATCA, CRS and EU DAC definitions.

A 'source of relevant foreign income' is as defined by the Income Tax (Trading and Other Income) Act 2005, s 830, that is to say, it is income which arises from a source outside the UK, and is chargeable under any of the provisions specified in s 830(2) (or would be if it were not for either remittance basis or the relief in certain circumstances for unremittable foreign income).

A 'source of employment income' is as defined by the Income Tax (Earnings and Pensions) Act 2003, s 7(2) ('ITEPA 2003'), that is to say, earnings, any amount treated as earnings, or any amount which counts as employment income.

An 'asset' is as defined by the Taxation of Chargeable Gains Act 1992, s 21, that is to say, all forms of property, including:

(a)   options, debts and incorporeal property generally;

(b)   currency, with the exception (subject to express provision to the contrary) of sterling;

(c)   any form of property created by the person disposing of it, or otherwise coming to be owned without being acquired.

The terms 'connected' and 'control' are used several times in the Regulations and take their meaning from the Corporation Tax Act 2010, ss 1122 and 1124, respectively.

In relation to a body corporate ('company A'), 'control' means the power of a person ('P') to secure:

(a)   by means of the holding of shares or the possession of voting power in relation to that or any other body corporate; or

(b)   as a result of any powers conferred by the articles of association or other document regulating that or any other body corporate, that the affairs of company A are conducted in accordance with P's wishes.

In relation to a partnership, 'control' means the right to a share of more than half the assets, or of more than half the income, of the partnership.

See the International Tax Compliance Regulations 2015.

CLIENT TERMS OF ENGAGEMENT

7.9

Focus

All client-facing organisations which have concluded that they could be affected by AEOI and/or the other issues that are dealt with in this book – particularly those organisations that are or could be an RFI under FATCA or CRS – should review their engagement letters or other document setting out the terms of their client engagements.

An organisation's review of its engagement letters should include those of all existing clients, as well as any standard engagement for use when engaging with new clients.

For example, an organisation may well need to consider whether or not it wishes to provide advice and assistance to its clients in relation to FATCA and CRS, in what circumstances and upon what terms. It will then need to spell that out in its engagement letters.

STAFF TRAINING

7.10   All client-facing organisations which have concluded that they could be affected by AEOI and/or the other issues that are dealt with in this book – particularly those organisations that are or could be an RFI under FATCA or CRS – should consider whether some or all staff need to be provided with training about the issues.

CLIENT ON-BOARDING PROCEDURES

7.11   All client-facing organisations which have concluded that they could be affected by AEOI and/or the other issues that are dealt with in this book – particularly those organisations that are or could be an RFI under FATCA or CRS – should consider whether their client on-boarding procedures are fit for purpose.

In particular, they may need to consider whether they will be able to obtain the right information to enable them to fulfil any due diligence and/or obligations that they may have under AEOI (see **Chapter 9** (due diligence) and **Chapter 12** (reporting)).

CLIENT CARE

7.12   Each organisation will need to consider whether it has done enough to keep clients suitably informed of what it is doing in relation to AEOI, and why it is doing it.

This is notwithstanding **7.1** to **7.12**, but also subject to **7.13**.

A CAUTIONARY TALE

7.13   On the one hand, it will be important to provide advice and assistance to clients as regards AEOI and the other issues that are dealt with in this book, where contractually and/or ethically obliged to do so.

On the other hand, it is also important to recognise that the wrong kind or advice or assistance must always be avoided.

For an extreme example of problems arising from the provision of the wrong kind of advice or assistance to a client, see the criminal prosecution of Adrian Baron (see **8.4**).

See **Chapter 8** generally in relation to other consequences from failing to comply with the AEOI rules.

Chapter 8

FATCA/CRS – What might happen to us, if we didn't comply?

SIGNPOSTS

- In addition to the penalties and other consequences that are referred to in this Chapter, many organisations will wish to consider whether they would want to suffer the adverse publicity which could result, in certain circumstances, from failing to comply with FATCA and/or CRS.

- The consequences of non-compliance with FATCA can, in exceptional cases, be extremely severe. See, for example, the custodial sentence which a US court imposed on banker, Adrian Baron, for criminal infringement of the FATCA regime and the associated loss of their banking licence and winding up of the bank for which he worked (see **8.4**).

- In the case of FATCA only and not CRS, some financial institutions could suffer severe consequences for their business if they are classified by the US authorities as a non-participating financial institution, which could arise from significant non-compliance with FATCA. They could then be included in a list of such institutions, which the US Treasury can choose to publicise. Such an organisation may also have to apply withholding tax to payments to US residents and US citizens (see **8.5** and **8.6**).

- There could also be other consequences for those involved with non-compliance either with FATCA or with CRS, for example, members of professional bodies such as the Chartered Institute of Taxation are bound by ethical standards and could face sanctions from their professional body for failing to comply with FATCA and/or CRS.

- In relation to FATCA, but not CRS, the competent authority has a power to enquire in relation to administrative errors or other errors, which could conceivably mean the US authorities could contact a UK reporting financial institution with queries. In practice, it is more likely that a UK reporting financial institution in that situation would be contacted with the queries by HMRC (see **8.1**).

- HMRC have powers to enquire by notice, where they suspect non-compliance either with FATCA or with CRS. The notice can be directed either at financial institutions as defined for the purposes of FATCA/CRS or in certain circumstances at a UK representative (see **8.2**).

- The International Tax Compliance Regulations 2015 contain what is in effect a targeted-anti-avoidance rule at reg 23. This enables the tax authorities to look through arrangements with a main purpose of avoiding obligations under FATCA and/or CRS (see **8.3**).

- The International Tax Compliance Regulations 2015, SI 2015/878 include extensive provisions for penalties to be charged in cases of non-compliance. Generally, there is a basic penalty of either £300 or £3,000 for various failures including not making a return, reporting inaccurate information, notifying reportable persons that information is going to be reported, not complying with an HMRC information notice, etc.

- The amount of the monetary penalties can become considerably higher if the failure continues after the basic penalty has been notified, as HMRC may then ask the tribunal to begin to apply 'daily default penalties'. In some cases, these could be up to £1,000 per day (see **8.11**).

- Most of the monetary penalties do not apply if one can persuade HMRC that there is a reasonable excuse for the non-compliance. Reasonable excuse is a common concept in UK tax law, including in relation to penalties generally. HMRC guidance includes a good deal of information about when HMRC consider that there is or is not a reasonable excuse (see **8.10**).

- It is possible to appeal against the penalties if one believes that they ought not to apply (see **8.15**).

- See **Chapter 18** regarding penalties for non-compliance with EU Directive 2018/822/EU ('EU DAC 6'). See **19.2** regarding penalties for non-compliance with country-by-country reporting.

POWER OF THE TAX AUTHORITIES TO ENQUIRE

Competent authority inquiry regarding administrative or other errors

8.1

Focus

The FATCA agreement states that the competent authority of either the US or the UK can make an inquiry directly to a reporting financial institution ('RFI') in the other's jurisdiction where it has reason to believe that 'administrative errors or other minor errors' may have led to incorrect or incomplete information reporting or resulted in other infringements of FATCA.

However, in practice it is likely, instead, that the 'receiving competent authority' might notify the 'providing competent authority' indicating that it suspected minor or administrative errors had been made. The providing competent authority would probably then apply its domestic law in order to resolve matters.

In other words, it is possible that a UK RFI could be contacted directly by the US authorities with a query about the way in which it has been dealing with its obligations under FATCA. However, it is much more likely that any such query will come from HMRC, with the latter possibly having been prompted to enquire by a query or information that it had received from the US authorities.

See the Competent Authority Arrangement between the Competent Authorities of the United States of America and United Kingdom of Great Britain and Northern Ireland, para 4.3.1, available at https://www.irs.gov/pub/irs-utl/ United%20Kingdom%20M1A%20CAA%20082815b.pdf.

Examples of minor errors could include:

- data fields missing or incomplete;
- data that has been corrupted;
- use of an incompatible format.

See **8.5** for examples of what would be regarded as significant non-compliance.

See HMRC's International Exchange of Information Manual IEIM405010 onwards.

See also **8.5** to **8.6** regarding the possibility of action in relation to 'significant non-compliance'.

See the FATCA agreement, Art 5(1).

HMRC information powers

8.2

Focus

HMRC have powers that they can use in relation to concerns that they may have about the way in which a person has dealt with its obligations under FATCA and/or CRS.

> An HMRC officer may require an RFI, UK representative, specified financial institution or specified relevant person to provide such information or documents as the officer reasonably requires as specified by written notice.
>
> The purpose of this is 'In order [for the HMRC officer] to determine whether or not the obligations arising under [the International Tax Compliance] Regulations have been complied with'. See reg 12G(1) of the International Tax Compliance Regulations 2015.

The information or documents required by this written notice must be provided:

(a)   within such period, being no less than 14 days; and

(b)   by such means and in such form, as is reasonably required by the HMRC officer.

See **4.15** regarding the meaning of 'specified financial institution'. See **7.4** regarding the meaning of 'specified relevant person'. See **Chapter 4** regarding the meanings of 'UK representative' and of 'reporting financial institution'.

Monetary penalties can apply if the notice is not complied with (see **8.7** onwards).

See the International Tax Compliance Regulations 2015. See particularly reg 12G inserted by the International Tax Compliance (Amendment) Regulations, SI 2017/598, regs 2, 8 with effect from 17 May 2017.

Anti-avoidance

8.3

> **Focus**
>
> In effect, the International Tax Compliance Regulations 2015 contain a targeted anti-avoidance rule at reg 23, which states that:
>
> •   if an RFI, UK representative, specified financial institution or specified relevant person enters into any arrangements; and
>
> •   the main purpose, or one of the main purposes, of entering into which is to avoid any obligation under the UK's FATCA/CRS rules as set out in the International Tax Compliance Regulations, then,
>
> the Regulations are to have effect as if the arrangements had not been entered into.

See **4.12** on UK representative, **7.3** on specified financial institution and **7.7** on specified relevant person.

See the International Tax Compliance Regulations 2015, reg 23.

CRIMINAL SANCTIONS

Criminal proceedings in relation to FATCA

8.4

Focus

In certain circumstances, failing to comply with FATCA can have extremely serious consequences, both for an RFI itself, and for some of the individuals who work for it.

Adrian Baron, a citizen of the UK and Saint Vincent and the Grenadines, was found guilty and a custodial sentence was imposed on him by a US court for failing to comply with FATCA. He worked for a bank called Loyal Bank Ltd.

As regards Loyal Bank Ltd itself, the bank's banking licence was revoked and, within a few weeks of that happening, the bank entered liquidation.

Mr Baron was the CEO of Loyal Bank Ltd, an offshore bank with offices in Saint Vincent and the Grenadines and Budapest, Hungary. Following an FBI sting operation, he was eventually charged with facilitating the bank's clients' efforts to 'impede, impair, obstruct and defeat the lawful governmental functions of the IRS in the ascertainment, computation, assessment and collection of revenue, specifically, failing to comply with FATCA'.

Regarding the case of *USA v Adrian Baron*, see, for example, US Department of Justice US Attorney's Office Eastern District of New York press release, 'First Ever Conviction for Failing to Comply with Foreign Account Tax Compliance Act (FATCA)', published on 11 September 2018, available at https://www.justice.gov/usao-edny/pr/former-executive-loyal-bank-ltd-pleads-guilty-conspiring-defraud-united-states-failing.

Regarding the impact on Loyal Bank Ltd, see, for example, a 15 November 2018 list of 'Frequently Asked Questions' issued by the joint liquidators, who are two partners in Deloitte & Touche in Barbados, available from the bank's website at https://www.loyalbank.com/.

CLASSIFICATION AS A NON-PARTICIPATING FINANCIAL INSTITUTION

Significant non-compliance

8.5

Focus

An entity that is non-compliant with FATCA may find itself classified as a non-participating financial institution, which is a concept that

89

exists in FATCA, but not in CRS or the EU Directive on Administrative Cooperation 2011/16/EU ('EU DAC').

For this to happen, there needs to be significant non-compliance.

The US tax authorities, 'the IRS', must make available a list of all reporting UK financial institutions and other partner jurisdiction financial institutions that are treated as non-participating financial institutions under this provision.

This is one of the potential consequences for a UK financial institution which the IRS deems to be guilty of significant non-compliance in relation to FATCA.

Another possible consequence is that under the FATCA agreement, 'a reporting United Kingdom financial institution … shall not be subject to withholding under section 1471 of the U.S. Internal Revenue Code *unless* such reporting United Kingdom financial institution is identified by the IRS as a Nonparticipating Financial Institution' (emphasis added) under the above provision.

Hence the IRS may presumably require the financial institution in question to withhold US tax from payments made to US residents and US citizens.

The FATCA agreement states that if the competent authority of either the US or the UK has determined that there is significant non-compliance with FATCA with respect to an RFI in the other's jurisdiction, it shall then notify the competent authority of the other party of this (ie the competent authority of the UK shall notify that of the US or vice versa). The notified competent authority shall then apply its domestic law to the issue.

However, if, in the case of a UK RFI, that does not resolve the non-compliance within a period of 18 months after notification of significant non-compliance is first provided, the US shall treat the reporting UK financial institution as a non-participating financial institution.

The following are examples of what would be regarded as significant non-compliance:

- repeated failure to file a return or repeated late filing;

- ongoing or repeated failure to register, supply accurate information or establish appropriate governance or due diligence processes;

- the intentional provision of substantially incorrect information;

- the deliberate or negligent omission of required information.

See **8.1** for examples of what would be regarded as minor errors.

See **12.10** regarding RFI reporting obligations in respect of payments to non-participating financial institutions.

See the FATCA agreement, Arts 4(1) and 5(2). See also HMRC's International Exchange of Information Manual IEIM401300 and IEIM405010 onwards.

Related entities that are non-participating financial institutions

8.6   It appears that a UK financial institution may risk being deemed non-compliant with FATCA if it has a related entity or branch operating in a jurisdiction where compliance with FATCA is prevented.

However, this will not be so provided where:

- the UK financial institution meets its obligations under FATCA in relation to each such related entity or branch;

- each such related entity or branch identifies itself to withholding agents as a non-participating financial institution;

- each such related entity or branch identifies its US accounts and reports the information with respect to those accounts as required under s 1471 of the US Internal Revenue Code to the extent permitted under the relevant laws pertaining to the related entity or branch; and

- each related entity or branch does not specifically solicit US accounts or accounts held by non-participating financial institutions, and the related entity or branch is not used by the UK financial institution to circumvent obligations under FATCA or the US tax code.

See **8.5** regarding significant non-compliance. See **11.3** and **11.4** regarding the meaning of 'entity' and 'related entity' under FATCA.

See the FATCA agreement, Arts 1(hh), (kk) and 4(5).

MONETARY PENALTIES

Overview of the UK's FATCA/CRS penalties

8.7

Focus

Under reg 13 of the International Tax Compliance Regulations 2015, an RFI or UK representative is liable to a penalty of £300, and in some situations **£3,000**, for a failure to comply with certain specified matters (see **8.8** and **8.9**).

> In certain circumstances, HMRC may also (or in some cases, instead) apply:
>
> - daily default penalties (see **8.11**);
>
> - penalties for inaccurate information (see **8.12**);
>
> - failure to comply with the FATCA agreement penalties (see **8.13**).
>
> Certain of these penalties do not apply if the person liable to the penalty satisfies HMRC or the tribunal that there is a reasonable excuse for the failure (see **8.10**).

Under reg 12H of the 2015 Regulations, where a partnership or trust becomes liable to a penalty under the UK's Automatic Exchange of Information ('AEOI') Regulations, the liability to the penalty falls upon a liable person of the particular financial institution or UK representative concerned.

'Liable person' means, in relation to:

(a)   a partnership, a partner of the partnership;

(b)   a trust which is not a collective investment scheme, a trustee of the trust; or

(c)   a trust which is a collective investment scheme, a trustee, manager or operator of the scheme.

For this purpose, 'collective investment scheme' means:

(a)   an investment trust within the meaning of the Corporation Tax Acts;

(b)   a venture capital trust within the meaning of Part 6 of the Income Tax Act 2007; or

(c)   any arrangements that are a 'collective investment scheme' within the meaning of the Financial Services and Markets Act 2000.

See the International Tax Compliance Regulations 2015.

Regarding the meaning of reporting financial institution, see **4.9**; on representative, see **4.12**; on specified financial institution, see **7.6**; and on specified relevant person, see **7.7**.

See **18.1** onwards as regards EU DAC 6 penalties.

Penalties under reg 13(1)

8.8   An RFI or UK representative which fails to comply with the obligations under the International Tax Compliance Regulations 2015, as set out in the following table, may be liable to a penalty of £300 under reg 13(1) of the 2015 Regulations.

See also **8.9** regarding penalties under reg 13(2) or (3).

Regulation governing the obligation	Nature of the obligation not complied with
Regulation 3	apply FATCA, CRS and EU DAC due diligence requirements – see **Chapter 9**
Regulation 6	make a return setting out the information required to be reported under FATCA, CRS/EU DAC – see **Chapter 12**
Regulation 9	carry out additional 2015 and 2016 FATCA due diligence and reporting obligations regarding payments to a non-participating financial institution*
Regulation 10	notify individual reportable persons – see **Chapter 7**
Regulation 12G	provide information reasonably required in an HMRC officer's written notice – see **8.2**

* In relation to a calendar year, an RFI's or UK representative's liability for penalties in respect of failure to comply with this obligation is capped at no more than £3,000. See reg 16. See **8.5** to **8.6** regarding non-participating financial institutions generally.

Regarding the meaning of reporting financial institution, see **4.9**, and for the meaning of UK representative, see **4.12**.

See **8.11** regarding the possibility that daily default penalties and increased daily default penalties are then added under regs 14 and 21.

Penalties under reg 13(2) or (3)

8.9   A specified financial institution or specified relevant person who fails to comply with the obligations under the International Tax Compliance Regulations 2015, as set out in the following table, may be liable to a penalty as follows under reg 13(2) or (3) of the 2015 Regulations.

See also **8.8** regarding penalties under reg 13(1).

Regulation governing the penalty	Regulation governing the obligation	Nature of the obligation not complied with	Penalty(ies)
Regulation 13(2)	Regulation 12B	a specified financial institution had to identify all of its specified clients	£3,000
Regulation 13(2)	Regulation 12C	a specified relevant person had to identify all of its specified clients	£3,000

Regulation governing the penalty	Regulation governing the obligation	Nature of the obligation not complied with	Penalty(ies)
Regulation 13(2)	Regulation 12D	a specified financial institution or specified relevant person had to notify all of its specified clients on or before 31 August 2017	£3,000
Regulation 13(2)	Regulation 12E	a specified financial institution or specified relevant person had to ensure any controlled overseas person was notified to specified individuals on or before 31 August 2017	£3,000
Regulation 13(3)	Regulation 12G	provide information reasonably required in an HMRC officer's written notice – see **8.2**	£300

Regarding the meaning of specified financial institution, see **7.6**; on specified relevant person, see **7.7**.

See **8.11** regarding the possibility that daily default penalties and increased daily default penalties are then added to those in the above table under regs 14 and 21.

Reasonable excuse

8.10

> **Focus**
>
> Many of the monetary penalties in relation to FATCA and CRS do not apply if HMRC can be persuaded that there is a reasonable excuse for the failure to comply.
>
> Reasonable excuse is a common concept in UK tax law. HMRC discuss the circumstances in which they will or will not accept that there is a reasonable excuse, at some length in their guidance.

The International Tax Compliance Regulations 2015 state that liability to certain penalties under regs 13, 14 or 16 do not arise if the person satisfies HMRC or (on an appeal notified to the tribunal) the tribunal that there is a reasonable excuse for the failure (see reg 17).

Specifically, the penalties to which this applies, are those arising under regs 13, 14 or 16. See **8.7**, **8.9** and **8.11** in relation to these.

If a person had a reasonable excuse for a failure but the excuse has ceased, the person is to be treated as having continued to have the excuse if the failure is remedied without unreasonable delay after the excuse ceased.

The Regulations also state that neither of the following is a reasonable excuse:

(a)   that there is an insufficiency of funds to do something;

(b)   that a person relies upon another person to do something.

Regulation 17 states a principle which applies commonly in the UK tax code.

For example, the corporation tax, income tax, capital gains tax, VAT and excise duties penalties in the Finance Act 2008, Sch 41 are subject to a similar 'reasonable excuse' waiver (see para 20 of that Schedule).

By way of further examples encompassing a wide range of taxes, see also the Finance Act 2009, Sch 55, para 23 in relation to penalties for failure to make returns or Sch 56, para 16 for failure to pay tax on time.

Reasonable excuse is a widely used concept in tax law. HMRC provide further guidance at https://www.gov.uk/tax-appeals/reasonable-excuses

HMRC's manuals and other published information give various examples of situations where HMRC will accept that the taxpayer has acted reasonably. See for example HMRC's Compliance Handbook Manual CH155650. See also HMRC's Enquiry Manual EM4109.

In HMRC's guidance about what to do if you 'Disagree with a Tax Decision', HMRC confirm that they 'will consider coronavirus as a reasonable excuse for missing some tax obligations'. See https://www.gov.uk/tax-appeals/print

The term reasonable excuse is not defined in statute. Unsurprisingly, the concept is the subject of considerable dispute.

As a result, what is or is not a 'reasonable excuse' has frequently been examined in the First-tier Tribunal ('FTT'). Despite this, there are far less decisions beyond the FTT and while the decisions of the FTT are persuasive, they are not binding.

In general, the burden of proving that there is a reasonable excuse falls on the taxpayer. See, for example, *Hansard v HMRC [2018] UKFTT 292 (TC)*, para 54.

Each case depends upon the circumstances in which the failure occurred. See, for example, *Perrin v HMRC* [2018] STC 1302, [2018] UKUT 156 (TCC), paras 70–73.

HMRC accept that where an AEOI return is made late owing to issues arising from the Covid-19 pandemic, the financial institution that makes the return late will have a reasonable excuse. See HMRC's International Exchange of Information Manual IEIM800000.

See **9.7** and **12.1** regarding an RFI's situation if it relies on a service provider in relation to its obligations under AEOI.

See International Tax Compliance Regulations 2015, reg 13 onwards.

See **18.5** as regards 'reasonable excuse' in relation to EU DAC 6 penalties.

Daily default penalties

8.11

Focus

If the failure in question continues after a reg 13 penalty has been notified to the person who is liable (see **8.7**), that person is then liable to a further penalty for each subsequent day on which the failure continues, of an amount not exceeding £60 for each such day.

In addition, this is then subject to the possibility of increased daily default penalties, which require the HMRC officer successfully to apply to the tribunal, if they are to apply.

Increased daily default penalties can apply if:

- a person is liable to a daily default penalty;
- with a penalty being assessed accordingly; and
- the failure in respect of which that assessment is made continues for more than a further 30 days beginning with the date on which notification of the daily default penalty was given.

Where that situation applies, an HMRC officer may then make an application to the tribunal for permission to assess an increased daily penalty.

The HMRC officer must notify the person liable to the penalty of this application to the tribunal at the time of making it.

If the tribunal then determines that an increased daily penalty may be assessed, then for each applicable day on which the failure continues, the person's liability to a daily default penalty shall be for that increased amount.

The increased daily penalty may not be for more than £1,000 for each applicable day.

If the tribunal determines that an increased daily penalty may be assessed, HMRC must notify the person liable to the penalty and in doing so must specify the future day from which the increased penalty is to apply.

See the International Tax Compliance Regulations 2015, regs 14 and 21.

Penalties for inaccurate information

8.12

Focus

An RFI or UK representative is liable to a penalty not exceeding £3,000 if in complying with the RFI's FATCA/CRS reporting obligations, the institution or representative provides inaccurate information, and condition A, B or C below are met.

(a)   Condition A is that the inaccuracy is:

    (i)   due to a failure to comply with the FATCA/CRS due diligence requirements; or

    (ii)   deliberate.

(b)   Condition B is that the RFI or UK representative knows of the inaccuracy at the time the information is provided but does not inform HMRC at that time.

(c)   Condition C is that the RFI or UK representative:

    (i)   discovers the inaccuracy sometime later; and

    (ii)   fails to take reasonable steps to inform HMRC.

See the International Tax Compliance Regulations 2015, reg 15.

FATCA agreement penalty: non-participating financial institutions

8.13

Focus

An RFI under the FATCA agreement faced additional due diligence (and reporting) obligations for the 2015 and 2016 calendar years in relation to payments to non-participating financial institutions (see **12.10**).

Under the International Tax Compliance Regulations 2015, there could be a penalty of no more than £3,000 (broadly) for failing to comply. See below.

An entity that is non-compliant with FATCA may find itself classified as a non-participating financial institution, which is a concept that exists in FATCA, but not in CRS or EU DAC. For this to happen, there needs to be significant non-compliance – see **8.5** to **8.6**.

If an RFI or a UK representative failed to comply with these obligations, it was liable to:

(a)   a penalty of £300 for each failure to report a payment; and

(b)   a penalty of £300 for each failure to set out a payment accurately in a report made under reg 9.

But in relation to a calendar year, the liability for these penalties was subject to a limit of £3,000.

See International Tax Compliance Regulations 2015 SI 2015/878 regs 9, 13(1) and 16.

HMRC PROCEDURE AND TIME LIMITS

8.14   If an HMRC officer decides to assess a penalty, 'The initial burden lies on HMRC to establish that events have occurred as a result of which a penalty is, prima facie, due'. See for example *Perrin v HMRC* [2018] STC 1302, [2018] UKUT 156 (TCC), para 69.

The 2015 Regulations state that if a person becomes liable to a penalty under any of regs 13 to 16 (see **8.7** onwards), an HMRC officer must notify the person.

An assessment of a penalty under:

●   reg 13(2) (see **8.9**);

●   reg 14 (daily default penalties – see **8.11**); or

●   reg 16(1)(a) (failure to report a payment to a non-participating financial institution – see **8.5** to **8.6**),

must be made within the period of 12 months beginning with the date on which the person became liable to the penalty (see reg 18(3)).

An assessment of a penalty under:

●   reg 13(1) (see **8.8**);

●   reg 15 (penalties for inaccurate information – see **8.12**); or

●   reg 16(1)(b) (failure to report accurately, when reporting a payment to a non-participating financial institution – see **8.13**),

must be made:

(a)   within the period of 12 months beginning with the date on which the inaccuracy or failure first came to the attention of an HMRC officer; and

(b)   within the period of six years beginning with the date on which the person became liable to the penalty.

See reg 18(4).

A penalty under the 2015 Regulations must be paid before the end of the period of 30 days beginning with the date mentioned in reg 22(2), being:

(a) the date on which the assessment of the penalty is notified; or

(b) if a notice of appeal is given, the date on which the appeal is finally determined or withdrawn.

See the International Tax Compliance Regulations 2015, regs 18 and 22.

APPEALING AGAINST A PENALTY

8.15

Focus

A person may appeal against a penalty assessment under the 2015 Regulations (see reg 19).

The appeal may be on the grounds that any of the penalties do not arise. Alternatively, in the case of penalties under regs 14 or 15 (see **8.11** and **8.12**) the appeal may be as to the amount of the penalty.

Notice of an appeal must state the grounds of appeal and must be given:

(a) in writing;

(b) before the end of the period of 30 days beginning with the date on which notification of the penalty was given;

(c) to HMRC.

On an appeal on the grounds that the penalty does not arise, that is notified to the tribunal – normally the FTT. The tribunal may confirm or cancel the assessment.

On an appeal as to the amount of the penalty that is notified to the tribunal, the tribunal may:

(a) confirm the assessment; or

(b) substitute another assessment that the HMRC officer had power to make.

The Regulations state that, subject to the Regulations themselves, the provisions of Part 5 of the Taxes Management Act 1970 relating to appeals have effect in relation to such appeals as they have effect in relation to an appeal against an assessment to income tax.

Where the FTT has determined a penalty against a person, the person may be able to appeal to the Upper Tribunal against the determination of the penalty.

See the International Tax Compliance Regulations 2015, regs 19 and 20.

See also HMRC's International Exchange of Information Manual IEIM660080.

Chapter 9

FATCA/CRS – Due diligence requirements under the UK's regulations

SIGNPOSTS

- Typically, under FATCA/CRS, a firm, business or other entity first needs to decide whether it is a 'reporting financial institution'. See **Chapter 4** on the meaning of reporting financial institution ('RFI').

- If the entity concludes that it is an RFI, it is likely that it will need next, to carry out the due diligence procedures that are stipulated under FATCA and CRS in relation to its 'financial accounts'. See **5.1** and **Chapter 5** generally on the meaning of financial account.

- General principles relating to due diligence under FATCA and CRS/EU DAC, are set out in this Chapter. **Chapter 10** considers due diligence specifically in relation to financial accounts held by individuals. **Chapter 11** considers due diligence due diligence in relation to financial accounts held by entities. See **9.1**.

- The results of the RFI's due diligence exercise should then enable it to decide whether and what it needs to report under FATCA and CRS. It should then do that within the appropriate timeframe for doing so. See **Chapter 12**.

- It is therefore advisable that an RFI follows the recommended steps (see **9.2**).

- The main purpose of the due diligence procedures that such an RFI must carry out, is to identify reportable accounts. The due diligence should be recorded and kept as evidence (see **9.3**).

- Self-certification and other documentation may only be relied on for the purposes of due diligence if the RFI knows or has reason to know that self-certification or other documentation is reliable (see **9.4**).

- As is described in **Chapters 10** and **11**, in certain circumstances the rules relating to due diligence of particular kinds of accounts require that further due diligence procedures such as electronic record search or enhanced review are undertaken (see **Chapter 10** and **Chapter 11**).

- In practice, due diligence that goes beyond the procedures described in **9.4**, often tends mainly to consist of reviewing available information and documentation to find any signs of US or reportable jurisdiction 'indicia' relating to an account holder – for example, a US or reportable jurisdiction mailing address or telephone number, say (see **9.5**).

- However, HMRC want RFIs to adopt a 'wider approach' by which they capture and maintain information on the tax residence of account holders, irrespective of whether or not that account holder is a reportable person for any given reportable period (see **9.8** and **9.9** regarding the meaning of 'reportable person', and see **9.6**).

- Hence the due diligence procedures should seek to identify whether an account is a reportable account (among other matters). A reportable account is an account held by one or more reportable persons (persons who are resident in a participating jurisdiction or the US or else a US citizen) or by a passive non-financial entity ('NFE') or non-financial foreign entity ('NFFE') with controlling persons who are resident in a reporting jurisdiction or the US or US citizens. Only reportable accounts need to be reported. Only accounts identified by the due diligence procedures as such are reportable accounts (see **9.7** and **9.8**).

- An entity's controlling persons are the natural persons who exercise control over it (see **9.10**).

- Certain dormant and de minimis accounts can be excluded both from due diligence and from reporting, provided an election is made to do so. The election needs to be made separately in respect of each reporting year to which it is to apply (see **9.11**).

- Rules called the account balance aggregation and currency rules must be applied to the due diligence and reporting processes (see **9.12**).

- Throughout this Chapter, where reference is made to 'CRS/EU DAC', this is in relation to the CRS rules as they apply to the UK through the EU/EUDAC. See **Chapter 2** regarding the impact of Brexit on this.

- An RFI under the FATCA agreement faced additional due diligence and reporting obligations for the 2015 and 2016 calendar years in relation to payments to non-participating financial institutions (see **9.16**; see also **12.10**).

OVERVIEW

9.1

Focus

General principles relating to due diligence under FATCA and CRS/EU DAC, are set out in this Chapter.

Chapter 10 considers due diligence specifically in relation to financial accounts held by individuals.

Chapter 11 considers due diligence in relation to financial accounts held by entities.

RECOMMENDED STEPS FOR AN ENTITY THAT MUST CARRY OUT FATCA/CRS DUE DILIGENCE

9.2

Focus

The following steps are suggested for an entity that falls within (or suspects that it might fall within) the definition of 'financial institution' for FATCA/CRS purposes:

(1)   identify the reportable population;

(2)   review client onboarding procedures;

(3)   identify and carry out remediation of 'pre-existing accounts';

(4)   conduct due diligence;

(5)   carry out reporting.

Each of these steps is described in more detail below.

---

(1)   Identify the reportable population

    (a)   Is the entity itself a financial institution for FATCA/CRS purposes?

        (i)   If it is not, the entity may still need to decide on its own categorisation for FATCA/CRS purposes because it may receive self-certification requests from financial institutions which hold its financial accounts – is the entity, for example, a passive NFE or a passive NFFE, say? See **4.1** and **11.7** onwards for further details.

        (ii)   If the entity truly cannot decide whether or not it is a financial institution, it may perhaps be better to err on the side of

103

caution and to proceed as if it is. However, this will then require it to proceed with the remainder of (1) and potentially with (2) to (5) below – which could prove time-consuming and costly. It is better therefore, if possible, to reach a firm conclusion about whether the entity is a financial institution.

(b)   Do the entity's clients or customers include reportable persons? Do they hold reportable accounts with the entity?

See **9.8** and **9.9** regarding reportable persons.

(i)   An entity may not need to answer that question (and may be able to ignore (2) to (5) below) if it has concluded that it is not a financial institution for FATCA/CRS purposes – subject to the following though.

(ii)   An entity that is not itself a financial institution may still need to work out its clients' situations if the entity will be advising its clients about Automatic Exchange of Information ('AEOI') – for example, if the entity is a firm of solicitors or accountants which advises its clients about AEOI, say.

(iii)   An entity that is a financial institution but is unsure whether or who its reportable persons are and whether it has reportable accounts, will almost certainly need to carry out at least some of (2) onwards to enable it to answer those questions.

(2)   Review client onboarding procedures

In addition to ensuring compliance with KYC (know-your-client) and AML (anti-money laundering) Regulations and performing the necessary risk assessments, the compliance management process should also undertake tax classification for FATCA, CRS and EU DAC.

As a minimum, it is likely that the following data will be required for each client or customer: name, residence address, jurisdiction(s) of residence for tax purposes, TIN (tax identification number) with respect to each reportable jurisdiction, date of birth.

Additionally, high-value accounts that are subject to more rigorous review procedures will drive additional requirements. See **9.3** onwards.

Generally, it will also be necessary to review the entity's standard terms of business to ensure that these are appropriate in light of AEOI.

(3)   Identify and carry out remediation of 'pre-existing accounts'

There are two distinct elements to this process:

(a)   identification of the customers who are in-scope for FATCA, CRS and EU DAC;

(b)   processing remediation for in-scope clients or customers.

As a minimum, the remediation process will need to ensure that equivalent information and documentation is held in relation to in-scope clients or customers to that referred to above regarding client onboarding procedures.

Where there are gaps in existing AML/KYC and any other data, then clients and customers may need to be contacted for further information and possibly required to complete a self-certification statement. This will include contacting clients or customers whose status for FATCA/CRS needs to be clarified or confirmed.

Again, it will often be necessary to review the entity's terms of business with its existing clients to ensure that these are appropriate in light of FATCA/CRS. In some cases, the terms of business may need to be amended.

(4)   Conduct due diligence

See **9.3** onwards.

(5)   Carry out reporting

See **Chapter 12**.

BROAD APPROACH TO CARRYING OUT FATCA, CRS/EU DAC DUE DILIGENCE PROCEDURES

9.3

Focus

The essence of the FATCA and CRS/EU DAC due diligence requirements is that work must be carried out whose aim is to determine whether each of the financial institution's financial accounts is reportable. The information so obtained, then enables the financial institution to report as necessary.

This work must be recorded and kept as evidence that the work was duly carried out.

In addition, there are more detailed requirements, depending on the particular type of account and of account holder. These are described in **Chapter 10** (regarding account holders who are individuals) and **Chapter 11** (regarding entities).

A reportable account is defined as an account held by one or more reportable persons or by a passive NFE (or a passive NFFE) with one or more controlling persons that is a reportable person, subject to two tests:

---

(1)   to understand different obligations based on customer segments;

(2)   to determine ultimate beneficial ownership: There is a requirement to look through passive (shell) entities to report on the ultimate beneficial owners.

See **9.8** and **9.9** regarding the meaning of 'reportable person'.

The information required to be reported includes identity and residence information; TIN; account details; reporting entity; and account balance/value etc.

One differentiator is that 'date of birth' is required for CRS and EU DAC reporting but is not a necessary data element for FATCA reporting.

A financial institution or a third party undertaking due diligence procedures for a financial institution must retain records of the documentary evidence, or a notation or record of the documents reviewed and used to support an account holder's status for a minimum period.

The minimum period is five years from the end of the period in which the account was last included in a return, or five years from the end of the period in which the due diligence process was last relied upon to treat the account as not being reportable.

The documentary evidence can be retained as originals, photocopies or in an electronic format.

FATCA introduced a number of account due diligence requirements, which can be categorised as (i) new account due diligence and (ii) pre-existing account due diligence.

Under FATCA, a new account is an account that is opened on or after 1 January 2014. A pre-existing account is an account that was in existence on or before 31 December 2013.

Under EU DAC, hence so far as the UK is concerned under CRS too, a new account is an account that is opened on or after 1 January 2016. A pre-existing account is an account that was in existence on or before 31 December 2015. See the International Tax Compliance Regulations 2015, SI 2015/878, reg 3(4A).

In certain circumstances, EU DAC gives the RFI the option of treating as a pre-existing account any new accounts of an account holder with one or more pre-existing accounts (which therefore also applies in the case of the UK for the purposes of the CRS too). Again, see reg 3(4A).

These same categories (ie pre-existing and new accounts) are also required under CRS and EU DAC, however, there are some key differences. Under CRS and EU DAC, the pre-existing account due diligence process comprises two components:

- high-value individual accounts (aggregate over US $1m); and

- all other pre-existing accounts.

For lower value accounts, a permanent residence address test based on documentary evidence or residence determination based on an indicia search is required (conflicting indicia would need to be resolved by self-certification and/or documentary evidence).

For high-value accounts, a more rigorous search and enhanced due diligence procedures applies, including a paper record search and a 'reason to know' test by the relationship manager for the account.

For pre-existing entity accounts, the financial institution must determine whether the entity itself is a reportable person. See **9.8** and **9.9** regarding the meaning of 'reportable person'.

Financial institutions may use previously captured AML and KYC data and documentation to determine if the entity is reportable under FATCA, CRS or EU DAC.

A financial institution that is not required to retain copies of documentation reviewed under AML due diligence procedures will be treated, for the purposes of all the regimes, as having retained a record of such documentation if it retains a record in its files noting:

- the date the documentation was reviewed;

- each type of document;

- the document's identification number where present (for example, a passport number); and

- whether any indicia of residence in a reportable jurisdiction were identified.

See HMRC's International Exchange of Information Manual IEIM404080.

See the FATCA agreement, Annex I. See CRS, Sections II to VII and EU DAC, Annex I, Sections II to VII.

RELIANCE ON SELF-CERTIFICATION OR DOCUMENTARY EVIDENCE

9.4

Focus

When carrying out due diligence under any of FATCA, CRS or EU DAC, a reporting UK financial institution may not rely on a self-certification or documentary evidence if it knows or has reason to know that the self-certification or documentary evidence is incorrect or unreliable.

> There is no prescribed format for self-certification. It may form part of a financial institution's account opening documentation.
>
> Whatever form it takes, it must enable an RFI to know:
>
> - the account holder's jurisdiction(s) of residence for tax purposes;
> - whether he or she is a US citizen;
> - TIN for each jurisdiction where the account holder is tax resident; and
> - date of birth (except under FATCA).
>
> The self-certification should be signed by the account holder. The financial institution should seek to verify it's accuracy by reference to anti-money laundering or other information that it holds in relation to the account holder.

If self-certification is needed and cannot be obtained within 90 days of opening a new account, the account is reportable for the period until a valid self-certification is obtained. If there are no indicia of residence in any jurisdiction other than the UK, then the account is reportable only to the US under FATCA. If there are indicia of residence in reportable jurisdictions other than the UK, then the account is also reportable under EU DAC or CRS to those other jurisdictions.

Acceptable documentary evidence for the purposes of FATCA due diligence includes any of the following:

(1) a certificate of residence issued by an appropriate tax official of the country in which the payee claims to be a resident;

(2) with respect to an individual, any valid identification issued by an authorised government body (for example, a government or agency thereof, or a municipality), that includes the individual's name and is typically used for identification purposes;

(3) with respect to an entity, any official documentation issued by an authorised government body (for example, a government or agency thereof, or a municipality) that includes the name of the entity and either the address of its principal office in the country (or US territory) in which it claims to be a resident or the country (or US territory) in which the entity was incorporated or organised;

(4) any financial statement, third-party credit report, bankruptcy filing, or US Securities;

(5) for the purposes of FATCA only, with respect to an account maintained in a jurisdiction with anti-money laundering rules that have been approved by the IRS in connection with a qualified intermediary ('QI')

agreement (as described in relevant US Treasury Regulations), any of the documents other than a USA Form W-8 or W-9 referenced in the jurisdiction's attachment to the QI agreement for identifying individuals or entities;

(5) any financial statement, third-party credit report, bankruptcy filing, or securities regulators (in the case of FATCA, the Securities and Exchange Commission report).

A self-certification remains valid unless and until the financial institution knows, or has reason to know, that it is incorrect or unreliable. This could either be at the time a new account is opened or later, because of a change of circumstances.

If a reasonably prudent person in the position of the RFI would question the information provided then that is reason to know that the information may be incorrect or unreliable.

Where the RFI cannot rely on the original self-certification it must obtain either:

(1) a valid self-certification that establishes the residence(s) for tax purposes of the account holder; or

(2) a reasonable explanation and documentation (as appropriate) supporting the validity of the original self-certification (and retain a copy or a notation of such explanation and documentation).

An RFI may then treat the status of the account holder as unchanged until the earlier of:

- 90 calendar days from the date that the self-certification became invalid due to the change in circumstances;

- the date that the validity of the self-certification is confirmed (where appropriate); or

- the date that a new self-certification is obtained.

If confirmation of the original self-certification cannot be obtained within the 90 calendar-day period, the financial institution must then treat the account holder as resident for AEOI purposes both in the jurisdiction indicated by the original self-certification and in the jurisdiction indicated by the change of circumstances.

A self-certification obtained from an entity must be signed (or otherwise positively affirmed) by the person with authority to sign on behalf of the entity. This will include:

- an officer or director of a corporate entity;

- a partner of a partnership;

- a trustee of a trust;

- any person holding an equivalent title to any of the above; and

- any other person with written authorisation from the entity to sign documentation on behalf of the entity.

The self-certification must also be dated at the latest at the date of receipt by the financial institution and must contain the following information in respect of the entity:

- the name;

- the address;

- the jurisdiction(s) of tax residence; and

- the TIN with respect to each reportable jurisdiction.

The financial institution may also request the account holder entity to include its status in the self-certification as either a financial institution or an NFE.

The financial institution is 'expected' to provide the entity with sufficient information to enable it to answer this question, and may either provide guidance of its own for that purpose or a reference to HMRC's International Exchange of Information Manual.

See HMRC's International Exchange of Information Manual IEIM403140 to IEIM403200, and as regards entities, IEIM403340.

See the FATCA agreement, Annex I. See CRS, Section VII(A). See EU DAC, Annex I, Section VII(A).

WHAT IS FURTHER DUE DILIGENCE MAINLY LOOKING FOR?

9.5

Focus

In many circumstances, it may be possible to limit due diligence to self-certification and/or a review of the RFI's own records, where necessary supported by the obtaining of additional confirmatory documentation (see **9.12**).

In some situations, the RFI may itself decide that that approach is insufficient. In other situations, the rules applicable to the particular kind of account will require that electronic record search or enhanced review are undertaken (see **Chapter 10**).

Carrying out further due diligence then tends to consist of reviewing available information and documentation to try to identify (and where appropriate to investigate) US indicia or reportable jurisdiction indicia relating to each account holder.

This is more relevant for due diligence of individual accounts (see **Chapter 10**) than for due diligence of entity accounts (see **Chapter 11**).

Under FATCA, US indicia may include:

- a US place of birth;

- Identification of the account holder as a US citizen or resident;

- a current US residence or mailing address (including a US PO box);

- a current US telephone number;

- standing instructions to pay amounts from a foreign (meaning non-US) account to an account maintained in the US;

- a current power of attorney or signatory authority granted to a person with a US address;

- a US 'in-care-of' or 'hold mail' address that is the sole address with respect to the account holder.

Reportable jurisdiction indicia under CRS/EU DAC may include:

- one or more telephone numbers in a reportable jurisdiction;

- a current reportable jurisdiction residence or mailing address (including a reportable jurisdiction PO box);

- standing instructions (other than with respect to a depository account) to transfer funds to an account maintained in a reportable jurisdiction;

- currently effective power of attorney or signatory authority granted to a person with an address in a reportable jurisdiction;

- a hold mail instruction or in-care-of address in a reportable jurisdiction.

THE 'WIDER APPROACH' TO FATCA/CRS DUE DILIGENCE

9.6

Focus

HMRC say that the UK's AEOI Regulations adopt a 'wider approach' which requires RFIs to capture and maintain information on the tax residence of account holders irrespective of whether or not that account holder is a reportable person for any given reportable period.

The due diligence procedures in the agreements governing automatic exchange – FATCA, CRS and EU DAC – are designed to identify accounts which are held by the residents of the jurisdictions with which the UK is committed to exchange information.

They are also required to maintain this information for a period of five years from the end of the period in which the account was last included in a return, or five years from the end of the period in which the due diligence process was last relied upon to treat the account as not being reportable.

The financial institution will then have this information ready in case a new jurisdiction commits itself to exchange under CRS.

The Regulations impose an obligation on financial institutions without any discretion on their part to collect this information. It is argued that the financial institutions are therefore able to do this while remaining compliant with data protection legislation. See also **Chapter 20**.

See **9.8** and **9.9** regarding the meaning of 'reportable person'.

See HMRC's International Exchange of Information Manual IEIM404140.

WHAT ARE THE FATCA/CRS DUE DILIGENCE REQUIREMENTS?

9.7

Focus

Under both FATCA and CRS/EU DAC, an RFI (see **Chapter 4**) must establish and maintain due diligence arrangements that are designed to identify in respect of each financial account (see **5.1** on the meaning of 'financial account'):

- the territory in which an account holder is resident for the purposes of income tax, corporation tax or various other taxes, (as well as, as regards FATCA only, whether he or she is a US citizen); and

- whether it is a reportable account.

'Reportable account' means an account held by either:

- one or more reportable persons; or by

- a passive NFE or a passive NFFE with one or more controlling persons that is a reportable person, provided it has been identified as such pursuant to the required due diligence procedures. See **Chapter 11** regarding NFEs and NFFEs.

See **9.8** and **9.9** regarding the meaning of 'reportable person'.

An account only needs to be reported under FATCA/CRS, if it is a reportable account. See more below about the meaning of reportable account. See **Chapter 12** as regards reporting.

Note that the due diligence process is critically important here, because both under FATCA and under CRS/EU DAC, an account is not a reportable account, unless it has been identified as such during the due diligence process. See below.

For CRS/EU DAC, an account is treated as a reportable account beginning as of the date it is identified as such pursuant to the due diligence procedures in CRS, Sections II through VII and, unless otherwise provided, information with respect to a reportable account must be reported annually in the calendar year following the year to which the information relates. See CRS, Section II. See EU DAC, Annex I, Section II.

For FATCA, a reporting UK financial institution has due diligence and reporting obligations in relation to accounts which are a 'US reportable account'. Under the FATCA agreement, an account shall not be treated as a US reportable account if such account is not identified as such after application of the due diligence procedures that are set out in the FATCA agreement, Annex I.

An RFI must keep a record of:

- the steps taken to comply with this; and

- the information collected in the course of identifying the matters referred to above.

The records must be kept for a period of:

(a) in respect of an account identified as a reportable account, five years beginning with the end of the year in which the account is last included in an AEOI return; or

(b) in respect of an account which is not a reportable account, five years beginning with the end of the last year in which the RFI relied upon the due diligence procedures to treat the account as not being a reportable account.

The due diligence procedures must comply with the relevant agreement. That is to say:

- in relation to EU DAC, the procedures set out in Annexes I and II to EU DAC;

- in relation to CRS, the procedures set out in Sections II to VII of the CRS; and

- in relation to FATCA, the procedures set out in Annex I to the FATCA agreement.

However, certain definitions in EU DAC specifically apply to the UK's AEOI rules instead of those in CRS.

Furthermore, where a provision of the CRS does not specify a deadline for the requirements of that provision to be satisfied but there is an equivalent provision in Annex I of EU DAC which does specify a deadline, then that deadline applies for the purposes of the provision in the CRS.

An RFI under the FATCA agreement faced additional due diligence (and reporting) obligations for the 2015 and 2016 calendar years in relation to payments to non-participating financial institutions (see **12.10**).

The UK's Regulations applying CRS and EU DAC continue to treat the UK as an EU Member State, despite Brexit. See **Chapter 2**.

An RFI may use a service provider to undertake its due diligence requirements, but in such cases those obligations continue to be the obligations of the institution.

The remainder of this Chapter includes explanation of how in certain circumstances due diligence procedures must include electronic record search and/or paper record search. In each case, records maintained by the financial institution must be searched.

See for example Annex I(II)(B) of the FATCA agreement: 'The Reporting United Kingdom financial institution must review *electronically searchable data maintained by* the Reporting United Kingdom financial institution ...' (emphasis added).

It is important to be aware that for these purposes, information is not regarded as maintained by the financial institution if it has been archived and is not used by the business. Only when such information is retrieved by the financial institution from the archive so that it can be used by it will the information be regarded as maintained.

Electronic records are available for use (therefore 'maintained') by the financial institution to the extent that they are electronically searchable. Information, data or files are not electronically searchable merely because they are stored in an image retrieval system such as portable document format (pdf) or as scanned documents.

See HMRC's International Exchange of Information Manual IEIM402300.

See the International Tax Compliance Regulations 2015, SI 2015/878, regs 3 and 12.

See **9.1** onwards regarding carrying out due diligence and due diligence procedures.

ACCOUNT HOLDERS, REPORTABLE PERSONS, US SPECIFIED PERSONS AND REPORTABLE ACCOUNTS

9.8

Focus

'Account holder' means the person listed or identified as the holder of a financial account by the financial institution (see Chapter 4) that maintains the account. See **5.1** and **Chapter 5** generally on the meaning of 'financial account'.

Under CRS, the meaning of 'reportable person' is broadly as follows. If an account holder is identified as being tax resident in any of the jurisdictions with which the UK has agreed to exchange information on a reciprocal basis then they are a reportable person and the account is a reportable account. See HMRC's International Exchange of Information Manual IEIM402505. See **9.9** below for a more detailed definition of reportable person.

The FATCA agreement does not use the term reportable person. Arguably, the nearest equivalent in the FATCA agreement to reportable person is 'US specified person' which broadly means an account holder who is identified as being either US tax resident or a US citizen (or both). See **9.9** below for a more detailed definition of US specified person.

An account is treated as a reportable account as of the date it is identified as such pursuant to the due diligence procedures that financial institutions must follow. See this Chapter generally.

Note that an account is only a reportable account if either the due diligence procedures identify it as being such or it has to be treated as reportable because of an absence of due diligence evidence pointing to the contrary. See the FATCA agreement at Art 1(1)(z)(3)(dd) and CRS at Section VIII(D)(1).

Under FATCA, information about US reportable accounts has to be reported.

'US Reportable accounts' are financial accounts held by: one or more US persons (US citizens and US tax residents); plus financial accounts held by certain entities in which one or more US persons hold a substantial ownership or controlling interest.

Similarly, under CRS and EU DAC, information about Jurisdiction A reportable accounts has to be reported, where Jurisdiction A is a country that has committed to exchange information under CRS/ EU DAC.

> 'Jurisdiction A reportable accounts' are financial accounts held by: one or more persons who are resident in Jurisdiction A; plus certain entities in which one or more persons who are resident in a reportable jurisdiction hold a substantial ownership or controlling interest.
>
> A person may either be an individual or an entity.

The CRS and EU DAC state that a person, other than a financial institution, holding a financial account for the benefit or account of another person as agent, custodian, nominee, signatory, investment advisor, or intermediary, is not treated as holding the account for purposes of either CRS or EU DAC, and such other person is treated as holding the account. However, this statement does *not* appear as part of the definition of account holder in the FATCA agreement.

On the other hand, the UK's Regulations implementing FATCA (see the International Tax Compliance Regulations 2015, reg 2(2)(b)) state that an account is not a reportable account if:

(i)   the account holder is deceased or is a personal representative (within the meaning of s 989 of the Income Tax Act 2007);

(ii)   the account is held to comply with an order or judgment made or given in legal proceedings; or

(iii)   the funds held in the account are held solely as security for the performance of a party's obligation under a contract for the disposal of an estate or interest in land or of tangible moveable property.

In the case of a cash value insurance contract or an annuity contract, the account holder is any person entitled to access the cash value or change the beneficiary of the contract. If no person can access the cash value or change the beneficiary, the account holder is any person named as the owner in the contract and any person with a vested entitlement to payment under the terms of the contract. Upon the maturity of a cash value insurance contract or an annuity contract, each person entitled to receive a payment under the contract is treated as an account holder.

A difference between FATCA, on the one hand, and CRS and EU DAC on the other, is that for FATCA the definition of financial account excludes equity and debt interests in an investment entity where those interests are regularly traded on an established securities market. Under EU DAC/CRS, however, equity and debt interests in certain listed investment entities, for example, investment trust companies, are in the scope of AEOI. See HMRC's International Exchange of Information Manual IEIM403230.

9.9   The full definition under CRS of 'reportable person' is that it means a reportable jurisdiction person other than: (i) a corporation the stock of which is regularly traded on one or more established securities markets; (ii) any corporation that is a related entity or a corporation described in clause (i); (iii) a governmental entity; (iv) an international organisation; (v) a central bank; or (vi) a financial institution.

Under CRS, the term 'reportable jurisdiction person' means an individual or entity that is resident in a reportable jurisdiction under the tax laws of such jurisdiction, or an estate of a decedent that was a resident of the reportable jurisdiction. See CRS, Section VIII(D)(2) and (3).

The full definition of 'specified US person' is that it means a US person, other than: (i) a corporation the stock of which is regularly traded on one or more established securities markets; (ii) any corporation that is a member of the same expanded affiliated group, as defined in s 1471(e)(2) of the US Internal Revenue Code, as a corporation described in clause (i); (iii) the United States or any wholly owned agency or instrumentality thereof; (iv) any State of the United States, any US Territory, any political subdivision of any of the foregoing, or any wholly owned agency or instrumentality of any one or more of the foregoing; (v) any organisation exempt from taxation under s 501(a) of the US Internal Revenue Code or an individual retirement plan as defined in s 7701(a)(37) of the US Internal Revenue Code; (vi) any bank as defined in s 581 of the US Internal Revenue Code; (vii) any real estate investment trust as defined in s 856 of the US Internal Revenue Code; (viii) any regulated investment company as defined in s 851 of the US Internal Revenue Code or any entity registered with the Securities Exchange Commission under the Investment Company Act of 1940 (15 U.S.C. 80a-64); (ix) any common trust fund as defined in s 584(a) of the US Internal Revenue Code; (x) any trust that is exempt from tax under s 664(c) of the US Internal Revenue Code or that is described in s 4947(a)(1) of the US Internal Revenue Code; (xi) a dealer in securities, commodities, or derivative financial instruments (including notional principal contracts, futures, forwards, and options) that is registered as such under the laws of the US or any State; or (xii) a broker as defined in s 6045(c) of the US Internal Revenue Code. See the FATCA agreement, Art 1(1)(gg).

Under FATCA, the term 'US person' means a US citizen or resident individual, a partnership or corporation organised in the United States or under the laws of the United States or any State thereof, a trust if (i) a court within the United States would have authority under applicable law to render orders or judgments concerning substantially all issues regarding administration of the trust, and (ii) one or more US persons have the authority to control all substantial decisions of the trust, or an estate of a decedent that is a citizen or resident of the United States. This definition is to be interpreted in accordance with the US Internal Revenue Code. See the FATCA agreement, Art 1(1)(ff).

See the International Tax Compliance Regulations 2015.

See the FATCA agreement, including the definitions in Art 1. See CRS, including the definitions in Section VIII. See EU DAC, including the definitions in Annex I, Section VIII.

CONTROLLING PERSONS

9.10

Focus

Under AEOI (FATCA and CRS/EU DAC), it is necessary to report about financial accounts held by certain entities whose controlling persons are resident in a reportable jurisdiction or the US (plus US citizens).

For CRS and EU DAC, 'the term 'controlling persons' means the natural persons who exercise control over an entity. See also **6.3** regarding how this applies in the case of a trust.

For FATCA, 'controlling persons' means the natural persons who exercise control over an entity.

In the case of a trust, it means the settlor, the trustees, the protector (if any), the beneficiaries or class of beneficiaries, and any other natural person exercising ultimate effective control over the trust, and in the case of a legal arrangement other than a trust, such term means persons in equivalent or similar positions.

The term 'controlling persons' shall be interpreted in a manner consistent with the Recommendations of the Financial Action Task Force ('FATF').

Regarding FATF and its Recommendations, see http://www.fatf-gafi. org/publications/fatfrecommendations/?hf=10&b=0&s=desc(fatf_ releasedate).

Under both CRS/EU DAC and FATCA, financial institutions are required to report accounts that are subject to reporting, which is to say reportable accounts (see **9.6**).

Reportable accounts are accounts held by persons or, for CRS and EU DAC passive NFEs with controlling persons resident in an AEOI partner country and for FATCA passive NFFEs with controlling persons who are US citizens or US residents.

Persons subject to reporting for CRS are any persons resident in a CRS partner state (reportable jurisdiction). Similarly, persons subject to reporting for EU DAC (except for EU DAC 6) are any persons resident in an EU Member State. As such, not only natural persons resident in a CRS partner state or (for EU DAC) an EU Member State but also persons controlling passive NFEs (such as foundations, trusts and domiciliary companies) fall into the scope of CRS and/or EU DAC. The only kinds of exceptions granted by CRS and EU DAC are exchange-listed companies, governmental entities and similar.

As regards the phrase 'Member State', all references in EU law to Member States is treated as including the UK during the Brexit transition period. See **2.8** and **2.9**.

Under the CRS and EU DAC regimes, only the controlling persons of passive NFEs are reported but not those of active NFEs. Therefore, the first step should be to determine which legal entities are passive NFEs: passive NFEs are legal entities which do not qualify as active NFEs, as well as investment entities which are not domiciled in participating jurisdictions. See **Chapter 11** regarding the meanings of 'passive NFE' and 'active NFE'.

Under FATCA, if the entity account holder is a passive NFFE, the reporting UK financial institution must identify the controlling persons as determined under AML/KYC procedures, and must determine whether any such person is a citizen or resident of the US on the basis of a self-certification from the account holder or such person. If any such person is a citizen or resident of the US, the account shall be treated as a US reportable account.

In order to prevent the circumvention of CRS by using passive NFEs, CRS contains a very broad definition of controlling person.

See **6.6** to **6.8** regarding charities and the reporting of controlling persons.

See the CRS at Section VIII. See EU DAC, Annex I, Section VIII. See the FATCA agreement, Annex I.

DORMANT AND DE MINIMIS ACCOUNTS

9.11

> **Focus**
>
> Under the UK's FATCA/CRS Regulations, an RFI may elect that dormant and certain de minimis accounts are not a reportable account for a calendar year. It appears that this election also mean that those same accounts may also be excluded from the RFI's due diligence procedures. It also means that those accounts are not reportable.
>
> A separate election must be made for each calendar year for which the election is to have effect. The election is made in the FATCA/CRS return for each year.

An account is a dormant account for these purposes if:

(a)   the account holder has not initiated a transaction with regard to the account or any other account held by the account holder with the RFI in the previous three years;

(b)   the account holder has not communicated with the RFI regarding the account or any other account held by the account holder with the RFI in the previous six years;

(c)   the account is treated as a dormant account under the RFI's normal operating procedures; and

(d)   in the case of a cash value insurance contract, the RFI has not communicated with the account holder regarding the account or any other account held by the account holder with the RFI in the previous six years.

See the International Tax Compliance Regulations 2015, regs 2 and 3(5), (9). See HMRC's International Exchange of Information Manual IEIM401900.

See also **10.6** in relation to certain pre-existing individual accounts and **10.3** in relation to certain new individual accounts. See **10.12** and **10.13** for reasons why it may sometimes be prudent to carry out due diligence procedures even where technically it is not required.

ACCOUNT BALANCE AGGREGATION AND CURRENCY RULES

9.12

Focus

The UK's AEOI Regulations say that an RFI must use the account balance aggregation and currency rules that are described below, in one of the following appropriate agreements: the FATCA agreement, the CRS or EU DAC. See the International Tax Compliance Regulations 2015, reg 2(4), (5).

Individual accounts

9.13   For the purposes of determining the aggregate balance or value of accounts held by an individual, a reporting UK financial institution shall be required to aggregate all accounts maintained by the reporting UK financial institution, or related entities, but only to the extent that the reporting UK financial institution's computerised systems link the accounts by reference to a data element such as client number or TIN, and allow account balances to be aggregated.

Each holder of a jointly held account shall be attributed the entire balance or value of the jointly held account for purposes of applying the aggregation requirements.

Entity accounts

9.14   For purposes of determining the aggregate balance or value of accounts held by an entity, a reporting UK financial institution shall be required to take into account all accounts held by entities that are maintained by the reporting UK financial institution, or related entities, to the extent that the reporting UK financial institution's computerised systems link the accounts by reference to a data element such as client number or TIN and allow account balances to be aggregated.

Special aggregation rule applicable to relationship managers

9.15   For the purposes of determining the aggregate balance or value of accounts held by a person to determine whether an account is a high value account, a reporting UK financial institution shall also be required, in the case of any accounts that a relationship manager knows or has reason to know are directly or indirectly owned, controlled, or established (other than in a fiduciary capacity) by the same person, to aggregate all such accounts.

Under the UK's FATCA/CRS Regulations, in applying the account balance aggregation and currency rules, an account balance that has a negative value is treated as having a nil value. See the International Tax Compliance Regulations 2015, reg 2(6).

In determining the balance or value of an account denominated in a currency other than US dollars, the institution must translate the relevant dollar threshold amounts into the other currency by reference to the spot rate of exchange on the date for which the institution is determining the threshold amounts. See reg 2(7).

See the International Tax Compliance Regulations 2015, reg 2.

See the FATCA agreement, Annex I, Section VI(C). See CRS, Section III(C). See EU DAC, Annex I, Section VII(C).

9.16

Focus

An RFI under the FATCA agreement faced additional due diligence and reporting obligations for the 2015 and 2016 calendar years in relation to payments to non-participating financial institutions (see **12.10**).

Chapter 10

FATCA/CRS due diligence of individual accounts

SIGNPOSTS

- General principles relating to due diligence under FATCA and CRS/EU DAC, are set out in **Chapter 9**. This Chapter considers due diligence specifically in relation to financial accounts held by individuals. **Chapter 11** then considers due diligence in relation to financial accounts held by entities.

- The specific due diligence requirements relating to financial accounts of where the account holder is an individual depend on what kind of account it is. In particular, it could be a pre-existing individual account or a new individual account. Each of these could then be an account not requiring review, identification or reporting or an account that does require these things (see **10.2**).

- Certain new individual accounts may not require review, identification or reporting. The rules here are slightly different for FATCA and distinct from CRS/EU DAC. However, in both cases, due diligence, identification and reporting will apply unless an election is made for this not to be the case. The election must be made separately for each reporting year to which it is to apply (see **10.3**).

- In certain circumstances, cash value insurance contracts and annuity contracts may be assumed not to be reportable accounts (see **10.4**).

- A reporting UK financial institution must obtain self-certification from an account holder of a new individual account to which due diligence procedures are applicable. This must allow the financial institution to determine whether the account holder is resident in the US or a reporting jurisdiction (or for the purposes of FATCA only, a US citizen). Under FATCA only, if a self-certification cannot be obtained, the individual account holder is to be treated as a US person and the account treated as reportable (see **10.5**).

- There is a further distinction in the case of pre-existing individual accounts between a lower value account or a high value account, with differing requirements for each of these. Pre-existing individual accounts are individual accounts which existed on or before 31 December 2013 (in the case of FATCA), or on or before 31 December 2015 (in the case of CRS and EU DAC), as applicable.

- Certain pre-existing lower value or dormant accounts do not require review, identification or reporting. The rules here are slightly different for FATCA as distinct from CRS/EU DAC. However, in both cases, due diligence, identification and reporting will apply unless an election is made for this not to be the case. The election must be made separately for each reporting year to which it is to apply – hence it is of continuing importance (see **10.6**).

- For pre-existing lower value accounts that are not exempt from review, identification or reporting under the rules described in **10.6**, basic due diligence (see **10.8**) had to be carried out by 31 December 2015 under FATCA or by 31 December 2017 under CRS/EU DAC (see **10.7**).

- Under the basic due diligence procedures, the reporting financial institution was able simply to review whatever documentary evidence it held in its files about the client. This is meant to gather basic information about the account holder such as his or her tax residence status so that the reporting financial institution can determine whether reporting is required and, if it is, report accordingly.

  However, where that was insufficient, an electronic record search had to be carried out, either as well, or instead. These should identify whether there are either 'US indicia' or 'reportable jurisdiction indicia', which is to say things like a US or reportable jurisdiction mailing address or telephone number. If US indicia are identified, the account must then be treated as reportable under FATCA. If reportable jurisdiction indicia were identified, a further paper record search, self-certification or the obtaining of further documentation had to be carried out; if that proved inconclusive, the account had to be reported as an undocumented account (see **10.8**).

- Enhanced review due diligence procedures must be applied to high value accounts. This can be of continuing importance (see below). Enhanced review due diligence procedures are intended to identify whether there are either 'US indicia' or 'reportable jurisdiction indicia'. There are similar consequences to the above where US indicia or reportable jurisdiction indicia are or are not identified (see **10.8**).

- Care should be taken even where an account which was a pre-existing lower value account, as such an account can sometimes later become a high value account to which enhanced review due diligence procedures then become applicable (see **10.12**).

- If US indicia or reportable jurisdiction indicia were not identified, care should be taken from then on to be alert to any 'change of circumstances' that may occur later on whereby account then becomes reportable (see **10.13**).

OVERVIEW

10.1

Focus

General principles relating to due diligence under FATCA and CRS/EU DAC, are set out in **Chapter 9**. This Chapter considers due diligence specifically in relation to financial accounts held by individuals.

Chapter 11 then considers due diligence in relation to financial accounts held by entities.

DUE DILIGENCE OF INDIVIDUAL ACCOUNTS

10.2

Focus

Different individual account due diligence procedures apply to different kinds of individual accounts.

For example, due diligence procedures relating to pre-existing individual accounts are described in **10.6** onwards, and so on.

There are two kinds of individual accounts for the purposes of Automatic Exchange of Information ('AEOI'):

- pre-existing individual accounts;
- new individual accounts.

Pre-existing individual accounts are individual accounts which existed on or before 31 December 2013 (in the case of FATCA), or on or before 31 December 2015 (in the case of the CRS and EU DAC), as applicable.

New individual accounts are individual accounts which are opened on or after 1 January 2014 (in the case of FATCA), or on or after 1 January 2016 (in the case of the CRS and EU DAC), as applicable.

Each of these is then further categorised as one of the following:

- accounts not required to be reviewed, identified or reported; or

- accounts where review, identification or reporting is required.

Pre-existing individual accounts are also categorised between:

- lower value accounts; or

- high value accounts.

This latter distinction can be of continuing importance because additional review may be required where an account which was a pre-existing lower value account, later on becomes a high value account (see **10.12**).

Where it is necessary to determine the balance or value of an account in order to decide which of these categories it falls into, the balance is to be determined as of the last day of the calendar year or other appropriate reporting period.

Under the UK's FATCA/CRS Regulations, an account held by an individual as a partner of a partnership is treated as an entity account and is not treated as an individual account. See the International Tax Compliance Regulations 2015, SI 2015/878, reg 2(8).

See **10.2** and **10.3** regarding accounts not required to be reviewed, identified or reported; see **10.5**, **10.7** and **10.8** regarding lower value accounts; see **10.11** regarding high value accounts.

See the International Tax Compliance Regulations 2015, reg 2.

See the FATCA agreement, Annex I. See CRS, Section II onwards. See EU DAC, Annex I, Section II onwards.

NEW INDIVIDUAL ACCOUNTS – WHERE REVIEW IS NOT REQUIRED

10.3

Focus

Under FATCA, for accounts held by individuals and opened on or after January 1, 2014 ('new individual accounts'), the following accounts are not required to be reviewed, identified or reported:

- a depository account unless the account balance exceeds US $50,000; and

- a cash value insurance contract unless the cash value exceeds US $50,000.

However, under the UK's AEOI Regulations, the review and reporting of these accounts may still be required unless an election to the contrary is made each year. See the International Tax Compliance Regulations 2015, regs 2(2)(c), (3) and 3(5) (see **9.11**).

There is no equivalent list of accounts not requiring review under CRS and EU DAC, hence all new individual accounts to which CRS or EU DAC apply will need to be reviewed, and accordingly may need to be reported. However, this is subject to the making of the election referred to below.

See **10.12** and **10.13** for reasons why it may sometimes be prudent to carry out due diligence procedures anyway.

Under the UK's Regulations implementing CRS and EU DAC (see the International Tax Compliance Regulations 2015, regs 2(2)(c) and 3(5)), a dormant account (other than an annuity contract) with a balance that does not exceed US $1,000 is not a reportable account for a calendar year if there is an election by the institution which has effect for that year to treat all such accounts, or a clearly identified group of such accounts, as not being reportable accounts.

The election then also has the effect of removing the requirement to apply due diligence review under CRS or EU DAC. Note that the election must be made separately for each year to which it is to apply. See 9.11 regarding dormant accounts.

See the FATCA agreement, Annex I. See CRS, Section IV. See EU DAC, Annex I, Section IV.

ALTERNATIVE PROCEDURES FOR INDIVIDUAL BENEFICIARIES OF A CASH VALUE INSURANCE CONTRACT OR AN ANNUITY CONTRACT

10.4

Focus

Under CRS and EU DAC, a reporting financial institution may presume that an individual beneficiary (other than the owner) of a cash value insurance contract or an annuity contract receiving a death benefit is

> not a reportable person and may treat such financial account as other than a reportable account, unless the reporting financial institution has actual knowledge, or reason to know, that the beneficiary is a reportable person.

A reporting financial institution has reason to know that a beneficiary of a cash value insurance contract or an annuity contract is a reportable person if the information collected by the reporting financial institution and associated with the beneficiary contains reportable jurisdiction or EU Member State indicia as described in **8.15**.

As regards the phrase 'EU Member State', all references in EU law to Member States is treated as including the UK during the Brexit transition period. See **2.8** and **2.9**.

If a reporting financial institution has actual knowledge, or reason to know, that the beneficiary is a reportable person (see **9.8** and **9.9**), it must follow the procedures referred to in **8.10**.

See CRS, Section VII. See EU DAC, Annex I Section VII.

NEW INDIVIDUAL ACCOUNTS – WHERE REVIEW IS REQUIRED

10.5

Focus

With respect to new individual accounts where due diligence review is required (see **10.3** for circumstances where that may not be the case) upon account opening, the reporting UK financial institution must obtain a self-certification that allows it to determine whether the account holder is either tax resident in the USA (for the purposes of FATCA), resident in a reporting jurisdiction (for the purposes of CRS) or in an EU Member State (for the purposes of EU DAC) or, for the purposes of FATCA only, a US citizen.

The self-certification should include obtaining the individual account holder's tax identification number ('TIN').

Under the FATCA agreement, if the reporting UK financial institution is unable to obtain a valid self-certification, the reporting UK financial institution must treat the account as a US reportable account for the purposes of FATCA.

If the account holder is either tax resident in the US (under FATCA), tax resident in a reporting jurisdiction (under CRS), tax resident in an EU Member

State (under EU DAC) or a US citizen, the UK financial institution must ensure that the self-certification includes the account holder's TIN. In the case of a US TIN, this may be in the form of an IRS Form W-9 or other similar agreed form.

The reporting UK financial institution must confirm the reasonableness of this self-certification based on the information obtained by the reporting UK financial institution, including by reference to any documentation collected pursuant to anti-money laundering ('AML')/know your client ('KYC') procedures.

If the self-certification establishes that the account holder is resident in the US for tax purposes or a US citizen, the reporting UK financial institution must treat the account as a US reportable account under FATCA.

If the reporting UK financial institution becomes aware of a change of circumstances in relation to the original self-certification, the reporting UK financial institution must then obtain a new self-certification that establishes whether the account holder is now resident in the US (under FATCA), a reporting jurisdiction (under CRS) or an EU Member State (under EU DAC) for tax purposes or (for FATCA only) a US citizen.

As regards the phrase 'EU Member State', all references in EU law to Member States is treated as including the UK during the Brexit transition period. See **2.8** and **2.9**.

See the FATCA agreement, Annex I. See CRS, Section IV. See EU DAC, Annex I, Section IV.

PRE-EXISTING INDIVIDUAL ACCOUNTS – WHERE REVIEW WAS NOT REQUIRED

10.6

Focus

Under the FATCA agreement, the following accounts are not required to be reviewed, identified or reported:

(1) pre-existing individual accounts with a balance or value that does not exceed US $50,000 as of 31 December 2013;

(2) pre-existing individual accounts that are cash value insurance contracts and annuity contracts with a balance or value of US $250,000 or less as of 31 December 2013;

(3) pre-existing individual accounts that are cash value insurance contracts or annuity contracts, provided the law or regulations of the UK or the US effectively prevents the sale of cash value insurance contracts or annuity contracts to US residents, such

---

as if the relevant financial institution does not have the required registration under US law, and the law of the UK requires reporting or withholding with respect to insurance products held by residents of the UK;

(4)   any depository account with a balance or value of US $50,000 or less.

Accounts within (3) are also not required to be reviewed, identified or reported under CRS/EU DAC either. However, (1), (2), and (4) are not excluded from CRS/EU DAC so are potentially subject to review, identification and reporting.

Furthermore, dormant accounts (other than an annuity contract) with a balance that does not exceed US $1,000 are also not required to be reviewed, identified or reported under CRS/EU DAC.

Despite this, it is important to be aware, under the UK's Regulations that apply FATCA and CRS/EU DAC, the review and reporting of all of these accounts will still be required unless an election to the contrary is made (separately for *each year* to which the election is to apply). See the International Tax Compliance Regulations 2015, regs 2(2)(c), (3) and 3(5) (see **9.11**).

See also **10.12** and **10.13** for reasons why it may nevertheless be prudent to undertake due diligence in respect of some or all of these accounts, anyway.

As regards the phrase 'Member State', all references in EU law to Member States is treated as including the UK during the Brexit transition period. See **2.8** and **2.9**.

However, under CRS only, a pre-existing individual account that is a cash value insurance contract or an annuity contract is not required to be reviewed, identified or reported, provided the reporting financial institution is effectively prevented by law from selling such contract to residents of a reportable jurisdiction. The UK's Regulations implementing CRS (see the International Tax Compliance Regulations 2015) will still require review, identification and reporting unless an election under reg 2(2)(c) is made – see also reg 3(5) as regards the impact of this election on due diligence obligations.

Furthermore, under the UK's Regulations implementing CRS and EU DAC (see the International Tax Compliance Regulations 2015, regs 2(2)(c) and 3(5)), a dormant account (other than an annuity contract) with a balance that does not exceed US$1,000 is not a reportable account for a calendar year if there is an election by the institution which has effect for that year to treat all such accounts, or a clearly identified group of such accounts, as not being reportable accounts. The election then also has the effect of removing the requirement to apply due diligence review under CRS or EU DAC. Note that the election must be made separately for each year to which it is to apply. See **9.11** regarding dormant accounts.

See the FATCA agreement, Annex I. See CRS, Section III. See EU DAC, Annex I, Section III.

PRE-EXISTING INDIVIDUAL ACCOUNTS – WHAT WERE LOWER VALUE ACCOUNTS?

10.7

Focus

Under FATCA, an account with a balance that exceeded US $50,000 as of 31 December 2013 (or US $250,000 in the case of a cash value insurance contract or annuity contract) is a lower value account.

For CRS and EU DAC, 'lower value account' means a pre-existing individual account with an aggregate balance or value as of 31 December 2015 that does not exceed an amount denominated in the domestic currency of each Member State that corresponds to US $1,000,000. See below regarding the phrase 'Member State' after Brexit.

Under CRS and EU DAC, review of pre-existing lower value individual accounts had to be completed by 31 December 2017.

PRE-EXISTING INDIVIDUAL LOWER VALUE ACCOUNTS WHERE DUE DILIGENCE IS CARRIED OUT – BASIC DUE DILIGENCE

10.8

Focus

The due diligence requirements for a pre-existing individual account allow for a residence address test procedure for a lower value account. Subject to conditions, the reporting financial institution ('RFI') could treat the individual account holder as resident for tax purposes of the country where their current residence address is located.

If the RFI had in its records a current residence address for the individual account holder based on documentary evidence, the reporting financial institution may treat the individual account holder as being a resident for tax purposes of the jurisdiction in which the address is located for purposes of determining whether such individual account holder is a reportable person (see **9.8** and **9.9**).

The current residence address had to be substantiated by evidence. The type of acceptable evidence depends on the circumstances.

A 'care of' or post office box address would not generally be presumed to be the residential address (except in special circumstances such as that of military personnel).

Where an RFI is unable to establish the residence of an individual with a lower value account with the residence address test, or chooses not to apply the residence address test, it must review its electronically searchable data for indicia of the individual's residence.

The account holder is regarded as a resident of the US or a reportable jurisdiction (or in the case of FATCA a US citizen) if any US indicia or reportable jurisdiction indicia are found. See **10.9** regarding the various kinds of indicia.

For a lower value account, it may have been possible to rely on a current residence address supported by documentary evidence. Where that was not the case, an electronic record search had to be carried out.

Electronic record search will generally be looking for US or reportable jurisdiction indicia. See **9.3** and **9.5**. See **10.9**.

In addition to basic due diligence, enhanced review due diligence is sometimes required. Again, this will be looking for US indicia or reportable jurisdiction indicia (see **10.11**).

Under CRS and EU DAC, if a 'hold mail' instruction or 'in-care-of' address is discovered in the electronic search and no other address and none of the other indicia listed in **10.9** are identified for the account holder, the reporting financial institution must, in the order most appropriate to the circumstances, apply paper record search described in subparagraph, or seek to obtain from the account holder a self-certification or documentary evidence to establish the residence(s) for tax purposes of such account holder.

In certain circumstances the reporting financial institution may rely on its own databases instead of applying paper record search, where its own databases contain sufficient information. See CRS, Section III(C)(3) and EU DAC, Annex I, Section III(C)(3).

Under CRS and EU DAC, if the paper search fails to establish an indicium and the attempt to obtain the self-certification or documentary evidence is not successful, the reporting financial institution must report the account as an undocumented account.

If US indicia are identified in relation to the account, it must therefore be reported under FATCA. The FATCA agreement does not appear to require that further due diligence be carried out after that. However, see above regarding a 'change of circumstances'.

In effect, it may be prudent to carry out due diligence in relation to these accounts, even though the FATCA agreement, CRS and EU DAC seem to say that this is not required.

As regards the phrase 'Member State' in the above, all references in EU law to Member States is treated as including the UK during the Brexit transition period. See **2.8** and **2.9**.

See the FATCA agreement, Annex I. See CRS, Section III. See EU DAC, Annex I, Section III.

US, REPORTABLE JURISDICTION AND MEMBER STATE INDICIA IN RELATION TO INDIVIDUAL ACCOUNTS

10.9   Under AEOI, a reporting UK financial institution carrying out an electronic record search had to review electronically searchable data it maintained for any of the following indicia:

(a)   identification of the account holder as a resident of the US (for FATCA), reportable jurisdiction (for CRS) or EU Member State (for EU DAC) or for FATCA only a US citizen;

(b)   for FATCA only, 'unambiguous indication' of a US place of birth;

(c)   current US, reportable jurisdiction or EU Member State mailing or residence address (including a post office box or 'in-care-of' address);

(d)   current US, reportable jurisdiction or EU Member State telephone number;

(e)   standing instructions to transfer funds to an account maintained in the US, reportable jurisdiction or EU Member State;

(f)   currently effective power of attorney or signatory authority granted to a person with a US, reportable jurisdiction or EU Member State address; or

(g)   an 'in-care-of' or 'hold mail' address that is the sole address the reporting UK financial institution has on file for the account holder.

As regards the phrase 'EU Member State', all references in EU law to Member States is treated as including the UK during the Brexit transition period. See **2.8** and **2.9**.

See the FATCA agreement, Annex I. See CRS, Section III. See EU DAC, Annex I, Section III.

10.10   However, in the case of a pre-existing individual account that is a lower value account, an 'in-care-of' address outside the US shall not be treated as US indicia for the purposes of FATCA.

Notwithstanding a finding of US indicia, a reporting UK financial institution is nevertheless not required to treat an account as a US reportable account if:

(1)   Where account holder information unambiguously indicates a US place of birth, the reporting UK financial institution obtains or has previously reviewed and maintains a record of:

    (a)   a self-certification that the account holder is neither a US citizen nor a US resident for tax purposes (which may be on an IRS Form W-8 or other similar agreed form);

    (b)   a non-US passport or other government-issued identification evidencing the account holder's citizenship or nationality in a country other than the US; and

    (c)   a copy of the account holder's certificate of loss of nationality of the United States or a reasonable explanation of:

        (i)   the reason the account holder does not have such a certificate despite renouncing US citizenship; or

        (ii)   the reason the account holder did not obtain US citizenship at birth.

(2)   Where account holder information contains a current US mailing or residence address, or one or more US telephone numbers that are the only telephone numbers associated with the account, the reporting UK financial institution obtains or has previously reviewed and maintains a record of:

    (a)   a self-certification that the account holder is not a US citizen or resident for tax purposes (which may be on an IRS Form W-8 or other similar agreed form); and

    (b)   a non-US passport or other government-issued identification evidencing the account holder's citizenship or nationality in a country other than the US.

(3)   Where account holder information contains standing instructions to transfer funds to an account maintained in the US, the reporting UK financial institution obtains or has previously reviewed and maintains a record of:

    (a)   a self-certification that the account holder is not a US citizen or resident for tax purposes (which may be on an IRS Form W-8 or other similar agreed form); and

    (b)   documentary evidence, as defined in the FATCA agreement.

(4)   Where account holder information contains a currently effective power of attorney or signatory authority granted to a person with a US address, has an 'in-care-of' address or 'hold mail' address that is the sole address

identified for the account holder, or has one or more US telephone numbers (if a non-US telephone number is also associated with the account), the reporting UK financial institution obtains or has previously reviewed and maintains a record of:

(a)   a self-certification that the account holder is not a US citizen or resident for tax purposes (which may be on an IRS Form W-8 or other similar agreed form); or

(b)   documentary evidence as defined in the FATCA agreement, establishing the account holder's non-US status.

See the FATCA agreement, Annex I.

HIGH VALUE ACCOUNTS – 'ENHANCED REVIEW' DUE DILIGENCE

10.11

Focus

In certain circumstances relating to high value accounts, enhanced review procedures must be carried out.

The enhanced review procedures which the reporting UK financial institution must carry out consist of both:

- electronic record search; and

- paper record search.

Under FATCA, CRS and EU DAC, the enhanced review procedures are intended to identify whether there are 'US indicia' (in the case of FATCA), indicia relating to a reportable jurisdiction (in the case of CRS) or indicia relating to a Member State (in the case of EU DAC) (see **9.7**).

If there are, that account must therefore be reported under FATCA, CRS or EU DAC as applicable. See below regarding the phrase 'Member State' after Brexit.

The FATCA agreement, CRS and EU DAC each say that the full procedures do not need to be carried out more than once. However, see **10.13** regarding a 'change of circumstances'.

The paper record search can be reduced if the financial institution's database contains sufficient information to enable this. For further details of these searches, see the Annex I of the FATCA agreement, Annex I of CRS and/or Annex I of EU DAC as applicable.

Under FATCA, if an account was a high value account (see **10.11**) as of 31 December 2013, enhanced review procedures had to be carried out by 31 December 2014. If it becomes a high value account as of 31 December of a subsequent calendar year, enhanced review procedures have to be carried out by six months after the end of that calendar year.

Under CRS and EU DAC, if an account was a high value account as of 31 December 2015, enhanced review procedures had to be carried out by 31 December 2016 – see **10.7** regarding the deadline for review of a lower value account.

Under CRS and EU DAC, if an account was not a high value account as of 31 December 2015 but subsequently becomes a high value account, enhanced review procedures must be carried out within the calendar year following the year in which the account becomes a high value account.

As regards the phrase 'Member State', all references in EU law to Member States is treated as including the UK during the Brexit transition period. See **2.8** and **2.9**.

Once a high value account has been reported under FATCA, CRS or EU DAC, it needs then to continue being reported each subsequent year while the account continues in existence, unless and until the account holder ceases to be a reportable person (or ceases to be a specified US person in the case of FATCA).

See **9.8** and **9.9** regarding the meaning of 'reportable person'. See **9.8** and **9.9** as well as FATCA agreement, Art 1(8)(gg) on the meaning of specified US person.

CAUTION REQUIRED – ACCOUNTS THAT BECOME HIGH VALUE ACCOUNTS LATER ON

10.12   Under FATCA an account with a balance that exceeded US $50,000 as of 31 December 2013 (or US $250,000 in the case of a cash value insurance contract or annuity contract) is a lower value account. As such it is subject to the review procedures described in **10.8**.

Under FATCA, CRS and EU DAC, an account with a balance exceeding US $1 million as of 31 December 2013 (for FATCA) or 31 December 2015 (for CRS or EU DAC) is a high value account. As such, it is subject to 'enhanced review procedures'.

Furthermore, even if an account had a balance not exceeding US $1 million as of 31 December 2013 (for FATCA) or 31 December 2015 (for CRS or EU DAC) and later on has a balance exceeding US $1 million as of 31 December of a subsequent calendar year, it is a high value account. As such, it is subject to enhanced review procedures.

Under FATCA, this can mean that an account that had a balance of less than US $50,000 as of 31 December 2013 (US $250,000 for certain insurance products) but subsequently became a high value account is therefore subject to enhanced review procedures. See **10.11**.

See the FATCA agreement, Annex I. See CRS, Section III. See EU DAC, Annex I, Section III.

CAUTION REQUIRED – THE 'CHANGE OF CIRCUMSTANCES' RULES

10.13

Focus

If self-certification or any electronic search that may have been carried out did not identify US indicia (under FATCA), reportable jurisdiction indicia (under CRS) or Member State indicia (under EU DAC), the account may still need to be reported under AEOI if later on the RFI becomes aware that there has been a 'change of circumstances'. See **Chapter 2** regarding the phrase 'Member State' after Brexit.

In practice – even in cases where technically speaking due diligence is not required – it may therefore appear prudent to carry out a review each year to see whether there has been a change of circumstances.

In particular, a reporting UK financial institution must implement procedures to ensure that a relationship manager identifies any change in circumstances of an account. The reporting UK financial institution must treat as reportable any high value accounts assigned to a relationship manager (including any accounts aggregated with such account) if the relationship manager has actual knowledge that the account holder is a reportable person (or a specified US person in the case of FATCA).

See **9.8** and **9.9** regarding the meaning of 'reportable person'.

In view of this in the case of lower value accounts for which such indicia were not initially present, a reporting UK financial institution will need to ensure that it can show that it is alert to the possibility of a change of circumstances and that it identifies and reacts to a change of circumstances when it occurs.

Therefore, it may well be prudent to continue to carry out a due diligence review each year unless and until US, reportable jurisdiction or Member State indicia are eventually uncovered and accordingly reporting is eventually required. See **Chapter 2** regarding the phrase 'Member State' after Brexit.

If the first run of due diligence procedures does not identify US, reportable jurisdiction or Member State indicia, the account may still need to be reported under FATCA, CRS or EU DAC if there is a 'change of circumstances'. See **Chapter 2** regarding the phrase 'Member State' after Brexit.

See **10.11** regarding accounts which become a high value account as of 31 December of a subsequent calendar year (than 31 December 2014 for FATCA or 31 December 2015 for CRS or EU DAC).

See **9.8** and **9.9** as well as the FATCA agreement, Art 1(8)(gg) on the meaning of specified US person.

See the FATCA agreement generally. See CRS, Section III. See EU DAC, Annex I, Section III.

Chapter 11

FATCA/CRS due diligence of entity accounts (including NFEs and NFFEs)

SIGNPOSTS

- General principles relating to due diligence under FATCA and CRS/EU DAC, are set out in **Chapter 9**. **Chapter 10** then considered due diligence specifically in relation to financial accounts held by individuals. This Chapter considers due diligence in relation to financial accounts held by entities (see **11.1**).

- The specific due diligence requirements relating to financial accounts where the account holder is an individual depend on what kind of account it is. In particular, it could be a pre-existing entity account or a new entity account. Of these, a pre-existing entity account could either be an account not requiring review, identification or reporting or an account that does require these. A new entity account will invariably require review, identification or reporting (see **11.2**).

- An entity is a legal person or a legal arrangement such as a trust (see **11.3**).

- An entity is regarded as being a related entity of another entity if one entity controls the other or the two are under common control (see **11.4**).

- Whether entities are related entities of each other may be important for the account balance aggregation rules, the scope of the term reportable person, for determining if a non-financial entity ('NFE') can meet the criteria for being an active NFE. It also has a wider application for FATCA. This includes that in certain circumstances an entity that is a member of a related entity group will not be a financial institution. Related entity status can also have an impact on whether a UK financial institution has obligations in respect of an entity that is a non-participating financial institution (see **11.5**).

- All partnerships are entities for the purposes of FATCA and CRS/ EU DAC. The UK's FATCA/CRS Regulations treat an account of a partner in a partnership as an entity account (see **11.6**).

- Provided an election is made to that effect in respect of each reporting year to which it is to apply under the UK's FATCA/ CRS Regulations, a pre-existing entity account not exceeding US $250,000 on 31 December 2013 does not require review, identification or reporting under FATCA rules. A pre-existing entity account not exceeding US $250,000 on 31 December 2015 does not require review, identification or reporting under CRS rules. However, the same account will begin to require review, identification and reporting under CRS if it exceeds US $250,000 on a subsequent 31 December and under FATCA if it subsequently exceeds US $1,000,000 (see **11.7**).

- Where a pre-existing entity account that did not exceed US $250,000 on 31 December 2013 exceeds US $1,000,000 as of a subsequent 31 December, due diligence review for FATCA purposes must be completed by six months after the end of the calendar year in which it does so. Where a pre-existing entity account that did not exceed US $250,000 on 31 December 2015 exceeds US $250,000 as of a subsequent 31 December, due diligence review for CRS purposes must be completed by 12 months after the end of the calendar year in which it does so (see **11.8**).

- For pre-existing entity accounts where review is required, the procedure consists in the main of reviewing anti-money laundering ('AML')/know-your-client ('KYC') information and documentation that the reporting financial institution ('RFI') has already obtained to determine (1) if the entity is a specified US person or a reportable person (see **9.8** and **9.9**) and (2) if the entity is a passive NFE/non-financial foreign entity ('NFFE') with a controlling person who is a US resident, US citizen or participating jurisdiction resident (see **11.9**).

- If there is a change of circumstances which calls into question the status of an entity account, the RFI must carry out further due diligence in order to re-determine the status of the account (see **11.10**).

- Due diligence is intended to determine whether an account is a reportable account. In the case of a pre-existing entity account, it cannot be reportable unless (in the case of FATCA) it is held by one or more entities that are specified US persons or by passive NFFEs with one or more controlling persons who are US citizens or residents; or (in the case of CRS) it is held by one or more entities that are reportable persons (see **9.8** and **9.9**) under CRS/ EU DAC or by passive NFEs with one or more controlling persons who are participating jurisdiction residents. Even then, see **12.3** and **12.4** regarding various circumstances when an account may, nevertheless, still not be reportable (see **11.11**).

- Under FATCA only, an account is not a reportable account if it is held by an entity that is a participating foreign financial institution ('FFI'), a deemed-compliant FFI, an exempt beneficial owner, or an excepted FFI, as those terms are defined in relevant US Treasury Regulations (see **11.12**).

- In relation to a new entity account, an RFI must determine information including whether the account is held (for FATCA) by a specified US person or passive NFFE with one or more controlling persons that are US residents or citizens and (for CRS) whether the account his held by a reportable person (see **9.8** and **9.9**) or by a passive NFE with one or more controlling persons that are participating jurisdiction residents. It should do this using information which it holds or that is publicly available and in certain circumstances self-certification (see **11.13**).

- An entity that is not a financial institution is an NFE (for CRS) or an NFFE (for FATCA). An NFE or NFFE is either a passive NFE or NFFE or else it is an active NFE or NFFE (see **11.14**).

- For FATCA, a passive NFFE is simply an NFFE that is not an active NFFE. Similarly, for CRS an NFE that is not an active NFE is a passive NFE. However, CRS passive NFEs also include investment entities which are not domiciled in CRS participating jurisdictions or in EU Member States (see **11.15**).

- The FATCA agreement and CRS set out a lengthy list of entities which are respectively active NFFEs or active NFEs (see **11.16**).

OVERVIEW

11.1

Focus

General principles relating to due diligence under FATCA and CRS/ EU DAC, are set out in **Chapter 9**. **Chapter 10** considers due diligence specifically in relation to financial accounts held by individuals.

This Chapter considers due diligence in relation to financial accounts held by entities.

DUE DILIGENCE OF ENTITY ACCOUNTS

11.2

Focus

Different due diligence procedures apply to different kinds of entity accounts. See this Chapter generally.

An entity is a legal person or a legal arrangement. An individual is not an entity.

'Entity' covers companies as defined in the Corporation Tax Act 2010, s 1121. It also covers partnerships (see **11.6**) and trusts (see **Chapter 6**).

See **11.3** on the meaning of entity generally.

For reporting purposes, an entity will either be a financial institution or an NFE (for CRS or EU DAC) or NFFE (for FATCA).

There are two kinds of entity accounts for the purposes of Automatic Exchange of Information ('AEOI'):

- pre-existing entity accounts;
- new entity accounts.

Pre-existing entity accounts are entity accounts which existed:

- on or before 31 December 2013 for the purposes of FATCA; or
- on or before 31 December 2015 for the purposes of CRS and EU DAC.

New entity accounts are entity accounts which are opened:

- on or after 1 January 2014 for the purposes of FATCA; or
- on or after 1 January 2016 for the purposes of CRS and EU DAC.

WHAT IS AN ENTITY?

11.3

Focus

Under CRS and EU DAC, 'entity' means a legal person or a legal arrangement, such as a corporation, partnership, trust, or foundation.

For the purposes of the FATCA agreement, 'entity' means a legal person or a legal arrangement such as a trust.

An important difference between FATCA, on the one hand, and CRS and EU DAC on the other, is that for FATCA the definition of financial account excludes equity and debt interests in an investment entity where those interests are regularly traded on an established securities market. Under EU DAC/CRS, however, equity and debt interests in certain listed investment entities, for example, investment trust companies ('ITC'), are in the scope of AEOI.

When a financial institution is carrying out AEOI due diligence in relation an entity, it may rely upon an audited financial statement to establish that an account holder meets a certain income or asset threshold (but is not obliged to where the entity's status can be established from other information or documentation that it holds).

If a financial institution does rely upon an audited financial statement to establish a status for an account holder, it has reason to know that the status claimed is unreliable or incorrect only if the audited financial statement for the account holder or the notes or footnotes to the financial statement conflicts with the self-certification provided to it.

In relation to entities, it may sometimes be necessary to determine whether one entity is a related entity of another.

See CRS, Section VIII(E)(3), (4) and EU DAC, Annex I, Section VIII(E)(3), (4). See the FATCA agreement, Arts 1(hh), (kk) and 4(5).

WHAT IS A RELATED ENTITY, AND WHY DOES IT MATTER?

11.4

Focus

An entity is regarded as being related to another entity if one entity controls the other or the two entities are under common control – the 'related entity group'. For this purpose, control is taken as including the direct or indirect ownership of more than 50% of the vote and value in an entity. See HMRC's International Exchange of Information Manual IEIM404005.

An entity is a 'related entity' of another entity if either entity controls the other entity, or the two entities are under common control. For this purpose, control includes direct or indirect ownership of more than 50% of the vote and value in an entity.

In addition, under EU DAC, an entity is also a 'related entity' if the two entities are investment entities:

143

(1)   (a) the gross income of which is primarily attributable to investing, reinvesting, or trading in financial assets, if the entity is managed by another entity that is a depository institution, a custodial institution, a specified insurance company; or

(b)   which primarily conducts as a business one or more of the following activities or operations for or on behalf of a customer:

(i)   trading in money market instruments (cheques, bills, certificates of deposit, derivatives, etc), foreign exchange, exchange, interest rate and index instruments, transferable securities, or commodity futures trading;

(ii)   individual and collective portfolio management; or

(iii)   otherwise investing, administering, or managing financial assets or money on behalf of other persons; and

(2)   are under common management, and such management fulfils the due diligence obligations of such investment entities.

For the purposes of the FATCA agreement, an entity is a 'related entity' of another entity if either entity controls the other entity, or the two entities are under common control. For this purpose, control includes direct or indirect ownership of more than 50% of the vote or value in an entity. Notwithstanding the foregoing, the UK competent authority may treat an entity as not a related entity of another entity if the two entities are not members of the same expanded affiliated group as defined in s 1471(e)(2) of the US Internal Revenue Code.

See CRS Section VIII(E)(3), (4) and EU DAC, Annex I, Section VIII(E)(3), (4). See the FATCA agreement, Arts 1(hh), (kk) and 4(5).

11.5

Focus

Whether an entity is a related entity to another entity may be relevant:

●   for the account balance aggregation rules (see IEIM403560);

●   the scope of the term reportable person (see **9.8** and **9.9**; also see HMRC's International Exchange of Information Manual IEIM403440); and

●   for determining if an NFE can meet the criteria for being an active NFE (see HMRC's International Exchange of Information Manual IEIM404040).

Whether an entity is a related entity has a wider application for FATCA. See HMRC's International Exchange of Information Manual IEIM404005 for further details.

This includes that in certain circumstances an entity that is a member of a related entity group, will not be a financial institution.

> Related entities are also relevant on the basis that a UK financial institution may find that it has obligations in respect of any related entity that is a non-participating financial institution.

See HMRC's International Exchange of Information Manual IEIM403220 and IEIM403230.

See the International Tax Compliance Regulations 2015, SI 2015/878, reg 2.

See the FATCA agreement, Annex I. See CRS, Section V onwards. See EU DAC, Annex I, Section V onwards.

PARTNERS AND PARTNERSHIPS
11.6

> **Focus**
>
> All partnerships, including general partnerships, limited partnerships and limited liability partnerships, are treated as entities for the purposes of FATCA, CRS/EU DAC.
>
> Under the UK's AEOI Regulations, an account held by an individual as a partner of a partnership is treated as an entity account and is not treated as an individual account. See the International Tax Compliance Regulations 2015, reg 2(8).

For example, the FATCA agreement defines 'US person' as a US citizen or resident individual, a partnership or corporation organised in the US or under the laws of the US or any State thereof. See Art 1(1)(ff) of the FATCA agreement.

In CRS, 'reportable jurisdiction person' means 'an individual or entity that is resident in a reportable jurisdiction …'; 'entity' means a legal person or a legal arrangement, such as a corporation, partnership, trust, or foundation. See CRS, Section VIII(D)(3) and E(3).

See also the very similar (as compared with CRS) definitions of 'Member State person' and 'entity' in EU DAC, Annex I, Section VIII(D)(3) and E(3).

See HMRC's International Exchange of Information Manual IEIM400860.

PRE-EXISTING ENTITY ACCOUNTS – WHERE REVIEW WAS NOT REQUIRED
11.7

> **Focus**
>
> Under the FATCA agreement, pre-existing entity accounts with account balances that do not exceed US $250,000 as of 31 December 2013, are

not required to be reviewed, identified, or reported as US reportable accounts until the account balance exceeds US $1,000,000.

Under CRS/EU DAC, pre-existing entity accounts with account balances that do not exceed US $250,000 as of 31 December 2015, are not required to be reviewed, identified, or reported as US reportable accounts until the account balance exceeds US $250,000.

However, under the UK's AEOI Regulations, the review and reporting of these accounts may still be required unless an election to the contrary is made each year. See the International Tax Compliance Regulations 2015, regs 2(2)(c), (3) and 3(5). See **9.11**.

Under the UK's Regulations implementing CRS and EU DAC, an account that is a pre-existing entity account with an account balance or value that does not exceed US $250,000 as of 31 December 2015 is not a reportable account for a calendar year if there is an election by the institution which has effect for that year to treat all such accounts, or a clearly identified group of such accounts, as not being reportable accounts (International Tax Compliance Regulations 2015, regs 2(2)(c) and 3(5)). The election then also has the effect of removing the requirement to apply due diligence review under CRS or EU DAC. Note that the election must be made separately for each year to which it is to apply. See **9.11** regarding dormant accounts.

By contrast, pre-existing entity accounts that have an account balance or value that exceeds US $250,000 as of 31 December 2013, and pre-existing entity accounts that initially do not exceed US $250,000 but the account balance of which later exceeds US $1,000,000 must be reviewed in accordance with the procedures described in **11.8** and **11.9**.

See the FATCA agreement, Annex I. See CRS, Section V. See EU DAC, Annex I, Section V.

WHICH PRE-EXISTING ENTITY ACCOUNTS NEEDED DUE DILIGENCE?

11.8

Focus

For the purposes of FATCA:

- review of pre-existing entity accounts with an account balance or value that exceeded US $250,000 as of 31 December 2013, had to be completed by 31 December 2015;

- review of pre-existing entity accounts with a balance or value that did not exceed US $250,000 as of 31 December 2013, but exceeds US $1,000,000 as of 31 December of a subsequent year, must be completed within six months after the end of the calendar year in which the account balance exceeds US $1,000,000.

For the purposes of CRS and EU DAC:

- review of pre-existing entity accounts with an aggregate account balance or value that exceeded, as of 31 December 2015, the equivalent of US $250,000, had to be completed by 31 December 2017.

- review of pre-existing entity accounts with a balance or value that did not exceed US $250,000 as of 31 December 2015, but exceeds that amount as of 31 December of a subsequent year, must be completed within the calendar year after that in which the account balance exceeds that amount.

See the FATCA agreement, Annex I. See CRS, Section V(E). See EU DAC, Annex I, Section V(E).

DUE DILIGENCE PROCEDURES FOR PRE-EXISTING ENTITY ACCOUNTS

11.9

Focus

For those pre-existing entities accounts where review is required applying the criteria in **11.7**, a reporting UK financial institution must apply the following review procedures:

(1) review AML/KYC information and documents on whether the entity is a specified US person or reportable person;

(2) review AML/KYC information and documents on whether the entity is a passive NFE/NFFE with a controlling person who is US resident or citizen or participating jurisdiction resident.

Where appropriate, obtain self-certification on these issues.

First, the reporting UK financial institution must review information obtained for AML/KYC purposes to determine whether the entity is a specified US person (for FATCA) or a reportable person (for CRS or EU DAC).

If the AML/KYC information indicates that the entity is a specified US person or a reportable person, the entity must be treated as such unless the reporting UK financial institution determines otherwise using self-certification or other evidence to the contrary.

See **9.8** and **9.9** regarding the meaning of 'reportable person'. See **9.8** and **9.9** too, as well as the FATCA agreement, Art 1(8)(gg) on the meaning of specified US person.

Secondly, the reporting UK financial institution must review information obtained for AML/KYC purposes to determine whether the entity is:

- a passive NFFE with a controlling person who is a citizen or resident of the US; or

- a passive NFE with a controlling person who is a resident of a participating jurisdiction (for CRS) or of an EU Member State (for EU DAC).

For the purposes of FATCA, if the AML/KYC information indicates that the entity is a passive NFFE with a controlling person who is a citizen or resident of the USA, the entity must be treated as such unless the reporting UK financial institution determines otherwise using self-certification or other evidence to the contrary.

For the purposes of determining whether a controlling person of a passive NFFE is a citizen or resident of the US for tax purposes, a reporting UK financial institution may rely on:

(1)   information collected and maintained pursuant to AML/KYC procedures in the case of a pre-existing entity account held by one or more NFFEs with an account balance that does not exceed US $1,000,000; or

(2)   a self-certification (which may be on an IRS Form W-8 or W-9, or on a similar agreed form) from the account holder or such controlling person in the case of a pre-existing entity account held by one or more NFFEs with an account balance that exceeds US $1,000,000.

Similarly, for the purposes of CRS and EU DAC, if the AML/KYC information indicates that the entity is a passive NFE with a controlling person who is a resident of a participating jurisdiction (for CRS) or of an EU Member State (for EU DAC), the entity must be treated as such unless the reporting UK financial institution determines otherwise using self-certification or other evidence to the contrary.

For the purposes of determining whether a controlling person of a passive NFFE is a citizen or resident of the US for tax purposes, a reporting UK financial institution may rely on:

(1)   information collected and maintained pursuant to AML/KYC procedures in the case of a pre-existing entity account held by one or more NFFEs with an account balance that does not exceed US $1,000,000; or

(2)   a self-certification from the account holder or such controlling person.

See also **11.7** regarding obligations in respect of a non-participating financial institution for the 2015 and 2016 calendar years only.

As regards the phrase 'EU Member State', all references in EU law to Member States is treated as including the UK during the Brexit transition period. See **2.8** and **2.9**.

See the FATCA agreement, Annex I. See CRS. See EU DAC.

CHANGE OF CIRCUMSTANCES

11.10

Focus

If there is a change of circumstances with respect to a pre-existing entity account that causes the reporting UK financial institution to know or have reason to know that the self-certification or other documentation associated with an account is incorrect or unreliable, the reporting UK financial institution must re-determine the status of the account in accordance with the procedures set forth in **11.8** and **11.9**.

See the FATCA agreement, Annex I. See CRS, Section V(E). See EU DAC, Annex I, Section V(E).

WHICH PRE-EXISTING ENTITY ACCOUNTS THEN NEEDED REPORTING?

11.11

Focus

As regards pre-existing entity accounts, only accounts that are held by:

- one or more entities that are specified US persons; or
- passive NFFEs with one or more controlling persons who are US citizens or residents,

shall be treated as US reportable accounts for the purposes of FATCA.

As regards pre-existing entity accounts, only accounts that are held by:

- one or more entities that are reportable persons (under CRS or EU DAC); or
- passive NFEs (for CRS or EU DAC) with one or more controlling persons who are participating jurisdiction residents (for CRS) or EU Member State residents (for EU DAC),

shall be treated as reportable accounts for the purposes of CRS or EU DAC.

See **12.3** and **12.4** regarding various circumstances when an account may, nevertheless, still not be reportable.

In addition, the FATCA agreement required a reporting UK financial institution to report certain payments to a non-participating financial institution for the 2015 and 2016 calendar years only. Broadly, a non-participating financial institution is a financial institution of a jurisdiction which has not entered into an intergovernmental agreement ('IGA') with the US in respect of FATCA. See Art 4 of the FATCA agreement. See **12.10**.

As regards the phrase 'EU Member State', all references in EU law to Member States is treated as including the UK during the Brexit transition period. See **2.8** and **2.9**.

See **9.10** regarding controlling persons and **11.15** regarding passive NFFEs and passive NFEs.

See **9.8** and **9.9** as well as the FATCA agreement, Art 1(8)(gg) on the meaning of specified US person.

See the FATCA agreement Annex I. See CRS. See EU DAC.

11.12

Focus

As regards FATCA only, if the entity account holder is:

(a)   a US person that is not a specified US person;

(b)   a UK financial institution or other partner jurisdiction financial institution;

(c)   a participating FFI, a deemed-compliant FFI, an exempt beneficial owner, or an excepted FFI, as those terms are defined in relevant US Treasury Regulations;

(d)   an active NFFE (see **11.16**); or

(e)   a passive NFFE (see **11.15**), none of the controlling persons of which is a US citizen or resident,

then the account is not a US reportable account. It follows that no FATCA reporting is then required with respect to the account, with one exception (see below).

The exception is that in certain circumstances it was necessary to report to HMRC for 2015 and 2016 only for certain payments to a non-participating financial institution which could conceivably include payments to certain UK financial institutions. See Art 4(1)(b) and Annex I(V)(C)(4) of the FATCA agreement.

See **9.8** and **9.9** as well as the FATCA agreement, Art 1(8)(gg) on the meaning of specified US person.

See **4.14**, **4.15** and **4.16** regarding 'exempt beneficial owner' and 'deemed-compliant FFI' or 'deemed compliant financial institution'.

See also the FATCA agreement, Annex I. See **9.10** on controlling persons.

DUE DILIGENCE PROCEDURES FOR NEW ENTITY ACCOUNTS

11.13

Focus

Under FATCA, a reporting UK financial institution must determine whether each account holder is:

(a)   a specified US person;

(b)   a UK financial institution or other partner jurisdiction financial institution;

(c)   a deemed-compliant FFI, an exempt beneficial owner, or certain other kinds of FFI; or

(d)   an active NFFE or passive NFFE. In the case of a passive NFFE, it must also identify any controlling persons. See **9.10** on controlling persons.

Under FATCA, the reporting UK financial institution may determine these things using information that is publicly available or that is in its possession.

If not, it must obtain self-certification. See **9.5** regarding reliance on self-certification or other documentation.

Under CRS and EU DAC, the RFI must carry out specified review procedures to determine:

•   whether the account is held by one or more reportable persons; or

•   passive NFEs with one or more controlling persons who are reportable persons.

See below regarding the procedures that may be applied under CRS and EU DAC.

11.13 *FATCA/CRS due diligence of entity accounts*

Under CRS and EU DAC, to determine whether the account is held by one or reportable persons, the RFI must:

- obtain self-certification, which may be part of the account opening documentation, that allows the RFI to determine the account holder's residence(s) for tax purposes and confirm the reasonableness of such self-certification based on the information obtained by the RFI; and

- if the self-certification indicates that the account holder is resident in a reportable jurisdiction, the RFI must treat it as a reportable account unless it reasonably determines otherwise based on information which it holds or which is publicly available.

Under CRS and EU DAC, to determine whether the account is held by passive NFEs with one or more controlling persons who are reportable persons, the RFI must:

- obtain self-certification to determine whether the account holder is a passive NFE, unless the RFI reasonably determines this based on information which it holds or which is publicly available;

- use information which the RFI has collected – for example, as part of its AML/KYC due diligence – to determine the controlling persons of the account holder;

- obtain self-certification from the account holder or its controlling person to determine whether the controlling person is a reportable person.

See STEP Briefing Note, 'FATCA recalcitrant entity account reporting' (February 2017) which applies only to new entity account reporting for FATCA. STEP say that HMRC has confirmed the position for FATCA reporting where a financial institution has been unable to get a self-certification in respect of a new entity account.

STEP go onto say that where a financial institution has been unable to get a self-certification from an entity, it should use AML/KYC and publicly available information to establish whether it can be excluded from reporting, for example, as a deemed-compliant financial institution, UK government entity or active NFFE.

If it cannot, then the UK/US FATCA IGA requires it to treat it as a passive NFFE – this is a default category for any entity that is not an FFI or active NFFE. The financial institution should use AML/KYC data to try and identify any controlling persons.

STEP say the reporting should be:

- the entity by default as a passive NFFE;

- any controlling persons with US indicia;

- if no controlling persons can be identified, or those identified do not have US indicia, then they are not reported.

The undocumented account flag should not be ticked for these accounts; an undocumented account can only exist in CRS reporting, where the only information a financial institution holds is a 'hold mail' or 'in care of' address.

See **9.8** and **9.9** as well as the FATCA agreement, Art 1(8)(ff) and (gg) regarding the meanings of 'specified US person' and 'US person'.

'Partner jurisdiction' means a jurisdiction that has in effect an agreement with the US to facilitate the implementation of FATCA.

See **4.14**, **4.15** and **4.16** regarding 'exempt beneficial owner' and 'deemed-compliant FFI' or 'deemed-compliant financial institution'.

See **11.14** onwards regarding active and passive NFFEs.

See **9.8** and **9.9** regarding the meaning of 'reportable person'. See **9.10** on controlling persons.

See **Appendix I** for a list of jurisdictions that have committed to a first exchange under CRS.

See the FATCA agreement, Annex I. See CRS, Section VI. See EU DAC, Annex I, Section VI.

Non-financial entities ('NFEs') and non-financial foreign entities ('NFFEs')

11.14

Focus

An entity that is not a financial institution will be an NFE for the purposes of CRS and EU DAC and an NFFE for the purposes of FATCA.

NFEs (and NFFEs) are divided into two categories, active NFEs (and active NFFEs) and passive NFEs (and passive NFFEs) – see **11.15** and **11.16**.

Strictly in the FATCA agreement, 'NFFE' means any non-US entity that is not an FFI as defined in relevant US Treasury Regulations, and also includes any non-US entity that is resident in the UK or other partner jurisdiction and that is not a financial institution.

FFI means a 'foreign financial institution'. Broadly, for the purposes of FATCA, this is a financial institution that is a 'foreign' (which is to say a non-US) entity, other than a financial institution organised under the laws of a possession of the US.

See the FATCA agreement, Annex I. See the CRS, Section VIII. See EU DAC, Annex I, Section VIII.

Passive NFEs and passive NFFEs

11.15

Focus

Under FATCA, CRS and EU DAC, only the controlling persons of passive NFEs (or in the case of FATCA 'passive NFFEs') are reported but not those of active NFEs (or in the case of FATCA 'active NFFEs') – see **11.16**. See **9.10** on controlling persons.

Therefore, an RFI under AEOI (or its UK representative) will need to determine which of the entities among its account holders are passive NFEs or passive NFFEs.

For the purposes of FATCA, a passive NFFE is simply a NFFE that is not an active NFFE. See **11.16** regarding active NFFEs.

However, in CRS and EU DAC, passive NFEs are legal entities which do not qualify as active NFEs, as well as investment entities which are not domiciled in CRS participating jurisdictions and (for EU DAC) EU Member States – see **Appendix II** for a list of jurisdictions that have committed to a first exchange under CRS.

As regards the phrase 'EU Member State', all references in EU law to Member States is treated as including the UK during the Brexit transition period. See **2.8** and **2.9**.

See the FATCA agreement, Annex I. See the CRS. See EU DAC.

Active NFEs and active NFFEs

11.16

Focus

Under CRS and EU DAC, an NFE is an active NFE, and under FATCA an NFFE is an active NFFE, if the NFE or NFFE meets any of the criteria that are listed below.

---

(1) It is active by reason of income or assets. This requires less than 50% of its gross income for the preceding calendar year or other appropriate reporting period to be passive income and less than 50% of its assets held in the same period to be assets that produce or are held for the production of passive income.

HMRC say that 'passive income' is income that is derived from investing in assets rather than from activities carried on in the normal course of a trade or business. It includes the portion of income that consists of:

(a) dividends and other distributions of income;

(b) interest;

(c) income equivalent to interest;

(d) rents and royalties, other than rents and royalties derived in the active conduct of a trade or business conducted, at least in part, by employees of the NFE (or NFFE, as applicable);

(e) annuities;

(f) the excess of gains over losses from the sale or exchange of property that gives rise to passive income described previously;

(g) the excess of gains over losses from transactions (including futures, forwards, options and similar transactions) in any financial assets;

(h) the excess of foreign currency gains over foreign currency losses;

(i) net income from swaps;

(j) amounts received under cash value insurance contracts.

The context in which the income described above is received is also important. For example, where the NFE or NFFE is a dealer in financial assets, any such income as described above may be income from a trading activity. Where the income described above is received by a NFE or NFFE and is accounted for, or is taxable as, income from trading activities should not be included in gross income as passive income.

See HMRC's International Exchange of Information Manual IEIM 404020.

(2) Its stock is regularly traded on an established securities market (or is a related entity of an entity whose stock is regularly traded on an established securities market).

(3) It is a government entity, international organisation, central bank or a wholly owned subsidiary of such an entity (or in the case of an NFFE under FATCA, the NFFE is either a non-US government or the government of a US territory.

'US territory' means American Samoa, the Commonwealth of the Northern Mariana Islands, Guam, the Commonwealth of Puerto Rico, or the US Virgin Islands. See the FATCA agreement, Art 1(1)(b).

(4) It is holding company for NFEs or NFFEs that are members of a non-financial group. It will not qualify as an active NFE or active NFFE where these holdings are part of a business as an investment fund or vehicle whose purpose is to acquire or fund companies and then hold interests as capital assets for investment purposes.

(5) It is a start-up NFE or NFFE which is not yet operating a business and has no prior operating history, but is investing capital into assets with the

intention of operating a business other than that of a financial institution. This category only applies during the first 24 months after the date that the NFE or NFFE was first formed.

(6) It is an NFE or NFFE that has not been a financial institution in the last five years and which is in the process of liquidating its assets or is reorganising with a view to continuing or recommencing business operations other than as a financial institution.

(7) It is a treasury centre of a non-financial group engaging in financing and hedging transactions with or for related entities.

(8) It is a not-for-profit organisation set up for religious, charitable, scientific, artistic, cultural, athletic or educational purposes; or it is established and operated as a professional organisation, business league, chamber of commerce, labour organisation, agricultural or horticultural organisation, civic league or an organisation operated for the promotion of social welfare. In all cases the organisation must be exempt from income tax and its income and assets cannot be applied other than for the express purposes for which the organisation is established.

For the purposes of FATCA only, a NFFE is also an active NFFE where the NFFE is organised in a US territory and all the owners of the payee are bona fide residents of that US territory. See **11.16** on the meaning of 'US territory(ies)'.

In addition to the above, a professionally managed investment entity that is tax resident in a non-participating jurisdiction is always treated as a passive NFE for the purposes of CRS, even though it would be treated as a financial institution if it were resident in a participating jurisdiction (this ensures that it is not possible for controlling persons to avoid reporting by setting up such entities in non-participating jurisdictions).

See **11.14** regarding NFEs and NFFEs, and see **11.15** regarding 'passive NFEs' and 'passive NFFEs'. See **9.10** on controlling persons.

See HMRC's International Exchange of Information Manual IEIM404040. See CRS, Section VIII. See EU DAC, Annex I, Section VIII. See the FATCA agreement, Annex I.

Chapter 12

Making a report under the UK's FATCA/CRS regulations

SIGNPOSTS

- Typically, under FATCA/CRS, a firm, business or other entity first needs to decide whether it is a 'reporting financial institution'. See **Chapter 4** regarding the meaning of reporting financial institution ('RFI').

- If the entity concludes that it is an RFI, it probably needs next, to carry out the due diligence procedures that are stipulated under FATCA and CRS (see **Chapter 9**).

- The results of the RFI's due diligence exercise should then enable it to decide whether and what it needs to report under FATCA and CRS. It should then do that within the appropriate timeframe for doing so (see this Chapter).

- Reporting under the UK's FATCA/CRS Regulations must be done online, using HMRC's online system. It will be necessary first to register online with HMRC. For entities that are to report under FATCA, it will also be necessary beforehand, to obtain a global intermediary identification number ('GIIN') from the US tax authorities – the Inland Revenue Service ('IRS') (see **12.1**).

- The filing date for filing FATCA/CRS returns with HMRC for each year ending 31 December is the following 31 May (see **12.2**).

- There are rules in CRS/EU DAC only (ie not under FATCA), setting out the circumstances when low value and dormant accounts do not need to be reported for the purposes of CRS only (see **12.3**).

- There are rules in FATCA only (ie not under CRS/EU DAC), setting out the circumstances when certain accounts do not need to be reported, such as where the account holder is deceased or a personal representative, as well as certain kinds of escrow account individuals (see **12.4**).

- The Regulations specify the information that must be reported for the purposes of FATCA and/or CRS/EU DAC. This will normally include the name, address and tax identification number ('TIN') of the account holder (see **12.5** to **12.7**).

- There are rules that determine what must be reported in respect of account balances (see **12.8**).

- There are rules under CRS/EU DAC that determine whether and when an account holder's date and/or place of birth must be reported. Normally, neither of these things needs to be reported under FATCA (see **12.9**).

- Throughout this Chapter, where reference is made to 'CRS/EU DAC', this is in relation to the CRS rules as they apply to the UK through the EU Directive on Administrative Cooperation 2011/16/EU ('EU DAC'). See **Chapter 2** regarding the impact of Brexit on this.

- An RFI under the FATCA agreement faced additional due diligence and reporting obligations for the 2015 and 2016 calendar years in relation to payments to non-participating financial institutions (see **12.10**).

HOW TO REPORT UNDER THE UK'S FATCA AND CRS REGULATIONS

12.1

Focus

Financial institutions must use HMRC's online system to report to HMRC under FATCA and CRS agreements – in the case of the latter, as it is applied to the UK by EU DAC (see **Chapter 2**).

A financial institution that needs to file a FATCA/CRS return will first need to register with HMRC, for Automatic Exchange of Information ('AEOI').

HMRC warn that it is essential to register at least 24 hours before making an AEOI return. Registration can be carried out at https://www.gov.uk/guidance/register-for-automatic-exchange-of-information.

In order to register it is necessary to have a Government Gateway user ID and password. If you do not have a user ID, you can create one when you use the service.

UK financial institutions who want to directly upload their return of reportable accounts must submit their returns to HMRC using the UK submission schema. A portal to allow reporting to HMRC is hosted on the UK Government Gateway. This can be found at https://www.gov.uk/government/publications/foreign-account-tax-compliance-act-registration-guidance-fatca.

For financial institutions who have few or no reportable accounts there is a form-based system that will allow the financial institution to manually enter their reportable accounts.

If the financial institution will be reporting under FATCA for the US, it will need its GIIN when registering with HMRC for AEOI. A financial institution that needs a GIIN and that does not already have one will need to register with the US IRS in order to obtain it. This can be carried out at https://www.irs.gov/businesses/corporations/fatca-foreign-financial-institution-registration-system.

See HMRC's International Exchange of Information Manual IEIM404520 regarding certain kinds of entity which should not register with the IRS to obtain a GIIN.

If the financial institution does not already have a Government Gateway user ID and password and/or if it needs and does not yet have a GIIN, obtaining these can add to the 24 hours of preparation time that HMRC warn is needed ahead of making an AEOI return.

An RFI may use a service provider to undertake its reporting requirements, but in such cases those obligations continue to be the obligations of the institution.

An RFI under the FATCA agreement faced additional due diligence and reporting obligations for the 2015 and 2016 calendar years in relation to payments to non-participating financial institutions (see **12.10**).

See HMRC's 'How to Report Automatic Exchange of Information', published 16 April 2019, at https://www.gov.uk/guidance/how-to-report-automatic-exchange-of-information

See International Tax Compliance Regulations 2015, SI 2015/878, regs 7 and 12.

TIMING OF A REPORT UNDER THE UK'S FATCA AND CRS REGULATIONS

12.2

Focus

The filing date for filing FATCA/CRS returns with HMRC for each year ending 31 December is the following 31 May.

Unless the contrary is proved:

(a) the use of an electronic return system is presumed to have resulted in the making of the return only if this has been successfully recorded as such by the relevant electronic validation process;

(b) the time of making the return is presumed to be the time recorded as such by the relevant electronic validation process; and

(c) the person delivering the return is presumed to be the person identified as such by any relevant feature of the electronic return system.

See the International Tax Compliance Regulations 2015, regs 7 and 12.

MUST DORMANT AND DE MINIMIS ACCOUNTS BE REPORTED?

12.3

Focus

For the purposes of CRS/EU DAC only, an RFI may elect that certain dormant and de minimis accounts are not a reportable account for the purposes of CRS/EU DAC for a calendar year.

A separate election must be made for each calendar year for which the election is to have effect. The election is made in the FATCA/CRS return made to HMRC for each year (see the International Tax Compliance Regulations 2015, reg 2(2)(c)).

See **12.4** regarding certain accounts that may not need to be reported under FATCA.

In particular, this can be applied (under reg 2(2)(c)(i)) for the purposes of CRS/EU DAC to a dormant account as defined below that does not exceed an amount equivalent to US $1,000.

An account is considered to be dormant if:

(1) the account holder has not initiated a transaction in the past three years on that account or any other account he or she holds with the financial institution; and

(2) the account holder has not communicated in the past six years with the financial institution that maintains the account regarding that account or any other account he or she holds with the financial institution; or

(3) the account is considered to be dormant under the normal operating procedures of the financial institution that are applied for all accounts maintained by it provided these procedures are substantially similar to the requirements in (1) and (2) above.

In addition, certain pre-existing individual accounts, pre-existing entity accounts and new entity accounts can be made not reportable for the purposes of FATCA, by making the same election. Essentially, these are the accounts where review, identification and reporting are not required as described respectively in **10.3**, **10.6** and **11.7**.

However, see HMRC's International Exchange of Information Manual IEIM402740 regarding:

- the circumstances when a dormant account as defined above, ceases to be dormant; and

- a special rule relating to an account that consisting of a cash value insurance contract. Essentially, the election referred to above can also cause these not to be reportable for CRS/EU DAC (see reg 2(1)(ba) and 2(2)(c)(ii)).

See the International Tax Compliance Regulations 2015, reg 2. See also HMRC's International Exchange of Information Manual IEIM401900.

COULD THERE BE OTHER ACCOUNTS THAT DO NOT HAVE TO BE REPORTED?

12.4

Focus

For the purposes of FATCA only, an account is not a reportable account if:

(a) the account holder is deceased or is a personal representative;

(b) the account is held to comply with an order or judgment made or given in legal proceedings; or

(c) the funds held in the account are held solely as security for the performance of a party's obligation under a contract for the disposal of an estate or interest in land or of tangible moveable property.

For the purposes of CRS/EU DAC only, certain tax-favoured pension and savings accounts (for example, ISAs) are not reportable. These are listed in the International Tax Compliance Regulations 2015, Sch 2.

This is automatic. That is to say, these accounts are not reportable, regardless of whether the election referred to in **12.3** is made or not.

See the International Tax Compliance Regulations 2015 SI 2015/878, reg 2. See also HMRC's International Exchange of Information Manual IEIM401840 onwards.

WHAT HAS TO BE REPORTED UNDER FATCA/CRS?

12.5   Under FATCA or CRS/EU DAC, a reporting UK financial institution must report the following in respect of each of its reportable accounts (US reportable accounts in the case of FATCA):

(1)   the name, address and TIN (US TIN in the case of FATCA) of:

    (a)   each reportable person (for CRS/EU DAC) or each US specified person (in the case of FATCA) that is an account holder of such accounts; and

    (b)   of any passive non-financial entity ('NFE') (for CRS/EU DAC) or passive non-financial foreign entity ('NFFE') (for FATCA) which has controlling persons who are reportable persons (for CRS/EU DAC) or US persons (for FATCA);

    (c)   together with the name, address and TIN of those same controlling persons,

    (see **9.8** and **9.9** regarding the meaning of 'reportable person');

(2)   the account number (or functional equivalent in the absence of an account number);

(3)   the name and identifying number of the reporting UK financial institution;

(4)   the account balance or value (including, in the case of a cash value insurance contract or annuity contract, the cash value or surrender value) as of the end of the relevant calendar year or other appropriate reporting period or, if the account was closed during such year, immediately before closure;

(5)   in the case of any custodial account:

    (a)   the total gross amount of interest, the total gross amount of dividends, and the total gross amount of other income generated with respect to the assets held in the account, in each case paid or credited to the account (or with respect to the account) during the calendar year or other appropriate reporting period; and

    (b)   the total gross proceeds from the sale or redemption of property paid or credited to the account during the calendar year or other appropriate reporting period with respect to which the reporting UK financial institution acted as a custodian, broker, nominee, or otherwise as an agent for the account holder;

(6)   in the case of any depository account, the total gross amount of interest paid or credited to the account during the calendar year or other appropriate reporting period; and

(7)   in the case of any account not described in point (5) or of this point, the total gross amount paid or credited to the account holder with respect to the account during the calendar year or other appropriate reporting period with respect to which the reporting UK financial institution is the obligor or debtor, including the aggregate amount of any redemption payments made to the account holder during the calendar year or other appropriate reporting period.

All UK financial institutions that are within the scope of FATCA are required to register with the US IRS and obtain a GIIN. The GIIN will be required as an identifying number for FATCA reporting. Where a financial institution is reporting under any of the other AEOI agreements it must either report a GIIN or confirm it does not hold one.

See HMRC's International Exchange of Information Manual IEIM404520 regarding certain kinds of entity which should not register with the US IRS in order to obtain a GIIN.

The financial institution will also need to report a UK identifying number. In most cases this will be a unique tax reference ('UTR'). In some cases, it will be the national insurance number of the person filing the AEOI return. If none of these is available, that should be stated in the AEOI return. See HMRC's International Exchange of Information Manual IEIM402100.

CRS/EU DAC requires the TIN, date of birth and place of birth. However, certain specified circumstances will allow some or all of these to be omitted. See CRS/EU DAC. See **12.8**.

Where a financial institution does not hold information in its records on either the account holder's TIN or date of birth it is expected to make reasonable efforts to obtain the information by the end of the second calendar year following the year in which the account is identified as reportable. See HMRC's International Exchange of Information Manual IEIM402320.

HMRC consider that reasonable efforts could include:

- contacting the account holder by mail, in-person or telephone; and/or
- reviewing electronically searchable information maintained by a related entity

However, it is not considered to include closing, blocking or transferring an account, nor conditioning or otherwise limiting its use, simply because the account holder does not comply with a request for this information.

Under CRS/EU DAC, the information reported must also identify the currency in which each amount is denominated.

12.6 *Making a report under the UK's FATCA/CRS regulations*

Under the UK's AEOI Regulations, for the purposes of the information required to be reported under FATCA or CRS/EU DAC (see the International Tax Compliance Regulations 2015, reg 6(5)):

(a) interest includes any amount that is chargeable as interest under Part 4 of the Income Tax (Trading and Other Income) Act 2005;

(b) references to the balance or value of an account include a nil balance or value; and

(c) references to paying an amount include crediting an amount.

See FATCA agreement, Art 1(8)(gg) regarding the meaning of 'US specified person' under FATCA. See **9.8** and **9.9** and HMRC's International Exchange of Information Manual IEIM402010 regarding the meaning of 'reportable person' under CRS/EU DAC and its equivalent under FATCA. See **9.10** on 'controlling person(s)'.

Under the UK's FATCA/CRS Regulations, an account held by an individual as a partner of a partnership is treated as an entity account and is not treated as an individual account. See the International Tax Compliance Regulations 2015, reg 2(8).

As regards reporting under CRS/EU DAC, see HMRC's International Exchange of Information Manual IEIM400580 and IEIM402005.

See the International Tax Compliance Regulations 2015 SI 2015/878, reg 6.

See the FATCA agreement, Art 2(2)(a). See CRS, Section I. See EU DAC, Annex I, Section I.

WHAT IS A TIN FOR THE PURPOSES OF FATCA?

12.6 Under FATCA, 'US TIN' means a US federal taxpayer's identifying number. See the FATCA agreement at Art 1(1)(ll).

See HMRC's International Exchange of Information Manual IEIM402040 regarding the circumstances in which HMRC will or will not regard a failure by a UK financial institution to provide them with a US TIN in respect of a reportable account as a failure to comply with the UK's FATCA/CRS Regulations.

The IRS FAQs confirm that if a financial institution is unable to obtain a TIN, this will not automatically lead the IRS to conclude that there is significant non-compliance. Instead, the IRS will consult with HMRC so they can take account of valid reasons why TINs could not be obtained and the efforts made to collect them. See **8.5** to **8.6** regarding the meaning of significant non-compliance. See also HMRC's International Exchange of Information Manual IEIM405010 onwards.

See IRS FAQ3 at https://www.irs.gov/businesses/corporations/frequently-asked-questions-faqs-fatca-compliance-legal#reporting.

HMRC say that where a return will not be including a TIN, in respect of the calendar year 2020 and future years, it will be possible to report an account without a TIN to HMRC by entering nine zeros in the TIN field.

In addition to the above, HMRC will need the AEOI return to state the jurisdiction to which the information is reportable.

As regards reporting under CRS/EU DAC, see HMRC's International Exchange of Information Manual IEIM400580 and IEIM402005.

See the International Tax Compliance Regulations 2015 SI 2015/878, reg 6.

See the FATCA agreement, Art 2(2)(a). See CRS, Section I. See EU DAC, Annex I, Section I.

WHAT IS A TIN FOR THE PURPOSES OF CRS/EU DAC?

12.7   Under CRS/EU DAC, 'TIN' means a taxpayer's identification number (or functional equivalent in the absence of a TIN). See CRS, Section VIII(E)(5) and EU DAC, Annex I, Section VIII(E)(5).

Some jurisdictions do not issue a TIN and where that is the case there will be nothing to report unless they use other high integrity numbers with an equivalent level of identification. For individuals these include:

- social security number,
- national insurance number,
- citizen or personal identification code or number,
- resident registration number.

HMRC say that for 'most individuals' in the UK, the TIN will be their national Insurance number.

For entities, jurisdictions may use a business/company registration code or number where no TIN has been issued.

As regards reporting under CRS/EU DAC, see HMRC's International Exchange of Information Manual IEIM400580 and IEIM402005.

See the International Tax Compliance Regulations 2015, reg 6.

See the FATCA agreement, Art 2(2)(a). See CRS, Section I. See EU DAC, Annex I, Section I.

HOW MUST ACCOUNT BALANCES BE DETERMINED AND REPORTED?

12.8

Focus

In general, the balance to be reported will be the amount which the financial institution calculates for the purpose of reporting to the account holder.

The account balance value is the amount at the end of the reporting period.

It should be reported in the currency in which the account is denominated.

The report must also identify the currency in which the report itself is denominated.

See HMRC's International Exchange of Information Manual IEIM402120 and IEIM402280.

In the case of joint accounts, each account holder is attributed the entire balance.

In the case of an account holder who is resident in more than one jurisdiction, the entire balance and the entire amount credited must be reported to each of the jurisdictions in which he or she is resident.

Hence the same amount may need to be reported multiple times, either if there are multiple joint account holders or if the account holder is resident in multiple jurisdictions. See HMRC's International Exchange of Information Manual IEIM402140 and IEIM402160.

Where an account is closed, there are different rules for FATCA, as compared with the rules under CRS/EU DAC.

For FATCA, in all cases the account balance or value immediately before closure must be reported.

For CRS/EU DAC, the fact that the account has been closed must be reported but not the balance at closure. However, any amounts paid or credited to the account in the reporting period up to the date of closure remain reportable.

In addition, in the case of a custodial account under FATCA and CRS/EU DAC, it is also necessary to report:

- the total gross amount of interest paid or credited to the account;

- the total gross amount of dividends paid or credited to the account;

- the total gross amount of other income generated with respect to the assets held in the account paid or credited to the account. Other income for this purpose means any amount that would be considered income for the purposes of the Income Tax Acts 2007 other than interest or dividends;

- the total gross proceeds from the sale or redemption of financial assets paid or credited to the account.

See **6.3** regarding whether a trust may be a custodial institution with financial accounts that are custodial accounts.

In addition, in the case of a depository account under FATCA, it is also necessary to report:

- the payments and income paid or credited to the account during the calendar year up to the point of closure or transfer; and

- the amount or value withdrawn or transferred from the account in connection with the closure or transfer of the account.

In the case of any account other than a depository account or a custodial account, the additional information to be reported for each reporting period is the total gross amount of income paid or credited to the account holder in the reporting period. See HMRC's International Exchange of Information Manual IEIM402260.

For cash value insurance contracts this will include any part surrenders taken throughout the policy year.

For a purchased life annuity, it will include any amounts paid or credited to the policy holder.

FATCA has different reporting requirements for cash value insurance contracts and annuity contracts. See HMRC's International Exchange of Information Manual IEIM402170.

Once an account has been identified as a reportable account it remains so until there is a change that takes account out of the definition of reportable account. While the account remains a reportable account, it must be reported even where the balance or value of the account is zero or negative. See HMRC's International Exchange of Information Manual IEIM 402520.

As reporting under all of the AEOI regimes is dependent on the status of an account at the end on the reporting period, if an account ceases to be reportable during a reporting period, it simply does not need to be reported upon for that reporting period. See HMRC's International Exchange of Information Manual IEIM402175.

WHEN MUST DATE AND PLACE OF BIRTH BE REPORTED?

12.9

Focus

Under CRS/EU DAC (but not FATCA), date of birth is reportable for all new accounts.

In effect, the requirement to report place of birth only applies under CRS/EU DAC (but not FATCA) where the RFI was previously reporting place of birth information to HMRC under the EU Savings Directive ('EUSD') (see **1.2**).

> Where place of birth needs to be reported, the place of birth to be reported is the town or city and country of birth of the reportable account holder.

The requirement in some circumstances to report place of birth under CRS and EU DAC (but not FATCA) is subject to the condition at Section I, para E of CRS and Annex I, Section I, para E of EU DAC.

The relevance of reporting place of birth under CRS/EU DAC is restricted to reporting to 'other Member States'. See **Chapter 2** regarding how this applies in the case of the UK following Brexit.

Even in the case of an RFI which was previously reporting place of birth information under EUSD, place of birth only needs reporting if it is available in the electronically searchable data maintained by the RFI.

HMRC's interpretation of EU DAC (as regards CRS) is that it does not place a continuous requirement, after the repeal of EUSD, on RFIs to collect and report place of birth in respect of their new accounts.

Hence if such an RFI obtains place of birth details in respect of account holders of new accounts opened since the repeal of EUSD, the RFI should not report this place of birth information under AEOI.

It is therefore not merely that only RFIs within the scope for EUSD must report place of birth information under AEOI. It is also the case that only those RFIs *can* report place of birth information under AEOI.

See HMRC's International Exchange of Information Manual IEIM402180. See also **12.8**.

FATCA: PAYMENTS TO A NON-PARTICIPATING FINANCIAL INSTITUTION

12.10   An RFI under the FATCA agreement faced additional due diligence and reporting obligations for the 2015 and 2016 calendar years in relation to payments to non-participating financial institutions (see **7.8**).

There is no requirement to report the name and aggregate value of payments to non-participating financial institutions for the year 2017 or subsequent years.

See **Chapter 8** regarding penalties for failing to comply.

See also **8.5** to **8.6** regarding special rules regarding related entities that are non-participating financial institutions.

See the International Tax Compliance Regulations 2015, reg 9. See also HMRC's International Exchange of Information Manual IEIM402360 to IEIM402400.

Chapter 13

EU DAC 6 – the EU Mandatory Disclosure regime

SIGNPOSTS

- The UK became a party to the EU's 'DAC 6' Mandatory Disclosure rules as a result of its former membership of the EU. EU Directive 2018/822/EU ('EU DAC 6'), which amends the EU Directive on Administrative Cooperation 2011/16/EU ('EU DAC'), is intended to assist the tax authorities of EU Member States by ensuring that details of cross-border tax planning arrangements are disclosed to them (see **13.1**).

- The UK's DAC 6 Regulations (see SI 2020/25) came into force on 1 July 2020, applying retrospectively to transactions that have taken place since 25 June 2018 (see **13.2**).

- There can be significant penalties for failing to comply (see **Chapter 18**).

- A UK intermediary may need to report an arrangement to HMRC. Typically, this will be a professional of some kind who has advised on or otherwise facilitated the arrangement. If no intermediary is required to report, the obligation to report can then fall on a UK relevant taxpayer. The meanings of 'UK intermediary' and 'UK relevant taxpayer' are described in **Chapter 14** (see **13.3**).

- In order to be reportable, an arrangement must fall within the meaning of an 'arrangement' (see **13.4**).

- In order to be reportable, an arrangement must also fall within the meaning of a 'cross-border arrangement' (see **13.5**).

- A key element in assessing whether there is a 'cross-border arrangement' is that it must 'concern' multiple jurisdictions. If there are tax consequences in a particular jurisdiction as a result of the arrangement in question, the arrangement will normally concern that jurisdiction (see **13.6**).

- A UK relevant taxpayer must also include the arrangement reference number ('ARN') and certain other information about the arrangement in his or her annual tax return (see **Chapter 16**).

- In order to be reportable, an arrangement must also fall within one or more of the hallmarks that are described in **Chapter 17** (see **13.7**). In light of Brexit and, in particular, the EU-UK Trade and Cooperation Agreement of 31 December 2020, the UK's rules implementing EU DAC 6 will only now require that either of the category D hallmarks is met. The other DAC 6 hallmarks are therefore rendered irrelevant to the UK reporting under EU DAC 6.

- In the UK, the first reporting under EU DAC 6, which had been scheduled for Summer 2020, was delayed by six months until Winter 2020/2021, after the EU agreed a delay due to the worldwide Covid-19 pandemic (see **13.8**).

OVERVIEW

13.1

Focus

The EU introduced a Directive on Mandatory Disclosure rules aimed at increasing transparency to assist the tax authorities of EU Member States in detecting potentially aggressive cross-border tax planning and the like.

The EU introduced these 'DAC 6' rules as part of EU DAC, to which the UK was a party as an EU Member State.

The UK was a party to EU DAC, and therefore to EU DAC 6, as an EU Member State. Having left the EU on 31 January 2020, the UK remained a party to most EU law, including EU DAC and EU DAC 6, during at least the transition period (which ended on 31 December 2020).

In effect, EU DAC 6 applies to cross-border arrangements that are within the scope of the EU DAC 6 regime, and where the first step is taken after 25 June 2018.

In light of Brexit and, in particular, the EU-UK Trade and Cooperation Agreement of 31 December 2020, the UK's rules implementing DAC 6 will only now require that either of the category D hallmarks is met. The other DAC 6 hallmarks are therefore rendered irrelevant to UK reporting under EU DAC 6.

EU Directive 2018/822/EU (sometimes called 'DAC 6') amended EU DAC so as to include these Mandatory Disclosure rules. This imposed mandatory reporting of cross-border arrangements involving at least one EU Member State where these fall within one of a number of hallmarks.

In effect, EU DAC 6 may be considered an attempt to put OECD BEPS Action 12 into effect (see **1.5**). Under BEPS Action 12, taxpayers should disclose their aggressive tax planning arrangements to the tax authorities.

Certain elements of EU DAC 6 have similarities with the UK's Disclosure of Tax Avoidance Schemes ('DOTAS') regime. See, for example, the Finance Act 2004, ss 306 to 319. It also has similarities with the OECD's Mandatory Disclosure Regime ('MDR'). See, for example, the OECD's Model Mandatory Disclosure Rules for CRS Avoidance Arrangements and Opaque Offshore Structures.

The Finance Act 2019, s 84 gave HM Treasury powers to make regulations to give effect to the UK's participation in EU DAC 6. The Finance Act 2019 received Royal Assent during the period when Theresa May was the UK's prime minister and she was seeking to negotiate the UK's withdrawal from the EU, following the Brexit referendum of 2016. See **Chapter 2** regarding the impact of Brexit on the UK's participation in EU DAC 6.

The UK has issued a statutory instrument reflecting the UK's commitment to be subject to EU DAC 6. See the International Tax Enforcement (Disclosable Arrangements) Regulations 2020, SI 2020/25. See also the International Tax Enforcement (Disclosable Arrangements) (Amendment) (No. 2) (EU Exit) Regulations 2020, SI 2020/1649.

As regards EU DAC 6 itself, see EU DAC, at Art 8(3a) and Annex I.

WHEN DID THE RULES COMMENCE, AND WHY IS IT IMPORTANT TO COMPLY?

13.2

Focus

The Regulations implementing EU DAC 6 came into force in the UK on 1 July 2020. However, the rules are retrospective and transactions that have taken place since 25 June 2018 may need to be reported.

The deadlines for submitting EU DAC 6 reports are described in **Chapter 15**. This includes a description of the EU and the UK's deferral of the initial deadlines in view of the Covid-19 pandemic.

Significant penalties can be levied on those who fail to comply. The basic penalty is £5,000. However, in extreme cases, the penalty could be up to £1 million. See **Chapter 18**.

There may of course be other implications from failing to comply. For example, professionally qualified individuals may find that some professional bodies may take a dim view of members who fail to comply.

There could also be reputational issues if it becomes public knowledge that a particular professional or a particular firm has a history of failing to comply with EU DAC 6.

See the International Tax Enforcement (Disclosable Arrangements) Regulations 2020, SI 2020/25, issued under powers in the Finance Act 2019, s 84.

WHO HAS TO REPORT, AND IN WHAT CIRCUMSTANCES?

13.3

> **Focus**
>
> Briefly, EU DAC 6 requires intermediaries and taxpayers to report details of certain types of cross-border arrangements to tax authorities. It covers all taxes of any kind with the exception of VAT, customs and excise duties and compulsory social contributions.
>
> HMRC will issue an ARN when an arrangement is first reported. A UK relevant taxpayer must then include the ARN and certain other information about the arrangement in his or her annual tax return. See **Chapter 16**.
>
> In order to require reporting under EU DAC 6, an arrangement must be a 'reportable cross-border arrangement'. See **13.7** regarding the meaning of that phrase.
>
> See **Chapter 14** for more details about who has to report, including the meaning of 'intermediary' and 'taxpayer' for these purposes.
>
> See **13.4** regarding the meaning of 'arrangement'. See **13.5** regarding the meaning of 'cross-border arrangement'.
>
> In addition, as explained in **13.7**, EU DAC 6 reporting is only applicable if certain 'hallmarks' are engaged. See **Chapter 17** for further details of these.

WHAT IS AN ARRANGEMENT?

13.4

> **Focus**
>
> An arrangement can only be reportable, if it is within the meaning of that term for the purposes of EU DAC 6.

An 'arrangement' is defined as including 'any scheme, transaction, or series of transactions'. The definition is non-exhaustive, so is potentially broad in scope. See the Finance Act 2019, s 84(3).

HMRC say that the phrase 'series of transactions' means that an arrangement must be looked at holistically, rather than as a series of small steps or separate transactions.

Where there is a pre-existing arrangement which is extended, HMRC would not normally view this as a new arrangement, unless there is some material change to the arrangement – see HMRC's International Exchange of Information Manual IEIM630020.

See also **Chapter 14** and **Chapter 15** regarding EU DAC 6 reporting obligations. In particular, see **14.1** to **14.5** for further details about who must report under EU DAC 6.

WHAT IS A CROSS-BORDER ARRANGEMENT?

13.5

Focus

An arrangement can only be reportable, if it is within the meaning of a cross-border arrangement for the purposes of the UK's Regulations implementing EU DAC 6.

An arrangement is a 'cross-border arrangement' if it both 'concerns' either:

- more than one of the UK and at least one EU Member State; or

- the UK or an EU Member State and a third country,

and any one of the following tests in paragraphs (a) to (e) of Art 3(18) of EU DAC is met:

(a)   the participants are resident in different jurisdictions;

(b)   any one of the participants is resident in more than one jurisdiction simultaneously;

(c)   any one of the participants has business activities in another jurisdiction through a permanent establishment ('PE') and the arrangement is part or the whole of the business of the PE;

(d)   any one of the participants in the arrangement carries on an activity in another jurisdiction without being resident for tax purposes;

> (e)   the arrangement possibly impacts on the automatic exchange of information or the identification of beneficial ownership.
>
> See below regarding the meaning of 'concerns'.

If the above applies, it is then necessary to determine if one of the prescribed 'hallmarks' exists for a transaction.

In light of Brexit and, in particular, the EU-UK Trade and Cooperation Agreement of 31 December 2020, the UK's rules implementing EU DAC 6 will only now require that either of the category D hallmarks is met. The other DAC 6 hallmarks are therefore rendered irrelevant to UK reporting under EU DAC 6.

For the above purposes, the overseas territories and dependencies of the UK and EU Member States are considered to be separate jurisdictions and arrangements involving those jurisdictions should be analysed accordingly for EU DAC 6 reporting purposes.

In relation to entities that are subject to the UK Banking Code of Conduct ('the Banking Code'), HMRC warn that EU DAC 6 is wider in scope that the Banking Code. Accordingly, merely because an entity is compliant with the Banking Code, does not mean that it will automatically also be compliant with EU DAC 6.

See HMRC International Exchange of Information Manual IEIM630030. As regards HMRC's comments about the Banking Code, see IEIM641050.

See the International Tax Enforcement (Disclosable Arrangements) Regulations 2020, particularly reg 2, which applies the Regulations to the definition of 'reportable cross-border arrangement' in Art 3(19) of EU DAC.

WHEN DOES AN ARRANGEMENT 'CONCERN' MULTIPLE JURISDICTIONS?

13.6

Focus

As explained in **13.5**, an arrangement (see **13.4**) is only a cross-border arrangement if it 'concerns' multiple jurisdictions. It can only be reportable if it is a cross-border arrangement within the meaning of that phrase under EU DAC 6. See **13.5**.

A key element in assessing whether there is a 'cross-border arrangement' is that it must 'concern' multiple jurisdictions. If there are tax consequences in a particular jurisdiction as a result of the arrangement in question, the arrangement will normally concern that jurisdiction.

HMRC is of the view that in order for the arrangement to meet the criterion that it 'concerns' multiple jurisdictions (see **13.4** and **13.5**), those jurisdictions must be of some material relevance to the arrangement.

Whether any particular arrangement is of material relevance to, and therefore concerns, multiple jurisdictions will be a question of fact and degree.

If there are tax consequences in a particular jurisdiction as a result of the arrangement in question, the arrangement will normally concern that jurisdiction. However, HMRC may not consider that to be the case where the tax effect is 'more removed'.

HMRC cite as an example, a company that is resident in one jurisdiction but which carries on a trade through a permanent establishment in another jurisdiction.

Suppose the company enters into an arrangement through its permanent establishment, which only concerns the permanent establishment (and counterparties resident in the jurisdiction where the permanent establishment is) and has no implications for other jurisdictions?

HMRC say that the fact the company is resident in a different jurisdiction from the counterparties, does not mean that the arrangement concerns multiple jurisdictions.

An arrangement does not 'concern' more than one jurisdiction for these purposes either, if there are no immediate tax consequences from the arrangement. An example might be where an arrangement involves funds belonging to a person resident in member State A being moved from an account in country B to an account in country C, with no immediate tax consequences following the movement of funds.

However, this contrasts with an otherwise identical situation where if country C had not implemented the Common Reporting Standard ('CRS'), whereas country B had, and the effect of the arrangement was to undermine CRS by ensuring that the funds would not be reported, then the jurisdictions involved would be of material relevance to the arrangement. The arrangement would then concern multiple jurisdictions.

HMRC also confirm in their guidance that if an arrangement would otherwise only concern one jurisdiction, the fact that an intermediary involved in the arrangement is located in a different jurisdiction will not automatically mean that the arrangement is cross-border.

Example 13.1 – cross-border lawyer and banker

Parisco SA and Marseilleco SA are two French companies. They enter into an arrangement which only involves the transfer of assets within France.

Bill Smith, a UK lawyer provides some of the paperwork for the arrangement, while Londonbank Plc (a bank that is resident in the UK) only provides the account from which the funds are transferred.

Neither Bill Smith's involvement nor Londonbank Plc's involvement means that the arrangement itself is cross-border.

Example 13.2 – cross-border company transaction

Redcompany Ltd, a UK resident company, sells shares that it holds in Greencompany BV (an overseas company that is resident in an EU Member State). Redcompany Ltd sells these shares to another UK resident company, Bluecompany Ltd.

All of the parties to the transaction are initially of the opinion that there will be no tax consequences in the EU Member State in which Greencompany BV is resident, arising directly from this transaction. If that were the case, HMRC would not consider that this transaction was of material relevance to the EU Member State where Greencompany BV is resident.

However, an accountant researches the situation and finds that there are potential stamp duty consequences from the transaction, in the EU Member State where Greencompany BV is resident.

Nevertheless, it is still unlikely HMRC would consider that the arrangement concerned the EU Member State where Greencompany BV is resident, because that jurisdiction is not material to the arrangement.

Example 13.3 – tax-driven cross-border company transaction

Sharpcompany Ltd, a UK resident company, sells shares that it holds in another overseas company ('Targetco') that is resident in an EU Member State. Sharpcompany Ltd sells these shares to another UK resident company.

The circumstances are identical to those relating to Redcompany Ltd's disposal of shares in Greencompany BV in Example 13.2, except that the other UK resident company is buying these shares from Sharpcompany Ltd in order to obtain a tax advantage in the EU Member State where the overseas company is resident.

The EU Member State where Targetco is resident is therefore of material relevance to this transaction, and so the transaction would concern that EU Member State.

However, it is also necessary to consider whether at least one of the tests in paragraphs (a) to (e) of a Art 3(18) of EU DAC is met in order to determine whether the arrangement is 'cross-border' – see above.

Here Targetco would not normally be seen as a 'participant' in the arrangement unless it had some active involvement. The passive transfer of B's shares without the knowledge or consent of company B would not be sufficient to make it a participant.

Example 13.4 – unit trust with overseas investors

A new unit trust is established, managed and administered in Bournemouth in the UK. It is open to retail investors resident anywhere in the world.

The possibility that there could be overseas investors does not necessarily make this a cross-border arrangement, because the location of the investors is not material to the establishment of the vehicle.

Example 13.5 – unit trust with tax-motivated overseas investors

An otherwise identical new unit trust to that in Example 13.4 is established.

However, this unit trust has been set up, in light of advice from a tax adviser, and the intention behind the unit trust is to exploit a mismatch between the tax rules in two particular jurisdictions. The idea is that it will enable retail investors in one of those jurisdictions to obtain a tax advantage in the other jurisdiction.

This is therefore a cross-border arrangement.

Example 13.6 – cross-border company loan

A company ('the first company') that is resident in one jurisdiction makes a loan to a company ('the second company').

The second company pays interest to the first company, in relation to the loan.

As the interest may be deductible in one jurisdiction and taxable in another, this arrangement concerns both of those two jurisdictions. This is therefore a cross-border arrangement.

> **Example 13.7 – offshore trust**
>
> An individual who is resident in one jurisdiction settles funds into a trust. The trustees of this trust are resident in another jurisdiction and that is also where the funds of the trust are to be held.
>
> HMRC say that this is a cross-border arrangement, as funds move from one jurisdiction to another 'and this is a key part of the arrangement'.
>
> Notice that this is different from the unit trust in Example 13.4 where there was no cross-border arrangement because the location of the investors was not material to the establishment of that vehicle.

> **Example 13.8 – tax haven company**
>
> Oldco is a company that is resident in a zero-tax jurisdiction. Oldco has only one asset – a UK investment property.
>
> Oldco's profits from its property rental business are subject to UK tax. If Oldco sold the UK investment property, its capital gains or losses from the disposal would be subject to UK corporation tax under the rules for taxation of UK property.
>
> Oldco then transfers its ownership of the UK investment property to Newco, a UK resident company in the same group of companies as Oldco.
>
> There is no material tax consequence from this arrangement, so, as regards EU DAC 6 rules, this is not a cross-border arrangement.

See HMRC's International Exchange of Information Handbook IEIM630040 and IEIM630050.

WHAT IS A 'REPORTABLE CROSS-BORDER ARRANGEMENT'?

13.7

> **Focus**
>
> An arrangement can only be reportable, if it is within the meaning of a reportable cross-border arrangement for the purposes of EU DAC 6.
>
> A 'reportable cross-border arrangement' is a cross-border arrangement that contains at least one of the hallmarks set out in EU DAC – see EU DAC at Art 3(19). See **13.4** and **13.5** regarding the meaning of 'arrangement' and 'cross-border arrangement'.

However, in light of Brexit and, in particular, the EU-UK Trade and Cooperation Agreement of 31 December 2020, the UK's rules implementing EU DAC 6 will only now require that either of the category D hallmarks is met. The other DAC 6 hallmarks are therefore rendered irrelevant to UK reporting under EU DAC 6.

If the conditions listed in **13.5** and **13.6** apply, any one of the hallmarks that are described in **Chapter 17** exists for any transaction and this occurred in the timeframe described below, it is likely that it will be necessary to make a report under EU DAC 6.

HMRC say that the five categories of hallmark relate to features or characteristics that are commonly seen in aggressive tax planning. However, the presence of any of the hallmarks does not necessarily mean that an arrangement represents unacceptable tax planning. See HMRC's International Exchange of Information Manual IEIM640010.

EU DAC 6 applies to a reportable cross-border arrangement ('RCBA') in the following circumstances.

(a) the RCBA is, or continues to be, made available for implementation or ready for implementation on or after 1 July 2020,

(b) an RCBA in respect of which on or after 1 July 2020 an intermediary (as defined in EU DAC) provided, directly or by means of other persons, aid, assistance or advice with respect to designing, marketing, organising, making available for implementation or managing the implementation of the reportable cross-border arrangement, and

(c) an RCBA in respect of which the first step in the implementation was made on or after 25 June 2018.

See **14.3** to **14.5** regarding the meanings of 'UK intermediary' and 'intermediary'.

See the International Tax Enforcement (Disclosable Arrangements) Regulations 2020, reg 1 regarding the circumstances in which EU DAC 6 applies to an RCBA. See reg 12 regarding the application of the hallmarks.

See EU DAC 6.

EU DISCUSSIONS LEADING TO DEFERRAL OF THE INTRODUCTION OF EU DAC 6

13.8

Focus

In the UK, the first reporting under EU DAC 6 had been scheduled for Summer 2020. However, by mid-June 2020 the EU was understood to be considering a three-month deferral of the first reporting requirement under EU DAC 6. This was caused by the worldwide Covid-19 Pandemic.

The UK government subsequently deferred its first reporting deadlines under its EU DAC 6 regulations, by six months – with the first reporting therefore delayed until Winter 2020/2021.

See **Chapter 15**, and particularly **15.8** and **15.9** regarding the deadlines for EU DAC 6 reporting.

A number of EU Member States, including Belgium, Luxembourg and Sweden, announced that they would provide for, and, in the case of Hungary, was said to be considering, a deferral in their domestic legislation in connection with the original filing deadlines as laid down in EU DAC 6.

These announcements and statements by Member States followed and refer to the political agreement that was apparently reached behind closed doors on 3 June 2020 by the 27 ambassadors to the EU in the Council's COREPER II (the body preparing the Council meetings) on the European Commission's proposed amendment to EU DAC 6 of 8 May 2020 regarding a deferral of EU DAC 6 reporting.

See, for example, https://ec.europa.eu/taxation_customs/news/taxation-commission-proposes-postponement-taxation-rules-due-coronavirus-crisis_en.

Chapter 14

EU DAC 6 – Who must report?

SIGNPOSTS

- Any obligation to report under the UK's DAC 6 Regulations (see SI 2020/25) will fall either on a UK intermediary or, in certain circumstances, on a UK relevant taxpayer. An intermediary does not need to report if the intermediary can prove that the arrangement has been reported by another intermediary, either to HMRC or to an EU Member State (see **14.1**).

- The primary obligation to report falls on any UK intermediary. A UK relevant taxpayer can only be required to report, if he or she cannot prove that the arrangement was reported by an intermediary – either to HMRC or to an EU Member State (see **14.2**).

- Neither an intermediary nor a taxpayer has to report an arrangement to HMRC if he, she or it is required to report the arrangement to an EU Member State (see **14.2**).

- Where either an intermediary or a taxpayer wishes to avoid the need to report an arrangement by relying on having proof that another intermediary or taxpayer has reported it, that intermediary or taxpayer must be prepared for the possibility that HMRC asks to see suitable evidence to support this contention. In the right circumstances, an arrangement reference number ('ARN') may be sufficient evidence of this (see **14.2**).

- Intermediary means any person that (1) designs, markets, organises or makes available for implementation or manages the implementation of a reportable cross-border arrangement; or (2) directly or by means of other persons has undertaken to provide aid, assistance or advice with respect to the above and knows, or could reasonably be expected to know, that this was in respect of a reportable cross-border arrangement (see **14.2**).

- A UK intermediary is an intermediary that is resident in the UK, has a permanent establishment relating to the arrangement here, is incorporated in or governed by the laws of the UK or is registered with certain UK professional bodies (see **14.2**, **14.3** and **14.4**).

- A relevant taxpayer is any person to whom a reportable cross-border arrangement is made available for implementation, or who is ready to implement a reportable cross-border arrangement or has implemented the first step of such an arrangement (see **14.5**).

- A UK relevant taxpayer is a relevant taxpayer that is resident in the UK, has a permanent establishment relating to the arrangement here, receives income or generates profits or carries on activity in the UK (see **14.5**).

- In appropriate circumstances, employees of intermediaries or taxpayers do not need to report under the UK's Regulations implementing EU Directive 2018/822/EU ('EU DAC 6') (see **14.6**).

- An intermediary is not obliged to report where legal professional privilege prevents this. HMRC say that where a lawyer is marketing an arrangement, that lawyer cannot then assert legal professional privilege so as not to make a return in respect of it. The intermediary lawyer's client may waive legal professional privilege, thereby allowing the DAC 6 report to be made by the lawyer on their behalf (see **14.8** and **14.9**).

OVERVIEW

14.1

Focus

The obligation to report under EU DAC 6 falls on either a UK intermediary or in certain circumstances a UK relevant taxpayer.

The primary reporting obligation falls on intermediaries. A taxpayer will not need to report an arrangement under EU DAC 6, unless no intermediary reports the arrangement.

Note, however, that a taxpayer needs to be able to prove that an intermediary made a DAC 6 report (see **14.2**).

A UK intermediary who participates in a reportable cross-border arrangement must report where no intermediary is required to report either to HMRC or to the competent authority of an EU Member State.

Where there are multiple intermediaries, they must all report except where they have proof that the same information has already been reported to the authorities.

Where no intermediary has an obligation to report, that obligation may then fall on a taxpayer. This might be because there is no intermediary, or the intermediary does not have an EU connection, or a legal professional privilege defence applies to the intermediary (see **14.8** and **14.9**).

Under EU DAC 6 a cross-border arrangement is reportable if it meets one or more of the hallmarks that are listed in EU DAC 6. See **13.4** and **13.5** regarding arrangements and, in particular, cross-border arrangements; see **Chapter 17** regarding the hallmarks.

As regards the phrase Member State after Brexit, while until 31 January 2020 the UK was in the EU, it was itself an EU Member State. After the UK left the EU, it was subject to the transition period arrangements until 31 December 2020. Under the terms of the transition period, the UK was treated as if it were still an EU Member State for certain purposes – including as regards the EU Directive on Administrative Cooperation 2011/16/EU ('EU DAC') and EU DAC 6. See **Chapter 2**.

See HMRC's International Exchange of Information Manual IEIM622030 and IEIM650010.

THE CIRCUMSTANCES WHEN AN INTERMEDIARY OR TAXPAYER DOES NOT NEED TO MAKE A RETURN

14.2

Focus

An intermediary or taxpayer does not need to make a return if:

- the intermediary or taxpayer is required to report the reportable information to the competent authority of another EU Member State; or

- another intermediary or taxpayer who participated in the arrangement has made a return to HMRC or to the competent authority of another Member State.

In the case of the second of these two bullet points, the intermediary or taxpayer may only not make a return if that intermediary or taxpayer has evidence that the reportable information required to be reported has been filed or returned.

Evidence that reportable information has been filed or returned must comprise the ARN or equivalent reference number issued by the competent authority of another Member State. That may often be sufficient – see below.

HMRC say that receipt of an ARN from another intermediary is sufficient for an intermediary to be satisfied that that other intermediary has filed a DAC 6 report, 'unless they have any reason to suspect that the report has not been submitted'. HMRC say that the intermediary who wishes to rely on that does not need to review the DAC 6 report that the other intermediary has submitted in order to check whether all of the reportable information held by the reporting intermediary has been reported to HMRC. See HMRC's International Exchange of Information Manual IEIM659010, and see below.

However, HMRC also say that the exclusion only applies where the intermediary has evidence that the information that they hold has been reported in the other Member State, or has been reported by the other intermediary. HMRC accept that there may be practical difficulties for intermediaries in obtaining evidence that reports made by other intermediaries involved in the arrangement are sufficient in order for the exemption to apply. In HMRC's International Exchange of Information Manual IEIM621120, HMRC refer to their guidance in IEIM659000 and IEIM659010, which includes the following.

HMRC draw a distinction between the situation where a DAC 6 return has been made by a promoter as compared with that where a DAC 6 return has been made by a service provider.

HMRC say that an intermediary who is a promoter of an arrangement, can be expected to know the full details of the arrangement. Hence, where a DAC 6 return has been made by a promoter of an arrangement, other intermediaries are entitled to assume that the promoter has provided full details in the return that the promoter has made, of the information that needed to be reported to HMRC (or to other tax authorities). However, see below where the return is made by a service provider, as distinct from a promoter.

HMRC say that the only exception to this is where another intermediary knows that there is information which needed to be reported, but which the promoter has not reported. Examples could include if the other intermediary who is not the promoter provided advice directly to a relevant taxpayer, which the promoter would not have been aware of, or if the intermediary was responsible for marketing the arrangement to clients, so that the promoter did not know the identities of the relevant taxpayers.

HMRC say that the situation where a DAC 6 return is made by a service provider is different from that where the return is made by a promoter. A service provider may not have full information about the arrangement. Hence an intermediary cannot automatically assume that a report made by a service provider will be complete and correct.

It may not always be entirely clear whether an intermediary is a promoter or a service provider. HMRC expect an intermediary that receives an ARN from a second intermediary to consider in light of their knowledge of the arrangement, whether that second intermediary will be a promoter or a service provider. This may require the first intermediary to enter into discussions with the second intermediary. HMRC say that the situation may not always be clear but that the first intermediary should seek to make a 'reasonable judgement in the circumstances'. See HMRC's International Exchange of Information Manual IEIM 659010.

MEANING OF 'UK INTERMEDIARY'

14.3

Focus

According to EU DAC as amended, Art 3(21) 'intermediary' means any person that:

(1)   designs, markets, organises or makes available for implementation or manages the implementation of a reportable cross-border arrangement; or

(2)   directly or by means of other persons, has undertaken to provide aid, assistance or advice with respect to the above and knows, or could reasonably be expected to know, that this was in respect of a reportable cross-border arrangement.

It is possible to avoid being an intermediary under (2) above if one did not know or could not reasonably be expected to have known that one was providing services in relation to a relevant cross-border arrangement.

In accordance with the UK's Regulations implementing EU DAC as amended, Art 8ab(3) 'UK intermediary' means an intermediary in relation to whom the UK is:

(a)   the State where the intermediary is resident for tax purposes;

(b)   the State where the intermediary has a permanent establishment through which the services with respect to the arrangement are provided;

(c)   the State which the intermediary is incorporated in or governed by the laws of;

(d)   the State where the intermediary is registered with a professional association related to legal, taxation or consultancy services.

The EU Directive uses the phrase 'Member State', rather than 'State'. However, in light of Brexit and, in particular, the EU-UK Trade and Cooperation Agreement of December 2020, the UK's rules implementing EU DAC 6 have been amended dropping the word 'Member'. See the International Tax Enforcement (Disclosable Arrangements) (Amendment) (No. 2) (EU Exit) Regulations 2020, reg 2.

See **Chapter 2**.

The International Tax Enforcement (Disclosable Arrangements) Regulations 2020, SI 2020/25 apply the definitions of 'intermediary', 'relevant taxpayer', 'UK intermediary' and 'UK relevant taxpayer' that are in EU DAC (as amended by EU DAC 6), Arts 3 and 8ab. However, in light of Brexit and, in particular, the EU-UK Trade and Cooperation Agreement of December 2020, the UK's rules implementing EU DAC 6 have been amended removing the word 'Member' where the EU definitions of these terms use the phrase 'Member State'. See the International Tax Enforcement (Disclosable Arrangements) (Amendment) (No. 2) (EU Exit) Regulations 2020, reg 2. See **2.8**.

See HMRC's International Exchange of Information Manual IEIM621020 regarding the meaning of 'UK intermediary'.

As regards point (d) above, HMRC have confirmed that in the case of a person living and working outside the UK and the EU, who is an intermediary only by virtue of being registered with a professional association in the UK, in practice HMRC would not usually expect a report to be made where doing so would contravene domestic legislation on data protection in the jurisdiction in which they were based. See HMRC's International Exchange of Information Manual IEIM621110.

See HMRC's International Exchange of Information Manual IEIM621140 regarding the meaning of 'registered with a professional association'.

A person is not treated as an intermediary in relation to a reportable cross-border arrangement where:

(a)   he or she is an employee, and

(b)   his or her employer is an intermediary or relevant taxpayer in relation to the relevant cross-border arrangement.

See **14.6** regarding employees of intermediaries and/or taxpayers.

14.4

Focus

A service provider can argue that they are not an intermediary because they did not know and could not reasonably have been expected to know that they were involved in a reportable arrangement. See HMRC's International Exchange of Information Manual IEIM621050 and IEIM621060 regarding the distinction between a service provider and an intermediary and the meaning of 'reasonably expected to know'.

A promoter can argue that they are in effect a service provider, rather than an intermediary if they are 'providing assistance in respect of the marketing' of an arrangement, as distinct from marketing it. See HMRC's International Exchange of Information Manual IEIM621030 regarding the distinction between these.

See 14.5 below regarding the meaning of 'UK relevant taxpayer'.

MEANING OF 'UK RELEVANT TAXPAYER'
14.5

Focus

According to EU DAC as amended, Art 3(22) 'relevant taxpayer' means any person to whom a reportable cross-border arrangement is made available for implementation, or who is ready to implement a reportable cross-border arrangement or has implemented the first step of such an arrangement.

In accordance with EU DAC as amended, Art 8ab(7) 'UK relevant taxpayer' means a relevant taxpayer in relation to whom the UK is the Member State, specifically:

(a)   the Member State where the relevant taxpayer is resident for tax purposes;

(b)   the Member State where the relevant taxpayer has a permanent establishment benefiting from the arrangement;

(c)   the Member State where the relevant taxpayer receives income or generates profits, although the relevant taxpayer is not resident for tax purposes and has no permanent establishment in any Member State;

(d)   the Member State where the relevant taxpayer carries on an activity, although the relevant taxpayer is not resident for tax purposes and has no permanent establishment in any Member State.

The EU Directive uses the phrase 'Member State', rather than 'State'. However, in light of Brexit and, in particular, the EU-UK Trade and Cooperation Agreement of December 2020, the UK's rules implementing EU DAC 6 have been amended dropping the word 'Member'. See the International Tax Enforcement (Disclosable Arrangements) (Amendment) (No. 2) (EU Exit) Regulations 2020, reg 2. See **2.8**.

See **14.4** on the meaning of 'UK intermediary'.

HMRC consider that a person does not have to have implemented or have started to implement a reportable cross-border arrangement, nor do they have to have decided that they will implement the arrangement. Simply having an arrangement made available to them for implementation, or being ready to implement an arrangement, is sufficient. See HMRC's International Exchange of Information Manual IEIM622010.

While a relevant taxpayer may not be resident in the UK, in order for the taxpayer to have a reporting obligation under EU DAC 6, they must be a UK relevant taxpayer.

HMRC say that for the purposes of paragraph (c) above, receiving income or generating profits could include earning profits from a property business. For the purposes of paragraph (d) carrying on an activity could include carrying on a trade otherwise than through a permanent establishment. See HMRC's International Exchange of International Manual IEIM622020.

See also above regarding the meaning of 'relevant taxpayer'. See also HMRC's International Exchange of Information Manual IEIM622010.

Note that for the purposes of EU DAC, therefore all of the above (and of EU law generally), all references to a 'Member State' continued to be treated as including the UK, until 31 December 2020 under the Agreement on the withdrawal of the United Kingdom of Great Britain and Northern Ireland from the European Union and the European Atomic Energy Community (the 'Brexit withdrawal agreement'). See **2.8** and **2.9**.

However, in light of Brexit and, in particular, the EU-UK Trade and Cooperation Agreement of December 2020, the UK's rules implementing EU DAC 6 have been amended dropping the word 'Member'. See the International Tax Enforcement (Disclosable Arrangements) (Amendment) (No. 2) (EU Exit) Regulations 2020, reg 2. See **Chapter 2**.

See the International Tax Enforcement (Disclosable Arrangements) Regulations 2020, regs 2, 3, 4 and 13. See also **13.3**.

EMPLOYEES OF INTERMEDIARIES OR TAXPAYERS

14.6

Focus

For these purposes a person ('P') is not treated as an intermediary in relation to a reportable cross-border arrangement where:

(a)   P is an employee of an employer ('E'), and

(b)   E is an intermediary or relevant taxpayer in relation to the reportable cross-border arrangement.

The International Tax Enforcement (Disclosable Arrangements) Regulations 2020 provide that where an individual who is an employee takes actions which would otherwise mean that he or she is an intermediary, he will not be treated as an intermediary provided that either his employer or someone connected with his employer is treated as an intermediary or relevant taxpayer as regards the cross-border arrangement instead.

For this purpose, 'connected' means 'closely bound by financial economic or organisational links'. 'Employer' and 'employee' have the meanings given by the Income Tax (Earnings and Pensions) Act 2003, s 4.

See the International Tax Enforcement (Disclosable Arrangements) Regulations 2020, reg 13. See also HMRC's International Exchange of Information Manual IEIM621080.

See **14.3** and **14.4** regarding the meanings of 'UK intermediary' and 'intermediary'.

WHAT IF SOMEONE IS BOTH AN INTERMEDIARY AND A TAXPAYER?

14.7

Focus

HMRC say that in certain circumstances the same person could be both an intermediary and a relevant taxpayer. HMRC say that provided that all relevant information is reported, and there is no attempt to delay or avoid reporting, they will not seek to charge penalties where a person in this particular position reports as an intermediary instead of as a relevant taxpayer, or vice versa.

A UK intermediary or (subject to the above) a UK relevant taxpayer that participates in a reportable cross-border arrangement may need to make a return. See HMRC's International Exchange of Information Manual IEIM622030 and IEIM650010.

However, a UK relevant taxpayer does not need to file a return if an intermediary is required to report the reportable information either to HMRC or to the competent authority of another EU Member State.

See HMRC's International Exchange of Information Manual IEIM622050.

EU DAC 6 AND LEGAL PROFESSIONAL PRIVILEGE

14.8

Focus

Although a person or a firm may fall within the definition of a UK intermediary in relation to an arrangement that needs to be reported, legal professional privilege may sometimes mean that that person or that firm does not need to (indeed cannot) report the arrangement under EU DAC 6.

Nevertheless, where applicable, such an intermediary must notify UK intermediaries or UK taxpayers who have participated in reportable cross-border arrangements to which the privilege information relates of their reporting obligations under the Regulations.

> The intermediary lawyer's client may waive legal professional privilege, thereby allowing the DAC 6 report to be made by the lawyer on their behalf.

The International Tax Enforcement (Disclosable Arrangements) Regulations 2020 state that nothing contained in them requires a UK intermediary to disclose any privileged information. For this purpose, 'privileged information' means information with respect to which a claim to legal professional privilege, or, in Scotland, to confidentiality of communications, could be maintained in legal proceedings.

See HMRC's International Exchange of Information Manual IEIM621130.

See the International Tax Enforcement (Disclosable Arrangements) Regulations 2020, reg 7. See also **14.9**.

14.9   The EU DAC 6 rules allow for Member States (see **2.8** and **2.9** regarding the application of this to the UK following Brexit) to give intermediaries an exemption to report where such disclosure would breach any legal professional privilege under its laws.

The UK Regulations include a provision that a UK Intermediary is not required to disclose any 'privileged information'. The UK Intermediary to which this applies may then need to notify any other intermediary (or if none, the relevant taxpayer) 'as soon as reasonably practicable' of the reporting obligation.

'Privileged information' means information with respect to which a claim to legal professional privilege, or, in Scotland, to confidentiality of communications, could be maintained in legal proceedings.

It is understood that there have been ongoing discussions between The Law Society and HMRC regarding the interaction of legal professional privilege with obligations under EU DAC 6.

See EU DAC 6 and legal professional privilege published by The Law Society on 8 June 2020 at https://www.lawsociety.org.uk/support-services/advice/articles/dac-6-and-legal-professional-privilege/

HMRC say that where a lawyer is marketing an arrangement, that lawyer cannot then assert legal professional privilege so as not to make a return in respect of it.

The intermediary lawyer's client may waive legal professional privilege, thereby allowing the EU DAC 6 report to be made by the lawyer on their behalf.

See HMRC's International Exchange of Information Manual IEIM621130.

See the International Tax Enforcement (Disclosable Arrangements) Regulations 2020, reg 7. See also **14.8**.

EU DAC 6 – What must be reported, when and how?

- The general rule is that a DAC 6 return must be submitted within 30 days of the earliest of (i) the day after the arrangement is made available, (ii) is ready for implementation, and (iii) the first step in implementation is made. There is a further reporting trigger for intermediaries who are service providers who can be required to report within 30 days after they provide aid, assistance or advice re the arrangement.

- In addition to the general rule, there are rules about when initial reporting under EU DAC 6 was to take place. Initial reporting under the UK's DAC 6 Regulations (see SI 2020/25) was delayed by six months so that the earliest by which DAC 6 reporting could possibly be required was in early 2021. The precise dates are described in **15.9**.

- In specified circumstances, HMRC will accept that there is a reasonable excuse for lateness because of the 25 June 2018 commencement date for EU DAC 6, or owing to reliance on a service provider, or because of the Covid-19 pandemic (see **15.10** to **15.12**).

- The meanings of 'made available', 'ready for implementation', 'first step', and 'aid, assistance or advice' which are key to the trigger points referred to above, are explained in **16.13** to **16.17**.

HOW MUST REPORTS BE MADE?

15.1

Focus

HMRC promised ahead of the first reporting deadlines under EU DAC 6, that they would provide an online portal which intermediaries and taxpayers could then use to file their DAC 6 returns. See HMRC's International Exchange of Information Manual IEIM658000.

As at mid-June 2020, HMRC was understood to be developing an online portal to be used when making DAC 6 reports. HMRC had promised that this would be ready by no later than 1 July 2020. However, a deferral of reporting deadlines under the UK's DAC 6 rules was later announced – see HMRC's International Exchange of Information Manual IEIM800010.

WHAT IS REPORTABLE INFORMATION?

15.2

Focus

HMRC expected that the information to be reported, would include the following.

- identity of intermediaries and relevant taxpayers (including name, date, place and date of birth, tax residence, TIN and associated enterprises);

- details of the relevant hallmarks that make the arrangement reportable;

- a summary of the content of the arrangements;

- the date of the first step of implementation;

- details of the national provisions forming the basis of the arrangements;

- the value of the arrangements;

- any EU Member States that are likely to be concerned by the arrangements;

- identity of any other person in an EU Member State likely to be affected by the arrangements.

As regards the phrase 'EU Member State', all references in EU law to Member States is treated as including the UK during the Brexit transition period (see **2.8** and **2.9**).

See HMRC's International Exchange of Information Manual IEIM800010.

15.3   The information which the UK's DAC 6 Regulations, namely the International Tax Enforcement (Disclosable Arrangements) Regulations 2020, SI 2020/25, and the EU Directive on Administrative Cooperation 2011/16/EU ('EU DAC') itself, say is 'reportable information', is as follows.

(a)   the identification of intermediaries and relevant taxpayers, including their name, date and place of birth (in the case of an individual), residence for tax purposes, TIN and, where appropriate, the persons that are associated enterprises to the relevant taxpayer;

(b)   details of the hallmarks* set out in Annex IV of EU DAC that make the cross-border arrangement reportable (see **13.6**);

(c)   a summary of the content of the reportable cross-border arrangement, including a reference to the name by which it is commonly known, if any, and a description in abstract terms of the relevant business activities or arrangements, without leading to the disclosure of a commercial, industrial or professional secret or of a commercial process, or of information the disclosure of which would be contrary to public policy;

(d)   the date on which the first step in implementing the reportable cross-border arrangement has been made or will be made;

(e)   details of the national provisions that form the basis of the reportable cross-border arrangement;

(f)   the value of the reportable cross-border arrangement;

(g)   the identification of the Member State of the relevant taxpayer(s) and any other Member States which are likely to be concerned by the reportable cross-border arrangement;

(h)   the identification of any other person in a Member State likely to be affected by the reportable cross-border arrangement, indicating to which Member States such person is linked.

*In light of Brexit and, in particular, the EU-UK Trade and Cooperation Agreement of December 2020, the UK's rules implementing EU DAC 6 will only now require that either of the category D hallmarks is met. The other DAC 6 hallmarks are therefore rendered irrelevant to UK reporting under EU DAC 6. See **Chapter 17**. See **2.8** on Brexit.

15.4   If the arrangement does not rely on any particular tax legislation, then no legislative reference is needed here. That could be the case where an arrangement meets hallmark category D.

It is possible that some 'cross-border', arrangements may rely on legislation in more than one jurisdiction. Where this is the case, the relevant legislative provisions across all jurisdictions should be reported.

As regards the value of the reportable arrangement at point (f) above, this will depend on the transaction. Where a transaction is carried out between independent third parties at arm's length, the value of the transaction will be the amount paid. For any other transaction, the value of the transaction for the purposes of point (f) should reflect its market value, rather than the amount paid.

The value of the transaction is not necessarily the amount brought into account for tax purposes, nor does it mean the amount of any tax advantage.

As regards the phrase 'Member State', all references in EU law to Member States is treated as including the UK during the Brexit transition period (see **2.8** and **2.9**).

As regards whether a jurisdiction is 'likely to be affected' by the reportable cross-border arrangement', particular attention should be paid to whether there is a tax effect of the arrangement in that jurisdiction.

The identity of any other person likely to be affected by the arrangement as required at point (h) could include the counterparty to a transaction, even where that person is not a relevant taxpayer in their own right.

Focus

'TIN' means:

(i)   if the person is resident for tax purposes in the UK, the UTR allocated to that person by HMRC;

(ii)   if the person is resident for tax purposes outside the UK, the UTR allocated to that person by HMRC or, if they do not have one, the reference number allocated to that person by the tax authority in the country or territory in which they are resident for tax purposes; or

(iii) if no such reference number has been allocated, the national insurance number, if any.

See EU DAC at Art 2(2).

In the case of UK relevant taxpayers and intermediaries, their TIN will be their UTR or their national insurance number ('NINO').

See HMRC's International Exchange of Information Manual IEIM657000.

See also the International Tax Enforcement (Disclosable Arrangements) Regulations 2020, regu 6; see also EU DAC at Art 8ab(14).

REPORTING BY INTERMEDIARIES – THE IMPORTANCE OF KNOWLEDGE, POSSESSION OR CONTROL

15.5

Focus

In order for information to be reportable by an intermediary, that information must be in the intermediary's knowledge, possession or control.

An intermediary should be prepared where necessary to review the information that is in its knowledge, possession or control. However, HMRC do not consider that an intermediary would have to trawl through all of an organisation's computer systems to try and find all information held in relation to a relevant taxpayer 'just to see if it was relevant'.

HMRC say that any deliberate effort to split work and knowledge between people working on a particular arrangement, to try and avoid certain pieces of information being reported, will be ineffective. HMRC would still consider that the information was in the intermediary's knowledge, possession or control.

Where an intermediary does not hold certain information, it may seek to obtain it, either from other intermediaries or from relevant taxpayers.

See HMRC's International Exchange of Information Manual IEIM657010.

REPORTING BY INTERMEDIARIES – THE ONGOING REPORTING OBLIGATION

15.6

Focus

If the reportable cross-border arrangement is a marketable arrangement, the UK intermediary must make a return at the end of every three-month period. These returns must set out any new reportable information, within the terms of EU DAC, which has become available in respect of the reportable cross-border arrangement since that return or a previous return, in respect of:

- the details of relevant taxpayers and associated enterprises;

- the date on which the first steps of the arrangement were implemented by the various relevant taxpayers;

- the EU Member State(s) where the relevant taxpayers are resident, and any other Member States that the arrangement is likely to concern;

- the identification of any other persons in EU Member States that are likely to be affected by the arrangement.

When the UK government announced a deferral of reporting deadlines under EU DAC 6, it announced that the first such report would now need to be made by 30 April 2021 – see **15.9**.

'Marketable arrangement' means a cross-border arrangement that is designed, marketed, ready for implementation or made available for implementation without a need to be substantially customised – see Art 3(24) of EU DAC.

In order to be accepted, a return required under the Regulations must be made electronically and in whatever form is specified by HMRC.

See the International Tax Enforcement (Disclosable Arrangements) Regulations 2020, regs 3,4, 9, 10 and 13.

See also HMRC's International Exchange of Information Manual IEIM653000.

INITIAL REPORTING OBLIGATION FOR RELEVANT TAXPAYERS

15.7

Focus

A UK relevant taxpayer does not need to file a return if an intermediary is required to report the reportable information either to HMRC or to the competent authority of another EU Member State (see **13.2**).

A relevant taxpayer is exempt from having to submit a DAC 6 return, if either of the following conditions is met. The conditions are that either:

- the relevant taxpayer has a reporting obligation in another Member State in respect of the same reportable cross-border arrangement, and that Member State features before the UK when applying the list in Art 8ab(7) of EU DAC; or

- another relevant taxpayer 'agreed the arrangement with the intermediary', or, where there is no agreement with an intermediary, another relevant taxpayer manages the implementation of the arrangement. See HMRC's International Exchange of Information Manual IEIM622040.

This exemption only applies where the relevant taxpayer has evidence that the information they are required to report has been reported in the other Member State, or has been reported by the other relevant taxpayer. See **14.2** regarding 'evidence'.

Where a relevant taxpayer has obligations to file information in multiple Member States, EU DAC provides that they are only required to file the information in the Member State which appears first in the list in Art 8ab(7) of EU DAC. The list is as follows:

(a)   the Member State where the relevant taxpayer is resident for tax purposes;

(b)   the Member State where the relevant taxpayer has a permanent establishment benefiting from the arrangement;

(c)   the Member State where the relevant taxpayer receives income or generates profits, although the relevant taxpayer is not resident for tax purposes and has no permanent establishment in any Member State;

(d)   the Member State where the relevant taxpayer carries on an activity, although the relevant taxpayer is not resident for tax purposes and has no permanent establishment in any Member State.

However, where a relevant taxpayer *does* have an initial reporting obligation, as distinct from an annual reporting obligation, the report must be made within 30 days of the earliest of:

- the day after the reportable cross-border arrangement is made available to the relevant taxpayer,

- the day after the reportable cross-border arrangement is ready for implementation by the relevant taxpayer, and

- when the first step in the implementation of the reportable cross-border arrangement has been made in relation to the relevant taxpayer.

HMRC say: 'Where a relevant taxpayer holds information in relation to a reportable cross-border arrangement which an intermediary does not hold (for example, their full address or NINO), the relevant taxpayer may provide that information to the intermediary so that they can report the information, rather than requiring the relevant taxpayer to make an additional report.' See HMRC's International Exchange of Information Manual IEIM622030.

This seems to imply that a relevant taxpayer could be required to submit an additional DAC 6 return, if certain of the 'information that must be reported in relation to a reportable cross-border arrangement' (as set out in HMRC's International Exchange of Information Manual IEIM657000), is known to the relevant taxpayer but not to any intermediary with a DAC 6 reporting obligation.

See **15.11** regarding a situation in which the same person is both an intermediary and a relevant taxpayer.

See also **15.4** regarding the annual reporting requirement of a UK relevant taxpayer.

See HMRC's International Exchange of Information Manual IEIM622040 and IEIM654000.

DAC 6 REPORTING DEADLINES – GENERAL RULE

15.8

Focus

The general rule is that a DAC 6 return must be submitted within a period of 30 days beginning on the earliest of:

(i)   the day after the day the reportable cross-border arrangement is made available for implementation – see **15.14**,

(iii)   the day after the day the reportable cross-border arrangement is ready for implementation – see **15.15**, and

(iii)   the day the first step in the implementation of the reportable cross-border arrangement is made – see **15.16**.

In addition to the above, there is a further reporting trigger for intermediaries who are 'service providers'. As such, the general rule for

---

them is that they are required to file a report within the period of 30 days beginning on the day after they provide the aid, assistance or advice in respect of the arrangement. See **15.17** as regards the meaning of 'aid, assistance or advice'.

If the reportable cross-border arrangement is a marketable arrangement, the UK intermediary must make a return as described in **15.6** at the end of every three-month period beginning with the date of the first DAC 6 return submitted to HMRC by the intermediary.

However, this general rule is then subject to the other rules that are set out in **15.9**.

HMRC expect that in practice, it is likely that most reports from service providers will be made in accordance with the further reporting trigger that is referred to above, as a service provider may not know the point at which the arrangement is made available for implementation, is ready for implementation or when the first step of the implementation is taken.

The general rule is subject to the further rules in **15.9**, which in turn take on board the government's announcement of a six-month deferral of their implementation of DAC 6 in view of the Covid-19 pandemic (see **13.8**).

Some of the deadlines depend on 'trigger points' – for example, when an arrangement is 'made available', 'ready for implementation' or the 'first step' is made. See **15.14**, **15.15** and **15.16** regarding the meanings of each of these 'trigger points'.

There is also the further trigger point that is described above in relation to service providers – see **15.17** as regards the meaning of 'aid, assistance or advice'.

See also **15.10**, **15.11** and **15.12** as regards various circumstances where HMRC say they may be sympathetic if a DAC 6 return is submitted late.

See HMRC's International Exchange of Information Manual IEIM651000. As regards service providers, see IEIM652000.

DAC 6 REPORTING DEADLINES – OTHER RULES

15.9

Focus

Following discussion among EU Member States about whether to defer EU DAC 6 in view of the Covid-19 pandemic, the UK government deferred by six months the first reporting deadlines.

The revised deadlines are as follows:

- For arrangements where the first step in the implementation took place between 25 June 2018 and 30 June 2020, reports must be made by 28 February 2021, instead of by 31 August as originally required (see regs 3(3)(a) and 4(4)(a)).

- For arrangements which were made available for implementation, or which were ready for implementation, or where the first step in the implementation took place between 1 July 2020, and 31 December 2020, reports must be made within the period of 30 days beginning on 1 January 2021. Under the original rules, such arrangements would have had to be reported within 30 days of the reporting trigger point being reached (see regs 3(3)(c)(i)–(iii) and 4(4)(c)(i)–(iii)).

- For arrangements in respect of which a UK intermediary provided aid, assistance or advice between 1 July 2020 and 31 December 2020, reports must be made within the period of 30 days beginning on 1 January 2021. Again, under the original rules, such arrangements would have had to be reported within 30 days of the aid, assistance or advice being provided (see reg 3(3)(c)(iv)).

- Arrangements which become reportable on or after 1 January 2021 must be reported as normal.

- Where periodic reports are required in relation to marketable arrangements, the first such report must be made by 30 April 2021.

The normal 30-day deadline that is referred to above, is also deferred in the case of a UK intermediary that is a service provider, for whom the trigger for a report is the day after the day the UK intermediary provided, directly or by means of other persons, aid, assistance or advice with respect to designing, marketing, organising, making available for implementation or managing the implementation of the reportable cross-border arrangement. When the UK government announced a deferral of reporting deadlines under EU DAC 6, it announced that the first such report would now need to be made within the 30 day-period beginning on 1 January 2021.

See **13.8** regarding EU discussion about deferral of the introduction of EU DAC 6.

In view of the deferral owing to the Covid-19 pandemic that is referred to above, certain of the above deadlines differ from those in the UK's DAC 6 Regulations – that is under the International Tax Enforcement (Disclosable Arrangements) Regulations 2020.

The government stated that it intended to amend the Regulations to give effect to this deferral. However, the amendments to the Regulations were not in force by 1 July 2020, but HMRC said that no action would be taken for non-reporting during the period between 1 July and the date the amendments came into force.

In the event, the amending Regulations, namely the International Tax Enforcement (Disclosable Arrangements) (Coronavirus) (Amendment) Regulations 2020, SI 2020/713, were made and then laid before the House of Commons on 9 July 2020, and came into force on 30 July 2020.

Some of the deadlines depend on 'trigger points' – for example, when an arrangement is 'made available', 'ready for implementation' or the 'first step' is made. See **15.14**, **15.15** and **15.16** regarding the meanings of each of these 'trigger points'.

There is also the further trigger point that is described above in relation to service providers – see **15.17** as regards the meaning of 'aid, assistance or advice'.

See also **15.10**, **15.11** and **15.12** as regards various circumstances where HMRC say they may be sympathetic if a DAC 6 return is submitted late.

See HMRC's International Exchange of Information Manual IEIM800010.

LATENESS

Lateness arising because of the 25 June 2018 commencement of EU DAC 6

15.10

Focus

HMRC are aware that there may be difficulties arising from potentially having to look back at things that were done before HMRC's regulations and guidance in relation to EU DAC 6 were published (possibly having to look back to as long ago as 25 June 2018).

HMRC say where that results in a failure to comply with the regulations arising from a lack of clarity about a person's obligations under EU DAC 6, it is likely that that person will have a reasonable excuse for the failure. Where a person has a reasonable excuse, no penalty will be due.

See HMRC's International Exchange of Information Manual IEIM670000.

Lateness owing to reliance on a service provider

15.11　HMRC comment on a situation where an intermediary can show that it was late submitting a DAC 6 return because it relied on, and was subsequently let down by, an agreement with another intermediary that the latter would submit the return. HMRC say that in those circumstances, the first intermediary has a reasonable excuse for submitting the return late, provided the first intermediary rectifies the situation 'without unreasonable delay'.

See HMRC's International Exchange of Information Manual IEIM659000, IEIM659010 and IEIM621120.

Coronavirus – Covid-19

15.12

Focus

HMRC accept that where an Automatic Exchange of Information ('AEOI') (including DAC 6) return is made late owing to issues arising from the Covid-19 pandemic, the person that makes the return late will have a reasonable excuse.

See HMRC's International Exchange of Information Manual IEIM800000.

VARIOUS REPORTING TRIGGER POINTS

15.13

Focus

Some of the deadlines that are set out in **15.8** and **15.9** depend on 'trigger points', for example:

- when an arrangement is 'made available',

- 'ready for implementation'

- or the 'first step' is made.

See **15.14**, **15.15** and **15.16** regarding the meanings of each of these 'trigger points'.

There is also the further trigger point that is described in **15.8** and **15.9** in relation to service providers – see **15.17** as regards the meaning of 'aid, assistance or advice'.

Meaning of 'made available'

15.14

> **Focus**
>
> There are many different ways in which an arrangement may be made available, such as:
>
> - a taxpayer could approach a promoter seeking advice or ideas, and the promoter could make available an arrangement in response to that request; or
>
> - an arrangement could be made available in the course of other work between an intermediary and a client, if, for example, the intermediary identifies a potential need, and suggests the arrangement as a solution; or
>
> - an arrangement could be proactively made available to prospective clients through a marketing campaign.
>
> If the design of an arrangement has not yet been finalised at the time when an outline is first provided to the client, it cannot be said to have been 'made available' at that stage.

Instead, the design of an arrangement will normally be final before the arrangement can be said to be made available for implementation.

For example, if an intermediary discusses three ideas in outline with a client, the client expresses an interest in one of these ideas and the intermediary agrees to go away and work up that idea further in relation to the client's specific circumstances. The arrangement has not as yet been 'made available' to the intermediary's client.

If the intermediary then identifies a number of funding options and engages with potential lenders to identify a couple of options that are confirmed as viable, although final agreement has not yet been reached, as the client has still not decided which option to proceed with.

The designs are finalised, including receiving the tax analysis from the other jurisdiction that is involved. Although there could still be some tweaks to the design, it is unlikely that they will be material. In light of this, when the options are presented again to the client, they are now being made available for implementation for the purposes of EU DAC 6.

However, a person will not be treated as having had an arrangement made available to them if they have not expressed any interest in or engagement with the arrangement being offered. For example, a person who sees an advertisement for an arrangement, but does not follow up on it, will not have had the arrangement made available to them. Neither the client (ie as a taxpayer) nor an intermediary has an obligation to report at that stage.

See HMRC's International Exchange of Information Manual IEIM651010.

Meaning of 'ready for implementation'

15.15

Focus

An arrangement could be ready for implementation before it is made available for implementation – for example, if a promoter has finalised the design of an arrangement, but decided not to promote it to potential clients until a later date.

If the arrangement is sufficiently finalised that it could be implemented by a client, then it is 'ready for implementation' for the purposes of EU DAC 6.

See HMRC's International Exchange of Information Manual IEIM651020.

Meaning of 'first step'

15.16

Focus

The timing of the first step is a question of fact. HMRC provide an example involving two 'scenarios' illustrating this. See below.

The first scenario concerns a company which has designed an arrangement in-house which will involve the transfer of assets to an overseas subsidiary.

The transfer is such that hallmark category E3 will be met. It is still finalising the precise details of certain later steps in the transaction, but it does not want to risk delays so it incorporates a new company in the overseas jurisdiction ready for the transfer to happen as soon as the details are finalised.

In this first scenario, incorporating the subsidiary is the first step, for the purposes of DAC 6, in implementing the reportable arrangement.

In the second scenario, a company is considering transferring some assets to an overseas subsidiary, but has not yet worked out the details. It does not yet know whether the transaction would meet any of the hallmarks, as the design is at too early a stage.

However, to avoid delays at a later date, it decides to incorporate an overseas subsidiary now in case it does decide to go ahead.

HMRC consider that in this second scenario, the incorporation cannot properly be considered to be the first step, as the arrangement's design has not yet been agreed and no decision has been taken as to whether or not to go ahead with the arrangement.

See HMRC's International Exchange of Information Manual IEIM651030.

Meaning of 'aid, assistance or advice'

15.17

> **Focus**
>
> A further reporting trigger for intermediaries who are 'service providers' is explained in **15.11** above. The trigger point occurs when the service provider provides 'aid, assistance or advice' in respect of the arrangement.
>
> According to HMRC: 'Aid, assistance and advice are broad terms to cover a range of services that an intermediary might provide. Advice, aid or assistance' could include providing finance, expertise or knowledge, sharing experience or offering legal or accounting advice.'
>
> The point at which aid, advice or assistance is provided will depend on the facts of the particular case. HMRC provide the following examples.

- HMRC's first example concerns an accountant who is asked to, and duly researches and then provides, advice on the correct treatment of a transaction. The advice is provided promptly by email. HMRC say that the date of the email will be the date the advice is provided.

- However, HMRC say that if the same accountant had phoned the client to let them know the correct treatment, but delayed sending the final email to try to delay having to make a report. HMRC say that, in those circumstances, the advice was given when the phone call was made.

- In HMRC's next example, a lawyer provides advice on a complex arrangement.

  Over several months, the lawyer and the client meet several times to discuss the arrangement, and the lawyer provides several drafts of the advice.

  As the arrangement evolves, so does the content of the advice.

  They have a final meeting where the lawyer sets out what the advice will say, and barring minor adjustments, the final written advice reflects that discussion and is provided promptly thereafter.

HMRC say that although it could be argued that the meeting is the point where the advice is provided, in practice HMRC would accept that the 30-day reporting window started the day after the final written advice was sent, provided it was sent without undue delay.

However, if HMRC can see that there is evidence of a material delay in providing the final advice, this treatment will not necessarily apply.

- In HMRC's final example, a wealth manager makes a comment to a client during an informal catch-up about the possible benefits of transferring certain intangible assets to an overseas subsidiary. The wealth manager suggests that the client may want to look into this in more detail.

   HMRC say that although this could be considered to be providing advice, the reporting obligation is not yet triggered, as the arrangement itself is insufficiently clear. The details of the arrangement have not yet been worked out.

   However, if subsequently the client asks for more specific or detailed advice about how the arrangement might work, the reporting obligation could be triggered at a later date.

See HMRC's International Exchange of Information Manual IEIM652000 to IEIM652020.

Chapter 16

EU DAC 6 – Other obligations

SIGNPOSTS

- Where HMRC receive a DAC 6 report, they will respond by then issuing an arrangement reference number ('ARN') to the intermediary or taxpayer who sent them the report (see **16.1**).

- Where appropriate, a UK intermediary or a UK relevant taxpayer to whom an ARN is notified, must then notify the ARN to other UK intermediaries or UK relevant taxpayers to whom it is relevant within a 30-day period (see **16.1** and **16.3**).

- A UK relevant taxpayer must also include the ARN and certain other information about the arrangement in his or her annual tax return (see **16.2**).

- In certain circumstances, HMRC may issue an information notice requiring a UK intermediary or UK relevant taxpayer to provide them with information or documents in relation to an arrangement (see **16.4**).

ARRANGEMENT REFERENCE NUMBER

16.1

Focus

Where either a UK intermediary or a UK relevant taxpayer makes a report to HMRC under the DAC 6 Regulations (see SI 2020/25), HMRC must issue an arrangement reference number ('ARN') and notify it to that intermediary or taxpayer.

A UK intermediary or a UK relevant taxpayer to whom an ARN is notified must then notify the ARN to any other UK intermediary or UK relevant taxpayer of whom he or she is aware within a 30-day period (see **16.3**).

HMRC say that ARNs will be issued by them 'on receipt of a valid report'. The ARN will be provided immediately once the report has passed validation checks, such as ensuring that required fields are completed.

HMRC say that this will not include checking whether or not the arrangement is in fact reportable or checking whether the report is complete and accurate. Hence, acceptance of a report and issuance of an ARN by HMRC does not mean that HMRC accepts that all obligations under the Regulations have been complied with.

Furthermore, HMRC stress that issuance of an ARN does not mean that HMRC accepts or agrees with the tax treatment or tax consequences of the arrangement as described in the report.

The ARN is referred to in the online reporting tool as the arrangement ID. The two terms are synonymous.

The online reporting tool also provides users with a disclosure ID. The disclosure ID is not the same as the ARN.

In certain circumstances, an intermediary is obliged to provide the ARN to other intermediaries, as well as to relevant taxpayers.

It is important to note that disclosure IDs should not be shared or passed onto other people. They allow an intermediary to view the specific disclosure they made, and to correct it if, for example, they realise they made a mistake in the report.

See the International Tax Enforcement (Disclosable Arrangements) Regulations 2020, SI 2020/25, reg 8. See also HMRC's International Exchange of Information Manual IEIM656000.

A UK RELEVANT TAXPAYER'S ANNUAL REPORTING REQUIREMENT

16.2

Focus

Where a UK relevant taxpayer participates in a reportable cross-border arrangement, the UK relevant taxpayer must make a return for:

(a)   the tax year or accounting period in which the first of the following occurs:

    (i)   the reportable cross-border arrangement is made available for implementation to the relevant taxpayer;

    (ii)   the reportable cross-border arrangement is ready for implementation by the UK relevant taxpayer; or

---

>   (iii)   the first step in the implementation of the reportable cross-border arrangement is made in relation to the UK relevant taxpayer; and
>
> (b)   each subsequent tax year or accounting period in which there is a tax advantage (see below regarding the meaning of 'tax advantage' in EU DAC.
>
> The return must include:
>
> (a)   the ARN; and
>
> (b)   the tax-advantage.
>
> HMRC say this should normally be done in the blank space in the relevant taxpayer's tax return.

The return must be made:

(a)   where the UK relevant taxpayer is a company, on or before the filing date for the company's tax return; or

(b)   in any other case, on or before 31 January immediately following the tax year.

'Tax advantage' is defined in EU DAC so as to include deferral of a payment of tax or advancement of a repayment of tax – see, for example, the International Tax Enforcement (Disclosable Arrangements) Regulations 2020, reg 2(4)(e).

See the International Tax Enforcement (Disclosable Arrangements) Regulations 2020, reg 5. See also HMRC's International Exchange of Information Manual IEIM655000.

INTERMEDIARY'S (AND TAXPAYER'S) OBLIGATION TO NOTIFY ARN

16.3

> **Focus**
>
> A UK intermediary or UK relevant taxpayer who has been notified of an ARN must, within 30 days after the relevant date, notify that number to any person who the UK intermediary or UK relevant taxpayer knows or should reasonably be expected to know is an intermediary or relevant taxpayer in relation to that reportable cross-border arrangement.
>
> 'The relevant date' means the later of:
>
> (a)   the date on which the ARN was notified to the UK intermediary or UK relevant taxpayer; and

> (b)   the date on which the other intermediary or the other relevant taxpayer became an intermediary or relevant taxpayer in relation to that reportable cross-border arrangement.

HMRC will issue ARNs on receipt by them of a valid DAC 6 return. See HMRC's International Exchange of Information Manual IEIM656000.

An intermediary who has not itself submitted a DAC 6 return, may find that it is notified of an ARN by another intermediary (who may or may not have submitted a DAC 6 return).

See the International Tax Enforcement (Disclosable Arrangements) Regulations 2020, reg 8. See also 16.1.

OBLIGATION TO COMPLY WITH HMRC INFORMATION POWERS

16.4

Focus

An HMRC officer may require a person whom he or she reasonably suspects is a UK intermediary or UK relevant taxpayer to provide such information or documents as the officer reasonably requires as specified by written notice.

The information or documents required by the notice must be provided:

(a)   within such period, being no less than 30 days; and

(b)   by such means and in such form, as is reasonably required by the HMRC officer.

Penalties can apply if the notice is not complied with (see **18.1**).

See the International Tax Enforcement (Disclosable Arrangements) Regulations 2020, reg 11.

Chapter 17

EU DAC 6 – The hallmarks

SIGNPOSTS

- Under EU Directive 2018/822/EU ('EU DAC 6') a 'cross-border arrangement' is reportable if it meets one or more of the hallmarks that are listed in EU DAC 6 (and in this Chapter). See **13.4** and **13.5** on the meaning of 'arrangements' and, in particular, 'cross-border arrangements'; see this Chapter regarding the hallmarks in detail (see **17.1**).

- Under EU DAC 6 there are five categories of hallmark – categories A, B, C, D and E. See **17.2** and this Chapter generally.

- During the UK's negotiations with the EU that led to the EU-UK Trade and Cooperation Agreement of December 2020, the UK agreed that it would continue to apply at least those aspects of EU DAC 6 that derived from the OECD Mandatory Disclosure Rules ('MDR'). Hence, for UK reporting purposes, only the DAC 6 hallmarks under category D are to apply to UK reporting. See, for example, https://www.icaew.com/insights/tax-news/2020/dec-2020/dac-6-to-be-replaced-by-oecd-rules-for-uk-intermediaries-from-2021. See **2.8** on Brexit.

- Where a cross-border arrangement concerns an EU Member State, it is therefore conceivable that DAC 6 reporting could be required under the rules of that EU Member State, even if it is not now required under UK reporting under EU DAC 6. However, the rules applying in States other than the UK are outside the scope of this book.

- Even where UK reporting will not now be required, it may be important to consider whether other UK reporting is nevertheless required – for example, perhaps under the Disclosure of Tax Avoidance Scheme ('DOTAS') rules.

- Categories A, B and subcategories 1(b)(i), 1(c) and 1(d) of C can only apply if the main benefit test is met (see **17.2**).

- Categories D and E and the remainder of C (that is subcategories 1(a), 1(b)(ii), 2, 3 and 4) can apply regardless of whether the main benefit test is met by an arrangement (see **17.2**).

- The main benefit test is met if a tax advantage is the main benefit or one of the main benefits that a person may reasonably be expected to derive from the arrangement. It is an objective test, which is to say, it is irrelevant whether the person was seeking a tax advantage or not (see **17.6**).

- Category A concerns the sorts of commercial characteristics typically seen in a marketed tax avoidance scheme (see **17.7**).

- Category B concerns the sorts of tax structured arrangements seen in avoidance planning (see **17.11**).

- Category C concerns cross-border payments and transfers (see **17.15**).

- Category D concerns arrangements which undermine tax reporting/transparency (see **17.3**).

- Category E concerns transfer pricing: non-arm's length or highly uncertain pricing or base erosive transfers (see **17.20**).

WHY ARE THE EU DAC 6 HALLMARKS IMPORTANT?

17.1

Focus

The obligation to report under EU DAC 6 falls on either a UK intermediary or in certain circumstances a UK relevant taxpayer. This is subject to various issues that are explained in **Chapter 13** onwards.

Under EU DAC 6 a cross-border arrangement is reportable if it meets one or more of the hallmarks that are listed in EU DAC 6. See **13.4** and **13.5** regarding the meaning of 'arrangements' and, in particular, 'cross-border arrangements'; see this Chapter regarding the hallmarks.

See HMRC's International Exchange of Information Manual IEIM622030, IEIM650010 and IEIM640010.

OVERVIEW OF THE HALLMARKS UNDER EU DAC 6

17.2

Focus

Under EU DAC 6 there are five categories of 'hallmark': categories A, B, C, D and E. During the UK's negotiations with the EU that led to the EU-UK Trade and Cooperation Agreement of 24 December 2020, the UK agreed that it would continue to apply at least those aspects of EU DAC 6 that derived from OECD MDR. Hence, for UK reporting purposes, only the hallmarks under category D apply to UK reporting. See **2.8** on Brexit.

Where a cross-border arrangement concerns an EU Member State, it is therefore conceivable that DAC 6 reporting could be required under the rules of the State, even if it is not now required under UK reporting under EU DAC 6. However, the rules applying in States other than the UK are outside the scope of this book.

For categories A, B and C 1(b)(i), 1(c) and 1(d) only, the hallmark can only apply if it can be established that the main benefit or one of the main benefits from an arrangement is the obtaining of a tax advantage.

Hallmarks under categories D and E are not subject to the main benefit test, and so whether the effect of an arrangement is to generate a tax advantage, and whether or not any such tax advantage represents the whole or main benefit of the arrangement, will not be relevant.

The hallmarks are as follows.

Categories	Hallmark
Category A Commercial characteristics seen in marketed tax avoidance scheme*	– confidentiality clause in a transaction not to disclose how a tax advantage is secured (see below regarding the meaning of 'tax advantage'); or – fee arrangements paid on the amount of tax saved; or – standardised documentation and/or structure
Category B Tax structured arrangements seen in avoidance planning*	– acquiring a loss buying company and the use of losses – conversion of income into capital – round tripping of funds using conduits/entities without substance
Category C Cross-border payments and transfers*	1. Payments to a recipient that: (a) is not tax resident in any jurisdiction; or (b) (i) resident in a jurisdiction with zero or close to zero corporation tax; or (ii) an EU blacklisted country;

Categories	Hallmark
	(c) the payment is fully exempt from tax where the recipient is resident; or
	(d) the payment benefits from a preferential tax regime where the recipient is resident.
	2. Depreciation of the same asset in more than one jurisdiction
	3. Double tax relief claimed in more than one jurisdiction in respect of the same income
	4. Transfer of assets where material difference in amount treated as payable
Category D Arrangements which undermine tax reporting/ transparency	– legislation on automatic exchange of financial account information circumvented – non-transparent legal or beneficial ownership chains used
Category E Transfer pricing: non-arm's length or highly uncertain pricing or base erosive transfers	– unilateral transfer pricing safe harbour rules used – transfer of rights to hard-to-value intangibles – cross-border transfer of functions/risks/assets projected to result in a more than 50% decrease in earnings before interest and taxes during the next three years

* The main benefit test must be satisfied for any arrangement for hallmarks under categories A, B and subcategories 1(b)(i), 1(c) and 1(d) of category C (only) to apply (see **17.3**).

See 17.4 as regards each hallmark in detail.

HALLMARKS THAT CAN APPLY TO UK REPORTING UNDER EU DAC 6

Hallmark category D

17.3

Focus

Hallmarks under category D are not subject to the main benefit test, and so whether the effect of an arrangement is to generate a tax advantage, and whether or not any such tax advantage represents the whole or main benefit of the arrangement, will not be relevant.

The hallmarks under category D are:

- D1 undermining reporting obligations;
- D2 obscuring beneficial ownership.

There is substantial common ground between the EU DAC 6 hallmarks under category D, on the one hand, and the OECD's Mandatory Disclosure Rules ('MDR'), on the other. Indeed, the preamble to EU DAC 6 makes clear that the MDR, and the guidance and commentary which accompany those rules, are a source of illustration and interpretation for hallmarks under category D of EU DAC 6.

Accordingly, where hallmark D and the MDR cover similar ground, HMRC will interpret hallmark D in line with the MDR.

See HMRC's International Exchange of Information Manual IEIM645000.

D1 undermining reporting obligations

17.4   This hallmark will apply to an arrangement, if that arrangement has the effect of undermining or circumventing financial account reporting obligations under EU DAC or equivalent agreements on the Automatic Exchange of Information ('AEOI'), or which take advantage of the absence of AEOI. This therefore includes reporting obligations under the OECD's Common Reporting Standard ('CRS').

HMRC consider that the UK's agreement with the US to implement FATCA is not an equivalent agreement since it does not provide similar reciprocity as AEOI under EU DAC and CRS.

Therefore, HMRC's view is that an arrangement which seeks to avoid reporting under FATCA would not be reportable under this hallmark of EU DAC 6.

However, see **8.3** regarding the possibility that an attempt to avoid falling within FATCA might fail owing to the anti-avoidance provisions in the International Tax Compliance Regulations 2015, SI 2015/878, reg 23.

Applying comments in the MDR, HMRC conclude that the hallmark will apply 'where a reasonable person in the position of a professional adviser with a full understanding of the terms and consequences of the Arrangement and the circumstances in which it is designed, marketed and used, would come to [the] conclusion' that an arrangement is intended either to circumvent or to exploit a gap in the CRS rules.

The test is an objective one. However, the intent of those involved is relevant.

It is important to consider the arrangement as a whole – not merely any particular step forming part of the arrangement.

Merely because carrying out a transaction results in no report being made under CRS, does not mean that the hallmark applies, provided what is done is in line with the policy intent of the CRS rules. For example, funds held in a French bank account by a UK resident would be reportable under CRS. If the UK resident uses those funds to purchase a property in France, this would not in itself have the effect of undermining CRS, because real estate is specifically excluded from reporting under CRS.

This contrasts with a situation where a promoter advises someone to move funds from a jurisdiction where CRS is in force to one where it is not, with the intention that CRS will therefore be avoided. That is clearly within hallmark D1.

Arrangements which will be caught by hallmark D1 include those employing the following features:

(a)   the use of an account, product or investment that is not, or purports not to be, a financial account;

(b)   the transfer of assets to jurisdictions that are not within AEOI;

(c)   the reclassification of income and capital so that it is somehow not subject to AEOI;

(d)   the transfer or conversion of a financial institution or a financial account or assets so that they are not subject to AEOI;

(e)   the use of legal entities, arrangements or structures that eliminate or purport to eliminate reporting under AEOI;

(f)   arrangements that undermine or exploit weaknesses in AEOI, including the use of jurisdictions with inadequate or weak regimes of enforcement or transparency.

Even though the arrangement itself may fall within hallmark D1, a person who simply processes a transaction, but who does not have insight into the arrangement as a whole or its expected effect, is not required to report it.

The following features may suggest that the hallmark applies:

- a transaction that is highly structured where the avoidance of CRS reporting is the logical explanation for that;

- a transaction that, other than avoiding CRS, is otherwise uncommercial;

- ownership structures which result in beneficial owners holding assets just below the threshold of reporting; or

- the refusal by a financial account holder to provide an explanation for a transaction or structure.

See HMRC's International Exchange of Information Manual IEIM645010.

D2 obscuring beneficial ownership

17.5   This hallmark will apply to arrangements that involve non-transparent legal or beneficial ownership chains which use persons (whether legal or real), legal arrangements or structures:

(a)   that do not carry on a substantive economic activity (for example, an activity that is supported by adequate staff, equipment, assets and premises); and

(b)   that are incorporated, managed, resident, controlled or established in any jurisdiction other than the jurisdiction of residence of one of the beneficial owners; and

(c)   where the beneficial owners are made unidentifiable.

The test in paragraph (c) is whether beneficial owners can reasonably be identified by relevant tax authorities, such as HMRC. The identity of the beneficial owners does not have to be publicly available.

Examples include where undisclosed nominee shareholders are used, or where control is exercised indirectly. A further example concerns the use of jurisdictions where there is no requirement to keep information on beneficial ownership, or no mechanism to obtain it.

The test must be applied from the standpoint of a hypothetical, informed observer.

Institutional investors, and entities wholly owned by one or more institutional investors, are not considered to be structures which obscure beneficial ownership.

Actively traded shares of widely held entities held in nominee name by brokers and custodians do not typically trigger this hallmark.

'Beneficial ownership' and 'beneficial owner' include 'any natural person who exercises control over a Legal Person or Legal Arrangement'. HMRC interpret these terms in accordance with the MDR commentary.

If a person successfully identifies a structure's beneficial owners in pursuit of that person's obligations under anti-money laundering legislation, this generally means that hallmark D2 does not apply as regards that structure.

In relation to trusts, where the beneficiaries are named, or identified by class, the beneficiaries would not necessarily be considered to be made unidentifiable for the purposes of this hallmark.

Similarly, where there is the possibility of beneficiaries being added to a trust in the future, this would not necessarily trigger this hallmark. An exception is where people are deliberately excluded from the trust to try to avoid being identified.

See HMRC's International Exchange of Information Manual IEIM645020.

See the OECD's Model Mandatory Disclosure Rules for CRS Avoidance Arrangements and Opaque Offshore Structures, including the commentary at III. This may be viewed at https://www.oecd.org/tax/exchange-of-tax-information/model-mandatory-disclosure-rules-for-crs-avoidance-arrangements-and-opaque-offshore-structures.pdf.

See also HMRC's International Exchange of Information Manual IEIM645000 onwards.

HALLMARKS UNDER EU DAC 6 THAT DO NOT APPLY TO UK REPORTING

The main benefit test

17.6

Focus

The main benefit test must be satisfied for any arrangement for hallmarks under categories A, B and subcategories 1(b)(i), 1(c) and 1(d) of category C (only) to apply. It is irrelevant to the hallmarks under category D which can apply to UK reporting under EU DAC 6, and is also irrelevant to the other EU DAC 6 hallmarks.

The main benefit test is an objective test. That is to say, it does not matter if a person was seeking a tax advantage or what other benefits they may have been seeking. What is important is whether a tax advantage is the main benefit or one of the main benefits that a person may reasonably be expected to derive from the arrangement.

In the UK's Regulations applying EU DAC 6, namely the International Tax Enforcement (Disclosable Arrangements) Regulations 2020, SI 2020/25, all of the DAC 6 hallmarks were originally to apply to UK reporting, including those for which the main benefit test was a requirement. The Regulations were amended as a result of agreement in December 2020 of the EU-UK Trade and Cooperation Agreement. See **2.8** on Brexit.

Under the amended Regulations, only the hallmarks under category D are to apply to UK reporting under EU DAC 6. Hence, the main benefit test does not apply to UK reporting. See the International Tax Enforcement (Disclosable Arrangements) (Amendment) (No. 2) (EU Exit) Regulations 2020, SI 2020/1649.

Where a cross-border arrangement concerns an EU Member State, it is conceivable that DAC 6 reporting could be required under the rules of the State, even if it is not now required under UK reporting under EU DAC 6. However, the rules applying in States other than the UK are outside the scope of this book.

Even where UK reporting will not now be required, it may be important to consider whether other UK reporting is nevertheless required – for example, perhaps under the DOTAS rules, particularly regarding arrangements that meet the profile of the main benefits test.

In order to obtain a tax advantage as the main benefit, it needs to be a significant or an important element, rather than merely incidental. See HMRC's International Exchange of Information Manual IEIM641010 to IEIM641040.

'Tax advantage' is defined in the EU Directive on Administrative Cooperation 2011/16/EU ('EU DAC') so as to include deferral of a payment of tax or advancement of a repayment of tax – see, for example, the International Tax Enforcement (Disclosable Arrangements) Regulations 2020, SI 2020/25, reg 2(4)(e).

In particular, tax advantage includes:

(a)   relief or increased relief from tax;

(b)   repayment or increased repayment of tax;

(c)   avoidance or reduction of a charge to tax or an assessment to tax;

(d)   avoidance of a possible assessment to tax;

(e)   deferral of a payment of tax or advancement of a repayment of tax; and

(f)   avoidance of an obligation to deduct or account for tax.

See reg 2(4): 'where the obtaining of the tax advantage cannot reasonably be regarded as consistent with the principles on which the relevant provisions that are relevant to the cross-border arrangement are based and the policy objectives of those provisions.'

Broadly 'tax', for this purpose, includes all taxes levied by or on behalf of a Member State other than VAT, customs and excise duties and social security contributions such as National Insurance contributions. See reg 2(1).

In determining whether the main benefit test is met, it is necessary to look at the arrangement as a whole. If the tax rules allow a particular tax advantage (such as a deduction for a payment, say) that may indicate that the tax advantage is consistent with policy objectives. However, the advantage may still not be consistent with the principles of the legislation, if it is reasonable to conclude that the overall outcome is not what was intended under the tax regime as a whole.

On the other hand, there may be commercial reasons for a transaction (a payment, say) which may mean that gaining a tax advantage is not a main benefit of the arrangement, and so the arrangement would not be reportable. See HMRC's International Exchange of Information Manual IEIM641030.

See the International Tax Enforcement (Disclosable Arrangements) Regulations 2020, reg 12.

See EU DAC', Annex IV (as inserted by EU DAC 6).

HALLMARK CATEGORY A

17.7

Focus

Hallmarks under category A are subject to the main benefit test. Accordingly, these hallmarks will not apply to an arrangement unless one of the expected main benefits is the obtaining of a tax advantage which is not in line with the policy intent of the applicable legislation.

The hallmarks under category A are:

- A1 confidentiality;

- A2 fee related to tax advantage;

- A3 standardised documentation and structures.

Those who are familiar with the DOTAS regime will notice that these are pretty similar to certain of the DOTAS hallmarks. If you are considering whether one or more of the EU DAC 6 category A hallmarks applies to an arrangement (or arrangements), it could be that you should also be considering whether disclosure is required under DOTAS – either instead of or as well as under EU DAC 6.

Under the amended Regulations which eventually resulted from the UK's negotiations with the EU that led to the EU-UK Trade and Cooperation Agreement of December 2020, only the hallmarks under Category D are to apply for UK reporting under EU DAC 6. Hence, the hallmarks under category A do not apply to UK reporting. See the International Tax Enforcement (Disclosable Arrangements) (Amendment) (No. 2) (EU Exit) Regulations 2020. See **2.8** on Brexit.

Where a cross-border arrangement concerns an EU Member State, it is therefore conceivable that DAC 6 reporting in relation to the hallmarks under category A could be required under the rules of the State, even if it is not now required under UK reporting under EU DAC 6. However, the rules applying in States other than the UK are outside the scope of this book.

A1 confidentiality

17.8   For the purposes of the hallmark, confidentiality could consist of wanting to keep details of an arrangement from HMRC or from other intermediaries. Either can fall within this hallmark.

This hallmark specifically looks at confidentiality around how the arrangements could secure a tax advantage. Commercial confidentiality conditions that do not relate to how the arrangement secures a tax advantage will not be caught under this hallmark.

Evidence of a confidentiality condition includes:

- non-disclosure agreements;

- written correspondence including a requirement, which may be explicit or implicit, that details of the arrangement should not be disclosed or shared more widely; or

- evidence from users or potential users or verbal or other agreements, implied or otherwise, of confidentiality requirements.

However, evidence may also be more circumstantial. It could include things like discouraging users or potential users from retaining promotional material or other details of the arrangement's operation.

There is no exhaustive list of things to take into account when considering whether the confidentiality hallmark in category A(1) is triggered.

See HMRC's International Exchange of Information Manual IEIM642010.

A2 fee related to tax advantage

17.9   This hallmark can only apply where there is an intermediary.

See HMRC's International Exchange of Information Manual IEIM642020.

A3 standardised documentation and structures

17.10   Under the UK's DOTAS legislation and regulations certain kinds of arrangements are specifically excluded, for example, ISA and Enterprise Investment Scheme arrangements (see the Tax Avoidance Schemes (Prescribed Descriptions of Arrangements) Regulations 2006, SI 2006/1543, reg 11(2)).

These kinds of arrangements are not specifically excluded from EU DAC. However, HMRC considers that in practice they will not fall within EU DAC because they will not meet the main benefits test. This is because that would require one of the main benefits of the arrangement to be the obtaining of a tax advantage which is inconsistent with the policy intent of the legislation.

HMRC say that considerable standardisation of a product does not necessarily mean that the hallmark is not potentially met. Where there is considerable customisation, albeit with standardised features, the hallmark will not be met.

HMRC cite the International Swaps and Derivatives Association ('ISDA') master agreement that is used for many derivatives contracts. They say that this is commonly subject to considerable amendment as a result of commercial negotiations between parties.

HMRC also cite the use of precedent documents in the production of legal documentation, which they say would not normally trigger this hallmark, as the documents are commonly subject to detailed consideration of the clients' circumstances, and customised accordingly.

See HMRC's International Exchange of Information Manual IEIM642030.

Regarding DOTAS generally, see the Finance Act 2004, s 306 onwards, and various regulations including, for example, the Tax Avoidance Schemes (Information) Regulations 2012, SI 2012/1836.

HALLMARK CATEGORY B

17.11

Focus

Hallmarks under category B are subject to the main benefit test. Accordingly, these hallmarks will not apply to an arrangement unless one of the expected main benefits is the obtaining of a tax advantage which is not in line with the policy intent of the applicable legislation.

The hallmarks under category B are:

- B1 loss buying;

- B2 conversion of capital into income;

- B3 circular transactions.

If you are considering whether one or more of the EU DAC 6 category B hallmarks apply to an arrangement (or arrangements), it could be that you should also be considering whether disclosure is required under DOTAS – either instead of or as well as under EU DAC 6.

Under the amended Regulations which eventually resulted from the UK's negotiations with the EU that led to the EU-UK Trade and Cooperation Agreement of December 2020, only the hallmarks under category D are to apply for UK reporting under EU DAC 6. Hence, the hallmarks under category B do not apply to UK reporting. See the International Tax Enforcement (Disclosable Arrangements) (Amendment) (No. 2) (EU Exit) Regulations 2020. See **2.8** on Brexit.

Where a cross-border arrangement concerns an EU Member State, it is therefore conceivable that DAC 6 reporting in relation to the hallmarks under category B could be required under the rules of the State, even if it is not now required under UK reporting under EU DAC 6. However, the rules applying in States other than the UK are outside the scope of this book.

B1 loss buying

17.12   This hallmark requires a participant to acquire a loss-making company, discontinue its main activity and use its losses in order to reduce its own tax liabilities. This includes through a transfer of those losses to another jurisdiction or by the acceleration of the use of those losses.

In doing so, the participant needs to have taken 'contrived steps', if the hallmark is to apply.

Whether the actions taken are contrived steps, is as determined from the point of view of a hypothetical, informed observer.

See HMRC's International Exchange of Information Manual IEIM643010.

B2 conversion of capital into income

17.13   This hallmark applies to arrangements which convert income into capital, gifts or other categories of revenue which are taxed at a lower level or exempt from tax.

The hallmark makes it clear that it can apply where there is conversion of income from one form into another that is taxed at a lower level or exempt from tax.

HMRC cite as an example where employment income is converted into dividend income in circumstances where dividend income would be taxed at a lower rate than employment income.

Employee share options are not within the hallmark, provided that the circumstances are not contrived or 'not normal commercial practice'.

Whether the hallmark applies, is as determined from the point of view of a hypothetical, informed observer.

HMRC say that where a company with distributable reserves is wound up, the directors may make a decision about whether the company should pay up a dividend before it enters liquidation (or not). They may do so, aware that their decision has particular tax consequences.

However, HMRC say it would be reasonable for an informed observer to conclude that hallmark B2 does not apply in that situation.

By contrast, a contrived arrangement which relies on the liquidation of a series of phoenix companies to extract income from an investment that remains in the same ultimate ownership could reasonably be considered by the same informed observer to fall within hallmark B2.

HMRC also consider a situation where a company is sold at a price which includes accumulated earnings, with the whole of the sale proceeds therefore being taxed as a capital receipt in the hands of the sellers. By contrast, if the accumulated earnings had been paid out as a pre-sale dividend, the dividend would instead have been taxed as the sellers' income.

HMRC say that this is a commercial choice between two alternative methods of realising value from the company, not the conversion of income into capital. They say it is clear in these circumstances that the sellers are exercising that choice in a way which is consistent with the underlying intent of the legislation. Hallmark B2 does not apply.

In HMRC's view, share buybacks do not fall within hallmark B2 unless some aspect is contrived.

An 'excluded indexed security' can be advantageous for UK tax purposes in certain circumstances because such a security can fall outside the 'deeply discounted securities' anti-avoidance legislation.

A security that qualifies as an excluded indexed security under UK tax law requires a direct link to the value of a chargeable asset and hence gains on that security are taxed as chargeable/capital gains.

However, HMRC say that the structuring of a security to qualify as an excluded indexed security should not fall within hallmark B2, provided that the situation as a whole is consistent with the principles of the relevant tax provisions.

See HMRC's International Exchange of Information Manual IEIM643020.

B3 circular transactions

17.14 This hallmark includes circular transactions resulting in the 'round-tripping' of funds.

In addition, any one of three additional conditions must be met:

- there are interposed entities without primary commercial function; or
- there are transactions that offset or cancel each other; or
- there are other similar features to these.

The hallmark commonly applies to arrangements whereby funds are routed via an offshore jurisdiction, despite having a domestic origin, in order to benefit from preferential tax treaty terms or other similar benefits.

This may be seen with respect to certain types of foreign direct investment ('FDI'), where a beneficial tax treatment applies to such FDI.

See HMRC's International Exchange of Information Manual IEIM643030.

HALLMARK CATEGORY C

17.15

Focus

The main benefit test only applies to certain hallmarks under category C, namely para 1(b)(i), 1(c) and 1(d).

If you are considering the applicability or not of one or more of the particular EU DAC 6 category C hallmarks (specifically para 1(b)(i), 1(c) and 1(d)), that are subject to the main benefit test, it could be that you should also be considering whether disclosure of the arrangement with which you are concerned is required under DOTAS – either instead of or as well as under EU DAC 6.

For the other hallmarks under this category, the main test does not apply so, for those hallmarks, whether the effect of an arrangement is to generate a tax advantage, and whether or not any such tax advantage represents the whole or main benefit of the arrangement, will not be relevant.

The hallmarks under category C are:

- C1 deductible cross-border payment made between two associated enterprises

  This category is then divided into various subcategories, which are explained in detail below. The main benefit test applies to certain of these, but not to others;

- C2 depreciation of the same asset in more than one jurisdiction;

- C3 relief from double taxation.

Under the amended Regulations which eventually resulted from the UK's negotiations with the EU that led to the EU-UK Trade and Cooperation Agreement of December 2020, only the hallmarks under category D are to apply for UK reporting under EU DAC 6. Hence, the hallmarks under category C do not apply to UK reporting. See the International Tax Enforcement (Disclosable Arrangements) (Amendment) (No. 2) (EU Exit) Regulations 2020. See **2.8** on Brexit.

Where a cross-border arrangement concerns an EU Member State, it is therefore conceivable that DAC 6 reporting in relation to the hallmarks under category C could be required under the rules of the State, even if it is not now required under UK reporting under EU DAC 6. However, the rules applying in States other than the UK are outside the scope of this book.

C1 deductible cross-border payment made between two associated enterprises

17.16   For this hallmark to apply, there needs to be a deductible cross-border payment made between two associated enterprises, and any of the following applies.

(a)   the recipient is not resident for tax purposes in any tax jurisdiction;

(b) although the recipient is resident for tax purposes in a jurisdiction, that jurisdiction either:

    (i) does not impose any corporate tax or imposes corporate tax at the rate of zero or almost zero; or

    (ii) is included in a list of third-country jurisdictions which have been assessed by Member States collectively or within the framework of the OECD as being non-cooperative (a 'blacklisted country');

(c) the payment benefits from a full exemption from tax in the jurisdiction where the recipient is resident for tax purposes;

(d) the payment benefits from a preferential tax regime in the jurisdiction where the recipient is resident for tax purposes.

An intermediary will not necessarily know whether a payment is deductible. If an intermediary does not know, and could not reasonably be expected to know this (which depends on the particular facts and circumstances), then the intermediary will not be required to make a report under the Regulations.

Similarly, an intermediary may not know where a recipient is tax resident. If the intermediary does not know, and could not reasonably be expected to know this, the intermediary may not be required to report. However, HMRC will not accept that the intermediary is not required to report in cases where the intermediary attempts to 'remain wilfully ignorant' of the residence of a recipient.

As regards C1(a), care is needed where the recipient is a permanent establishment ('PE'), as the concept of corporate residence does not apply to a PE. Consequently, it will be necessary to look at the residence position of the company of which the PE is a part for the purposes of that hallmark.

In the case of a jurisdiction whose tax code does not have a concept of tax residency, if the recipient is located in such a jurisdiction by reason of incorporation or by that place being the location of its central management and control, the recipient is treated as if it were resident in that location. In those circumstances, C1(a) would not then apply, although another hallmark, such as C1(b)(i), perhaps might.

As regards C1(b)(i), in HMRC's view a tax rate is 'almost zero' if it is less than 1%. This applies to the headline rate of tax, rather than to the effective tax rate a company faces.

In assessing whether C1(b)(ii) applies (that is the recipient is resident in a jurisdiction that is a blacklisted country), the assessment should be made at the time that the reporting trigger point is met (see **15.11**). That is to say, one of the following:

- the point when the arrangement is made available for implementation;

- the point when the arrangement is ready for implementation;

- the point when the first step of the implementation of the arrangement is made;

- the point at which the aid, assistance or advice in respect of the arrangement is provided by the intermediary.

Where the first step in the arrangement was taken on or after 25 June 2018, but before 1 July 2020, the arrangement will only be reportable in respect of (b) (ii) where the jurisdiction in question appears on the relevant list(s) *both* on the date that the relevant one of the above reporting trigger points is reached, and also on 1 July 2020.

Where the countries on the lists subsequently change, HMRC say that there is no need to re-evaluate whether or not the hallmark is met.

The list may be viewed at https://www.consilium.europa.eu/en/policies/eu-list-of-non-cooperative-jurisdictions/.

As regards C1(c), it is the nature of the payments, rather than the status of the recipient that must be exempt. Hence an exempt body such as a pension fund will not automatically be caught.

For the purposes of hallmark C1(d), a tax regime should be considered to be preferential if it is listed as harmful in accordance with the criteria of the OECD's Forum on Harmful Tax Practices or by the EU Code of Conduct Group.

For lists of tax regimes that have been assessed by these groups, see https://www.oecd.org/tax/beps/harmful-tax-practices-peer-review-results-on-preferential-regimes.pdf; and see also: https://www.consilium. europa.eu/register/en/content/out?typ=SET&i=ADV&RESULTSET =1&DOC_TITLE=&CONTENTS=&DOC_ID=9639%2F18&DOS_ INTERINST=&DOC_SUBJECT=&DOC_SUBTYPE=&DOC_ DATE=&document_date_from_date=&document_date_from_date_ submit=&document_date_to_date=&document_date_to_date_ submit=&MEET_DATE=&meeting_date_from_date=&meeting_date_ from_date_submit=&meeting_date_to_date=&meeting_date_to_date_ submit=&DOC_LANCD=EN&ROWSPP=25&NRROWS=500&ORDERBY =DOC_DATE+DESC.

'Associated enterprise' means a person who is related to another person in at least one of the following ways:

(i)   a person participates in the management of another person by being in a position to exercise a significant influence over the other person;

(ii) a person participates in the control of another person through a holding that exceeds 25 % of the voting rights;

(iii) a person participates in the capital of another person through a right of ownership that, directly or indirectly, exceeds 25% of the capital;

(iv)   a person is entitled to 25 % or more of the profits of another person.

If more than one person is within (i) to (v), all of those persons are associated enterprises.

If the same persons participate, as referred to in points (i) to (iv), in the management, control, capital or profits of more than one person, all persons concerned shall be regarded as associated enterprises.

A person who acts together with another person on the voting rights or capital ownership of an entity is treated as participating in all of the voting rights or capital ownership of that entity that are held by the other person.

In indirect participations, the requirements under point (iii) are determined by multiplying the rates of holding through the successive tiers.

A person holding more than 50% of the voting rights is deemed to hold 100%.

As regards the above meaning of 'associated enterprise', see EU DAC at Art 3(23).

See HMRC's International Exchange of Information Manual IEIM644010 to IEIM644050.

C2 depreciation of the same asset in more than one jurisdiction

17.17   This hallmark may apply where deductions for the same depreciation are claimed in more than one jurisdiction.

The UK tax code does not provide for deductions for depreciation. Instead there is a system known as 'capital allowances'. HMRC view capital allowances as equivalent to depreciation for the purposes of this hallmark.

HMRC do not consider that the hallmark applies where a deduction for depreciation is claimed in both a jurisdiction where there is a PE (in which the asset is used), and in the jurisdiction where the company is resident, provided that the profits from the PE are taxed in both jurisdictions (subject to any double taxation relief).

See HMRC's International Exchange of Information Manual IEIM644060.

C3 relief from double taxation

17.18   This hallmark may apply where relief from double taxation in respect of the same item of income or capital is claimed in more than one jurisdiction.

However, HMRC take the view that this hallmark will not apply where two or more territories give double taxation relief in respect of the same income or capital, and that income or capital is taxed in each of those territories.

See HMRC's International Exchange of Information Manual IEIM644070.

C4 transfer of assets

17.19   This hallmark may apply where there are arrangements which include a transfer of assets and where there is a 'material difference' in the 'amount being treated as payable in consideration' for the assets in those jurisdictions involved.

HMRC consider that the 'amount being treated as payable in consideration' is the amount treated as payable for tax purposes, rather than the amount treated as payable for accountancy purposes.

HMRC also considers that there is no 'material difference' if it arises from just the normal operation of the tax legislation. However, there would be a material difference if, for example, it sought to exploit mismatches in the tax system to give an unintended outcome.

See HMRC's International Exchange of Information Manual IEIM644080 and IEIM644090.

See HMRC's International Exchange of Information Manual IEIM644010 onwards.

HALLMARK CATEGORY E

17.20

Focus

Hallmarks under category E are not subject to the main benefit test, and so whether the effect of an arrangement is to generate a tax advantage, and whether or not any such tax advantage represents the whole or main benefit of the arrangement, will not be relevant.

The hallmarks under category E are:

- E1 unilateral safe harbours;
- E2 hard-to-value intangibles;
- E3 cross-border transfers.

Under the amended Regulations which eventually resulted from the UK's negotiations with the EU that led to the EU-UK Trade and Cooperation Agreement of December 2020, only the hallmarks under category D are to apply for UK reporting under EU DAC 6. Hence, the hallmarks under category E do not apply to UK reporting. See the International Tax Enforcement (Disclosable Arrangements) (Amendment) (No. 2) (EU Exit) Regulations 2020. See **2.8** on Brexit.

Where a cross-border arrangement concerns an EU Member State, it is therefore conceivable that DAC 6 reporting in relation to the hallmarks

---

> under category E could be required under the rules of the State, even if it is not now required under UK reporting under EU DAC 6. However, the rules applying in States other than the UK are outside the scope of this book.

Hallmarks under category E relate to transfer pricing and seek disclosure of arrangements that are contrary to the OECD's Transfer Pricing Guidelines for Multinational Enterprises and Tax Administrations ('TPG').

Hallmark E does not apply to cross-border arrangements if the relevant taxpayer and its associated group companies would be exempted from the basic transfer pricing rule by Chapter 3 of Part 4 of the Taxation (International and Other Provisions) Act 2010 ('TIOPA 2010'). That provision exempts dormant and small and medium enterprises from having to apply the rules in Part 4, with certain exceptions.

If an arrangement is outside the transfer pricing rules in Part 4 for reasons other than being exempted by Chapter 3 of Part 4 of TIOPA 2010, the EU DAC 6 reporting requirements can still apply.

E1 unilateral safe harbours

17.21   A safe harbour is any rule which applies to a group of transactions or taxpayers which relieves them of certain transfer pricing requirements.

Advance pricing agreements ('APAs') made between tax authorities and companies or groups are not unilateral safe harbours. Instead they are agreements as to the correct pricing for transactions.

For similar reasons, advance thin capitalisation agreements are also not caught under the hallmark.

See IEIM646020.

E2 hard-to-value intangibles

17.22   This hallmark will apply to arrangements that involve the transfer of hard-to-value intangibles.

That is to say, intangibles or rights in intangibles for which, at the time of their transfer between associated enterprises:

(a)   no reliable 'comparables' exist; and

(b)   'at the time the transaction was entered into, the projections of future cash flows or income expected to be derived from the transferred intangible, or the assumptions used in valuing the intangible are highly uncertain, making it difficult to predict the level of ultimate success of the intangible at the time of the transfer'.

See the DAC at Article 23(3) for the meaning of 'associated enterprises'. See the TPG regarding the meaning of 'hard-to-value intangibles'.

Whether the hallmark applies is as determined from the point of view of a hypothetical, informed observer.

The key question is whether the hallmark is met at the time the obligation to report would have arisen. Hence, it could be that a decision is taken not to report that is based on projections or comparables which later on prove to have been incorrect or unreliable. In such a situation, it will not necessarily follow that the decision not to make a disclosure was incorrect.

See also HMRC's International Exchange of Information Manual IEIM646030.

E3 cross-border transfers

17.23   This hallmark applies to arrangements: 'involving an intragroup cross-border transfer of functions and/or risks and/or assets, if the projected annual earnings before interest and taxes (EBIT), during the three-year period after the transfer, of the transferor or transferors, are less than 50% of the projected annual EBIT of such transferor or transferors if the transfer had not been made.'

HMRC say that the UK's hallmark E3 rules require this hallmark to be considered at the level of the individual company, rather than at the level of the sub-group that is located within the same jurisdiction. However, HMRC recognise that other jurisdictions will take a different approach.

Whether the hallmark applies is as determined from the point of view of a hypothetical, informed observer.

The key question is whether, taking account of all the available facts and the circumstances as they are at the time, a reasonable person would consider that the earnings of the transferor during the three year period after the transaction would, on the balance of probabilities, be less than 50% of what they would otherwise have been.

HMRC accept that uncertainty is inherent in trying to make this prediction. Accordingly they say that where, later on, it becomes apparent that the transferor's EBIT is less than 50% of what it would have been, there will not be a failure to comply with EU DAC 6 regarding this hallmark, if the projections used in reaching a decision not to report were what a hypothetical, informed observer would reasonably have expected.

The test requires consideration of a projection of earnings over the three-year period after the transfer. HMRC anticipate that a company or its advisers will undertake such a projection when deciding whether to proceed with a transfer of business functions, risks or assets of the kind that is referred to in the terms of the hallmark. It is this projection which HMRC expect companies to use when they come to assess whether hallmark E3 applies, rather than a projection that the company might produce specifically for the purposes of the hallmark.

For certain entities the use of EBIT that is normally adopted in relation to hallmark E3, may not give a sensible measure of the operating profit of the entity. In such cases, it may be necessary to consider whether there is another measure which will give an equivalent view of the operating profits of the entity.

HMRC accept that hallmark E3 does not apply if a company projects both that it would make a loss, if it did not proceed with a transfer, and the same company projects that that loss would change to nil if it did proceed with the transfer.

See HMRC's International Exchange of Information Manual IEIM646040.

See TIOPA 2010, Part 4 as regards the UK's transfer pricing legislation.

See OECD's Transfer Pricing Guidelines for Multinational Enterprises and Tax Administrations 2017, available at https://read.oecd-ilibrary.org/taxation/ oecd-transfer-pricing-guidelines-for-multinational-enterprises-and-tax-administrations-2017_tpg-2017-en#page1.

See also HMRC's International Exchange of Information Manual IEIM646000 onwards.

Chapter 18

EU DAC 6 – Penalties for non-compliance

> **SIGNPOSTS**
>
> - The UK's Regulations that apply EU DAC 6, namely the International Tax Enforcement (Disclosable Arrangements) Regulations 2020, SI 2020/25, provide for a range of penalties to be applied, in relation to a range of different kinds of failure to comply with that regime. The penalties and situations to which they can apply, are summarised in **18.1**.
>
> - In most circumstances, the basic penalty is £5,000. However, if an HMRC officer considers that £5,000 is an inappropriately low penalty, HMRC can then apply to the tribunal for a penalty instead of up to £600 per day during the period during which the failure to comply continues (see **18.2**).
>
> - Penalties not exceeding £5,000 may be determined by an HMRC officer. That HMRC officer should consider the circumstances. For example, he or she should consider whether the failure to report had significant consequences which could reasonably have been foreseen, which would be likely to require a higher penalty than if that were not the case. The officer may agree a special reduction in the penalty or decide not to charge a penalty at all, in appropriate circumstances (see **18.3**; see also **18.6**).
>
> - In certain circumstances, a DAC 6 penalty that is determined by a tribunal can be for an amount not exceeding £1 million (see **18.3** and **18.6**).
>
> - There is a right of appeal to the First-tier Tribunal against a DAC 6 penalty. One can appeal on a point of law to the Upper Tribunal (see 18.4; see also **18.6**).
>
> - There will be no DAC 6 penalty if HMRC or the tribunal are persuaded that there is a reasonable excuse for the failure that is in question. In considering whether a person had a reasonable excuse, the HMRC officer or the tribunal must consider whether the person maintains such procedures as it is reasonable in all

> the circumstances to have in place to secure the identification of reportable cross-border arrangements and compliance with the UK's Regulations that are intended to apply EU DAC 6 (see **18.5**).
>
> - Reasonable excuse is a widely used concept in UK tax law. HMRC provide further guidance about what they consider a reasonable excuse in their manuals and elsewhere. See 18.5.
>
> - HMRC accept that where a DAC 6 return is made late owning to issues arising from the Covid-19 pandemic, the taxpayer or intermediary who makes the late return will have a reasonable excuse (see **18.5**).
>
> - Certain time limits apply to DAC 6 penalties. See **18.7** regarding time limits on DAC 6 penalties generally.

PENALTIES RELATING TO DAC 6

18.1

> **Focus**
>
> A range of penalties can apply for failing to comply with the UK's Regulations that seek to apply EU DAC 6 – the mandatory disclosure regime.
>
> The basic penalty is £5,000. Where a DAC 6 penalty does not exceed £5,000, it may be determined by an HMRC officer, without the need for that officer to apply to the tribunal.
>
> In certain circumstances a penalty can be considerable higher than this. Where an HMRC officer wishes to seek a higher penalty than £5,000, he or she must apply to the tribunal for it to apply such a higher penalty. See elsewhere in this Chapter.

The primary penalty regime in relation to failure to comply with DAC 6 is set out in reg 14(1) to (5). The default position for any such failure is a one-off penalty of no more than £5,000. See reg 14(1)(a)(i).

Such a penalty of any amount up to £5,000 may be determined by HMRC (see **18.3**).

The following penalties may apply to a person who fails to comply with the DAC 6 Regulations. See also **18.3** in cases where a penalty of £5,000 is considered by HMRC to be 'inappropriately low'.

Person failing to comply:	reg governing the obligation[1]	Nature of the failure:	Penalty(ies):
UK intermediary	reg 3(1)	failure to make a return of reportable information	a penalty not exceeding: (i) £5,000; or (ii) an amount considered appropriate[2]
UK intermediary	reg 3(4)	failure to make a return of new reportable information	a penalty not exceeding £5,000
UK intermediary	reg 7(2)	failure to notify where legal professional privilege exclusion applies	a penalty not exceeding: (i) £5,000, or (ii) an amount considered appropriate[2]
Intermediary	reg 8(2)	Intermediary's failure to notify arrangement reference number	a penalty not exceeding £5,000
UK relevant taxpayer	reg 4(1)	failure to make a return of reportable information	a penalty not exceeding: (i) £5,000; or (ii) an amount considered appropriate[2]
UK relevant taxpayer	reg 5	failure to comply with a taxpayer's obligation to make an annual report	(i) £5,000 in respect of each reportable cross-border arrangement; or (ii) an amount considered appropriate[3]
Persons generally	reg 11	failure to comply with an information notice	a penalty not exceeding: (i) £5,000; or (ii) an amount considered appropriate[2]

[1] In all cases, the reg or regulations referred to are in the International Tax Enforcement (Disclosable Arrangements) Regulations 2020.

[2] In the case of a failure to comply with any of regs 3(1), 7(2), 4(1) or 11, if a penalty of £5,000 available to HMRC under reg 14(1)(a)(i) appears to an HMRC officer to be inappropriately low after taking into account all relevant considerations, a penalty of £600 per day may be applied under reg 14(1)(a)(ii) instead.

In certain circumstances a penalty under reg 14(1)(a)(ii) (combined with reg 16) can be of an amount 'not exceeding £1 million' – see reg 16(5). See also **8.2**.

[3] For a UK relevant taxpayer who has previously failed on only one occasion to comply with reg 5 during the previous 36 months, the penalty is £7,500 in respect of each reportable cross-border arrangement, increasing to £10,000 if he or she failed on more than one occasion in the previous 36 months.

In addition to the above, there may then be a further penalty or penalties not exceeding £600 for each day on which the failure continues. See reg 14(1)(b).

See the International Tax Enforcement (Disclosable Arrangements) Regulations 2020, reg 14.

See also HMRC's International Exchange of Information Manual IEIM660010 and IEIM660060.

HIGHER PENALTIES WHERE £5,000 IS INAPPROPRIATELY LOW

18.2

Focus

Where HMRC consider that the basic penalty for failing to comply with DAC 6 is inappropriately low, HMRC can apply to the First-tier Tribunal ('FTT') for daily penalties to be applied.

In certain circumstances, these can be substantial. Indeed, in appropriate circumstances, the FTT may increase the penalty to such amount as it deems appropriate, not exceeding £1 million in total.

A failure to comply with certain obligations under DAC 6 can give rise to a penalty where, if the amount of the penalty appears to an HMRC officer to be inappropriately low after taking into account all relevant considerations, the penalty can be revised instead to £600 for each day during the initial period. See below regarding 'initial period'.

'In exceptional circumstances', HMRC say a penalty of £5,000 will be inappropriately low and therefore a higher penalty will apply. HMRC also say: 'This would typically only occur where there is a failure which is deliberate, which has serious consequences, or where a person repeatedly fails to comply with their obligations, and a larger penalty is needed to deter future non-compliance.'

Where HMRC consider that such a high penalty is appropriate, HMRC then need to apply to the FTT for a penalty to be charged under reg 14(i)(a)(ii) instead of the default penalty under reg 14(1)(a)(i).

The FTT may determine the amount of such a penalty, up to £600 per day for the duration of the failure.

If the FTT considers that the total amount of a penalty of £600 per day is inappropriately low, having regard to all the facts and circumstances, the FTT may increase the penalty to such amount as it deems appropriate, not exceeding £1 million in total.

HMRC may only apply to the FTT to charge higher penalties in the case of:

- a failure to report under regs 3(1) or 4(1);

- a failure to notify where legal professional privilege applies under reg 7(2); or

- a failure to provide information under reg 11.

An HMRC officer who is considering seeking to apply a high penalty is instructed, first, to consult with the Exchange of Information policy team in Business, Assets and International.

See HMRC's International Exchange of Information Manual IEIM660030.

See **18.1**, including as regards which DAC 6 obligations this can apply to.

For these purposes 'the initial period' means the period:

(a)   beginning with the relevant day; and

(b)   ending on the earlier of:

    (i)   the day on which the penalty is determined; and

    (ii)   the last day before the failure ceases.

'The relevant day' is the day specified in relation to the failure in the following table.

Failure[1]	Relevant day[1]
A failure to comply with reg 3(1) (UK intermediary's obligation to make a return of reportable information)	The first day after the day by which the return needed to be made
A failure to comply with reg 4(1) (UK relevant taxpayer's obligation to make a return of reportable information)	The first day after the day by which the return needed to be made
A failure to comply with reg 7(2) (UK intermediary's obligation to notify where legal professional privilege exclusion applies)	The day after the day the notification should have been made
A failure to comply with reg 11 (HMRC notice to provide information)	The first day after the latest time by which reg 11 must be complied with as specified in the HMRC notice

[1]   In all cases the regulation or regulations referred to are in the International Tax Enforcement (Disclosable Arrangements) Regulations 2020.

It is important to note that in certain circumstances a penalty under reg 14(1)(a)(ii) (combined with reg 16) can be of an amount 'not exceeding £1 million' – see reg 16(5).

See the International Tax Enforcement (Disclosable Arrangements) Regulations 2020, reg 14. See also **18.1**.

DETERMINATION OF DAC 6 PENALTIES BY HMRC

18.3

Focus

Where HMRC wish to apply a penalty not exceeding £5,000 arising under the International Tax Enforcement (Disclosable Arrangements) Regulations 2020, reg 14(1)(a)(i), an HMRC officer may make a determination imposing such a penalty.

The HMRC officer will then set the penalty at such amount as, in the opinion of that officer, is correct or appropriate.

In deciding the amount of any penalty due in relation to a failure to comply with DAC 6, an HMRC officer is instructed to take into account all relevant facts. In particular, he or she should consider the reason for the failure.

This should include considering whether there is any evidence that the failure was deliberate or due to the careless behaviour of the person.

It should also include reviewing whether the person had previously failed to comply with obligations under these Regulations, and what steps, if any, the person had taken to comply with the legislation.

The HMRC officer should also consider whether failure to report had significant consequences which could have reasonably been foreseen. HMRC cite as an example, a lengthy failure to report an abusive tax avoidance scheme, which meant that HMRC was unable to take appropriate compliance action. HMRC say this would be likely to receive a higher penalty than a short failure to report, which had no impact on their ability to take compliance action.

HMRC may decide not to charge a penalty if it considers that to be appropriate in light of all the relevant facts. See HMRC's International Exchange of Information Manual IEIM660020. See also **18.6**.

A special reduction in the amount of a penalty may be agreed by an HMRC officer, where there are special circumstances that merit it. Special circumstances could include, but are not limited to, situations where a penalty has been charged for the same failure in another jurisdiction. See HMRC's International Exchange of Information Manual IEIM660110. See also **18.6**.

An HMRC officer may also make a determination imposing a penalty under reg 14(6), which is to say a penalty for a UK relevant taxpayer's failure to comply with a taxpayer's obligation to make an annual report (see **18.1**).

Furthermore, an HMRC may make a determination under reg 17 imposing a penalty under reg 14(1)(b), which is to say a further penalty or penalties not exceeding £600 for each day on which the failure continues after either a reg 14(1)(a)(i) or a reg 14(1)(a)(ii) penalty has previously been imposed. (See **18.6** regarding penalties under reg 14(1)(a)(ii).)

See the International Tax Enforcement (Disclosable Arrangements) Regulations 2020, regs 15, 18 and 19.

APPEALING AGAINST DAC 6 PENALTIES

18.4

Focus

The recipient of a DAC 6 penalty may appeal to the tribunal against that penalty.

There is a right of appeal to the FTT against such a penalty, whether under reg 14(1)(a)(i), reg 14(1)(b) or reg 14(6).

The FTT may then confirm the determination or set aside or reduce it.

Alternatively, the FTT can decide that the penalty is insufficient and increase it.

In addition to any right of appeal against the FTT's decision on a point of law under the Tribunals Courts and Enforcement Act 2007, s 11(2), the person liable to the penalty may appeal to the Upper Tribunal against the amount of the penalty.

See the International Tax Enforcement (Disclosable Arrangements) Regulations 2020, regs 15, 18 and 19.

MITIGATION OF DAC 6 PENALTIES – INCLUDING DEMONSTRATING A 'REASONABLE EXCUSE'

18.5

Focus

If an HMRC officer thinks it right because of special circumstances, the officer may reduce a penalty that arises under the DAC 6 Regulations.

Liability to a penalty under reg 14 does not arise if the person satisfies an HMRC officer or, on a determination by the FTT or an appeal notified to the tribunal, the tribunal that there is a reasonable excuse for a failure to do anything required to be done under these Regulations.

Reasonable excuse is a widely used concept in tax law. HMRC provide further guidance at https://www.gov.uk/tax-appeals/reasonable-excuses.

> HMRC stress that there is then a further requirement for a penalty to be excused owing to a reasonable excuse, which is that the failure must have been rectified without unreasonable delay once the reasonable excuse had ceased.
>
> In considering whether a person had a reasonable excuse, the HMRC officer or the tribunal must consider whether the person maintains such procedures as it is reasonable in all the circumstances to have in place to secure the identification of reportable cross-border arrangements and compliance with obligations under these Regulations.

Failure to have such procedures in place will not automatically mean that a penalty is due, but simply that a person will not be able to rely on having procedures in place as part of their defence. Having such procedures in place will not necessarily mean that a person has a reasonable excuse, either. See HMRC's International Exchange of Information Manual IEIM660090.

Businesses wishing to demonstrate that they have reasonable procedures will need to be prepared to provide evidence of that to HMRC, where appropriate. There is no definitive list of what are reasonable procedures. HMRC will have regard to all of the circumstances when considering whether that is the case. This will include in particular:

- the nature of the business;

- its size and scale of operations; and

- the general profile of its activities – for example, whether it has involvement in a lot of cross-border work.

Businesses may wish to consider such things as:

- training procedures for staff;

- escalation routes for potentially reportable arrangements; and

- governance around decisions on what is reportable.

Businesses should also consider the practicalities of reporting. See HMRC's International Exchange of Information Manual IEIM660100.

None of the following is a reasonable excuse:

(a)　that there is an insufficiency of funds to do something;

(b)　that the person relies on legal advice if:

　　(i)　the advice was given or procured by a person who is an intermediary within the meaning of EU DAC in relation to the reportable cross-border arrangement to which the failure relates;

　　(ii)　the advice was not based on a full and accurate description of the facts; or

(iii) the conclusions in the advice that the person relied upon were unreasonable.

HMRC are aware that there may be difficulties arising from potentially having to look back at things that were done before HMRC's regulations and guidance in relation to DAC 6 were published (possibly having to look back to as long ago as 25 June 2018). HMRC say that in the situation where there is failure to comply with the Regulations due to a lack of clarity about a person's obligations under DAC 6, it is likely that that person will have a reasonable excuse for the failure. Where a person has a reasonable excuse, no penalty will be due. See HMRC's International Exchange of Information Manual IEIM670000.

HMRC accept that where a DAC 6 return is made late owing to issues arising from the Covid-19 pandemic, the taxpayer or intermediary who makes the return late will have a reasonable excuse. See HMRC's International Exchange of Information Manual IEIM800000.

HMRC's manuals and other published information give various examples of situations where HMRC will accept that the taxpayer has acted reasonably. See, for example, HMRC's Compliance Handbook Manual CH155650. See also HMRC's Enquiry Manual EM4109.

It is also the case that a special reduction in the amount of a penalty may be agreed by an HMRC officer, where there are special circumstances that merit it. Special circumstances could include, but are not limited to, situations where a penalty has been charged for the same failure in another jurisdiction. See HMRC's International Exchange of Information Manual IEIM660110.

HMRC comment on a situation where an intermediary can show that it was late submitting a DAC 6 return because it relied on, and was subsequently let down by, an agreement with another intermediary that the latter would submit the return. HMRC say that in those circumstances, the first intermediary has a reasonable excuse for submitting the return late, provided the first intermediary rectifies the situation 'without unreasonable delay'. See HMRC's International Exchange of Information Manual IEIM659000, IEIM659010 and IEIM621120.

See the International Tax Enforcement (Disclosable Arrangements) Regulations 2020, regs 20 and 21.

DETERMINATION OF PENALTY BY FIRST-TIER TRIBUNAL

18.6

Focus

An HMRC officer may commence proceedings before the FTT for a penalty under reg 14(1)(a)(ii), which is to say where an HMRC officer considers a reg 14(1)(a)(i) penalty to be inappropriately low (see **18.2**) a penalty of £600 per day may be applied under reg 14(1)(a)(ii) instead.

In certain circumstances a penalty under reg 14(1)(a)(ii) can be an amount not exceeding £1 million – see reg 16(5). See also **18.1**.

The person liable to the penalty must be a party to the proceedings. The FTT may then determine a penalty accordingly.

Where it appears to an HMRC officer that a penalty under reg 14(1)(a)(ii) has been determined on the basis that the initial period begins with a day later than that which the officer considers to be the relevant day, the HMRC officer may commence proceedings for a re-determination of the penalty. See reg 16(6).

In addition to any right of appeal on a point of law, the person liable to the penalty may appeal to the Upper Tribunal against the determination of a penalty. The Upper Tribunal may then confirm, set aside or reduce or (if it considers the penalty insufficient) increase the penalty accordingly.

If the maximum penalty under reg 14(1)(a)(ii) appears inappropriately low after taking account of all relevant considerations, the penalty is to be of such amount not exceeding £1 million as appears appropriate having regard to those considerations.

See the International Tax Enforcement (Disclosable Arrangements) Regulations 2020, reg 16.

TIME LIMITS IN RELATION TO DAC 6 PENALTIES

18.7

Focus

Proceedings in relation to the DAC 6 penalties described in **18.1** onwards, under the UK's Regulations applying EU DAC 6, must be commenced, or a determination of a penalty must be made, before the latest of the following dates:

(a)   the date 24 months after the date on which the inaccuracy or failure first came to the attention of an officer of Revenue and Customs;

(b)   the date six years after the date on which the person became liable to the penalty; and

(c)   in the case of a determination by HMRC under reg 17 of a penalty under reg 14(1)(b) (see **18.3**), the date three years after the date of determination of a penalty under reg 14(1)(a).

The latter is therefore the date three years after the determination of a penalty either under reg 14(1)(a)(i) (see **18.3**) or under reg 14(1)(a)(ii) (see **18.6**).

A penalty that is assessed by HMRC must be assessed by the latest of the above three dates.

Where a penalty is to be determined by the FTT, HMRC must commence proceedings before the FTT by the latest of the three dates above.

The DAC 6 penalties that are described in **18.1** onwards, are due and payable at the end of the period of 30 days beginning with the date of determination of the penalty by the FTT or issue of the notice of determination, as the case may be.

See the International Tax Enforcement (Disclosable Arrangements) Regulations 2020, reg 18.

See also HMRC's International Exchange of Information Manual IEIM660070.

Chapter 19

Other forms of exchange under EU DAC

SIGNPOSTS

- The UK has contributed to and agreed to participate in various OECD projects that are designed to promote cross-border cooperation and 'fairness' between jurisdictions, in relation to taxation matters. For example, in 2014, the then Secretary to the Treasury, David Gauke, expressed the UK's support for the OECD BEPS Action Plan: 'We'll continue to work through the G20 and OECD — on the digital economy, on coherence, on substance and on transparency — to make sure that this area is properly reformed.'

  See https://www.gov.uk/government/speeches/david-gaukes-speech-to-the-lord-mayors-taxation-forum.

  See also the UK's participation in the OECD/Council of Europe Convention on Mutual Administrative Assistance in Tax Matters, as described in **20.4**.

- The OECD's BEPS Action Points (or 'BEPS Actions') are set out in **1.5**.

- The UK's efforts (as a consequence of its past EU membership) to comply with certain BEPS Actions are applied by the EU Directive on Administrative Cooperation 2011/16/EU ('EU DAC'). See, for example, EU Directive 2018/822/EU ('EU DAC 6'), which is intended to comply with BEPS Action 12, which concerns the disclosure by taxpayers of their 'aggressive tax planning arrangements' (see **Chapter 13** onwards).

- This Chapter describes two further regimes that are applied by EU DAC – specifically, the Exchange of Cross-Border Tax Rulings regime, which is applied by EU DAC, Art 8a, and Country-by-Country reporting ('CbC reporting'), which is applied by EU DAC, Art 8aa.

- The Exchange of Cross-Border Tax Rulings regime is intended to be consistent with BEPS Action 5, which includes the promotion of greater transparency in tax matters (see **19.1**).

- CbC reporting derives from BEPS Action 13 (see **19.2**).

EXCHANGE OF CROSS-BORDER TAX RULINGS
19.1

Focus

The Exchange of Cross-Border Tax Rulings regime is, for the most part, an obligation that HMRC and other tax authorities have to comply with, rather than a direct obligation for particular taxpayers. However, it may well be of interest to particular taxpayers to know that information about their tax 'rulings' is or could be shared with the tax authorities of EU Member States and with the European Commission.

HMRC say in their International Exchange of Information Manual IEIM510020 that automatic exchange of certain new rulings with the tax authorities of other jurisdictions than the UK began in April 2016, and with increased exchange from 1 January 2017 – see IEIM510500. HMRC say that they will also exchange past rulings and advance pricing agreements, in some cases back to those made in January 2010 – see IEIM510550.

'Ruling' is a term used in international taxation to refer to an agreement made between a tax authority and a taxpayer (referred to by HMRC as a 'customer'), upon which the taxpayer (or the customer) can rely. Under certain circumstances rulings should be shared with other tax authorities to increase transparency and help to tackle international tax avoidance and evasion.

In the case of HMRC, 'ruling' for these purposes includes statutory and non-statutory clearances, and other types of assurance about a customer's tax position, as well as things like advance thin capitalisation agreements.

Certain bilateral or multilateral advance pricing arrangements with third countries are excluded from automatic exchange if the double tax treaty under which the arrangement was concluded does not permit its disclosure to third parties. See Art 8a(3) of EU DAC.

Some rulings may be exchanged under OCED BEPS Action 5, and some also under EU DAC. See HMRC's International Exchange of Information Manual IEIM560010.

The OECD's work in relation to the wider base erosion and profit shifting ('BEPS') project included work on the exchange of information on tax rulings. In light of this, the EU passed Directive 2015/2376/EU ('DAC 3') amending EU DAC, which foresaw the mandatory automatic exchange of information on advance cross-border rulings and advance pricing agreements. See **1.5** regarding the OECD's work in relation to BEPs.

Whilst the UK was an EU Member State, exchange of tax-rulings principles were applied in the UK through the UK's participation in EU DAC. This continued to be the case during the Brexit transition period – when the UK continued to be treated largely as if it were an EU Member State for many purposes (see **Chapter 2**).

Article 8a of EU DAC says that EU Member States will exchange information relating to cross-border tax rulings. As explained in **Chapter 2**, these rules therefore applied to the UK while it was a member of the EU and also during the transitional period immediately following Brexit.

EU DAC says that, except in the case of rulings issued to persons conducting mainly financial or investment activities, Member States *may* exclude from exchange, information on advance cross-border rulings issued, amended or renewed before 1 April 2016 to a person or persons with a groupwide annual net turnover of less than EUR 40 million in the fiscal year preceding the date of issuance, amendment or renewal of the ruling in question. For this purpose, ruling includes advance pricing agreements.

HMRC say that even before that, they already spontaneously exchanged tax rulings with the other jurisdictions. The UK's international agreements, such as double taxation treaties allow and, in some cases, oblige the UK to do this.

The information must be provided to competent authorities of all other Member States (not just those affected by the ruling), as well as to the European Commission. However, the UK does not pass information to the European Commission that could enable the Commission to identify a particular taxpayer.

Some rulings may also (or sometimes instead) be made under OECD BEPS Action 5; see HMRC's International Exchange of Information Manual IEIM560010.

See EU DAC. See also HMRC's International Exchange of Information Manual IEIM500000 and IEIM550000 onwards.

COUNTRY-BY-COUNTRY REPORTING

19.2

Focus

The obligation for annual filing of the CbC report arises for multinational enterprise groups with a consolidated group turnover exceeding EUR 750 million in the fiscal year preceding the year to which the CbC report applies.

HMRC say that they will use the CbC report within the risk assessment process for cross border transactions, principally between members

> of the multinational group. See HMRC's International Exchange of Information Manual IEIM300180 and IEIM300190.
>
> HMRC may use the data for the following purposes only:
>
> - high-level transfer pricing risk assessment;
>
> - assessment of other BEPS-related risks; and
>
> - economic and statistical analysis, where appropriate.
>
> In addition, HMRC have agreed not to use CbC reporting data as a substitute for a detailed transfer pricing analysis of individual transactions and prices based on a full functional analysis and a full comparability analysis.
>
> CbC reports must be filed for accounting periods or their equivalent starting on or after 1 January 2016. The CbC report must be submitted within 12 months from the last day of the reporting fiscal year.
>
> CbC reporting essentially requires large multinational enterprises ('MNEs') to provide an annual return that breaks down the key elements of their activities among the jurisdictions in which they operate.

The OECD says that under BEPS Action 13:

> 'all large multinational enterprises (MNEs) are required to prepare a country-by-country (CbC) report with aggregate data on the global allocation of income, profit, taxes paid and economic activity among tax jurisdictions in which it operates. This CbC report is shared with tax administrations in these jurisdictions, for use in high level transfer pricing and BEPS risk assessments.'

> 'The lack of quality data on corporate taxation has been a major limitation to measuring the fiscal and economic effects of tax avoidance, making it difficult for authorities to carry out transfer pricing assessments on transactions between linked companies and even more difficult to carry out audits.'

Accordingly, the OECD has set out a CbC reporting implementation package, including model legislation and model Competency Authority Agreements.

Whilst the UK was an EU Member State, CbC reporting principles were applied in the UK through the UK's participation in EU DAC. This continued to be the case during the Brexit transition period – when the UK continued to be treated largely as if it were an EU Member State for many purposes (see **Chapter 2**).

Article 8aa of EU DAC says that EU Member States will exchange information relating to country-by-country reports ('CbC reports'). Further details about

CbC reporting are set out in Annex III of EU DAC. As explained in **Chapter 2**, these rules therefore applied to the UK while it was a member of the EU and also during the transitional period immediately following Brexit.

As well as reporting obligations, there are also 'notification' obligations. See HMRC's International Exchange of Information Manual IEIM300110 as regards directions relating to notification requirements.

The obligation to report generally falls on the ultimate parent entity ('UPE') of the MNE group. In certain circumstances it can fall instead on a UK entity ('UKE'), for example, where there is no UPE of the MNE group in the UK.

Where a UKE does not need to report, for example, because the UPE is to report instead, the UKE may nevertheless have notification obligations.

HMRC provide a series of examples illustrating where a UPE or UKE may or may not have reporting or notification obligations. See HMRC's International Exchange of Information Manual IEIM300120. This has come about in response to the OECD's work in relation to the wider BEPS project (see **1.2**). In particular, CbC reporting is in response to BEPS Action Point 13 (see **1.2**).

CbC reporting is one of the areas covered by the OECD's final report on Action 13: Transfer Pricing Documentation and Country-by-Country Reporting. See https://read.oecd-ilibrary.org/taxation/transfer-pricing-documentation-and-country-by-country-reporting-action-13-2015-final-report_9789264241480-en#page1.

HMRC say that their guidance in the International Exchange of Information Manual IEIM300000 onwards will help affected taxpayers to complete a CbC report, but where a taxpayer has an issue that is not addressed by this or the OECD's guidance, the taxpayer should contact their HMRC customer compliance manager ('CCM'). If the taxpayer has no CCM, email queries should be sent to msb.countrybycountryreportingmailbox@hmrc.gsi.gov.uk.

The OECD's and HMRC's schema guidance for reporting may be found at the International Exchange of Information Manual IEIM300080. In addition, there is guidance on the completion of CbC reports at the International Exchange of Information Manual IEIM300140.

A failure to comply with obligations under the CbC reporting rules could lead to the imposition of penalties. See HMRC's International Exchange of Information Manual IEIM300200.

A list of countries with which the UK will exchange CbC reports can be found at http://www.oecd.org/tax/beps/country-by-country-exchange-relationships.htm.

See the UK's enabling legislation in the Finance Act 2015, s 122 and regulations in the Taxes (Base Erosion and Profit Shifting) (Country-by-Country Reporting) Regulations 2016, SI 2016/237, as amended by SI 2017/497.

19.2 *Other forms of exchange under EU DAC*

See EU DAC. See also HMRC's International Exchange of Information Manual IEIM300000.

See OECD Action Overview, BEPS Action 13 Country-by-Country Reporting, at https://www.oecd.org/tax/beps/beps-actions/action13/#:~:text=The%20 BEPS%20Action%2013%20report,%2DCountry%20(CbC)%20Report.

Chapter 20

HMRC's legal framework for exchange

SIGNPOSTS

- In the early days of Automatic Exchange of Information ('AEOI') (specifically of FATCA), there was a concern that the exchange of taxpayer information between jurisdictions raised legal issues (see **20.1**).

- However, HMRC consider that they have a legal basis under the General Data Protection Regulation 2016/679/EU ('GDPR') for processing taxpayer information (see **20.3**).

- Furthermore, despite their legal obligation to protect taxpayer confidentiality, HMRC consider that there are 'legal gateways' that enable them to exchange information with other jurisdictions, by means of the various different kinds of exchange that are available to them (see **20.4** and **20.5**).

- Concerns are sometimes raised about whether reporting under the AEOI agreements has the potential to impact on the human rights of account holders in some circumstances. HMRC say that this is monitored and ask that any such concerns are raised with them. There is a procedure for redacting certain information in appropriate cases (see **20.6**).

- However, there is a possibility that HMRC could face legal challenges in relation to AEOI in the future (see **20.7**).

OVERVIEW

20.1

Focus

In the early days of FATCA, it was thought that AEOI 'raised a number of issues, including that FFIs established in [some] countries may not be able to comply with the reporting, withholding and account closure requirements because of [local] legal restrictions'.

See the Joint Statement from the United States, France, Germany, Italy, Spain and the United Kingdom regarding an intergovernmental approach to improving international tax compliance and implementing FATCA, published by HM Treasury on 8 February 2012.

See also **20.7** as regards more recent concerns about certain of the perceived 'issues'.

20.2

Focus

HMRC say that the legal basis for processing a taxpayer's personal data falls within Art 6(1)(c) and (e) of GDPR.

HMRC say it is necessary for them to do so, for example, in order to:

- comply with their legal obligations; and

- carry out their functions as the UK's tax authority.

See HMRC's Automatic Exchange of Information Privacy Notice, published 10 September 2019.

See GDPR.

DATA PROTECTION AND EU DAC

20.3   Article 25 of the EU Directive on Administrative Cooperation 2011/16/EU ('EU DAC') says that reporting financial institutions and the competent authorities of each Member State shall be considered to be data controllers for the purposes of the EU Data Protection Directive 95/46/EC.

Of course, the General Data Protection Regulation 2016/679/EU ('GDPR') has more recently superseded the EU Data Protection Directive. According to Eur-Lex, an entity that is run by the Publications Office of the European Union, it appears that Art 25 is subject to a 'subsequent related instrument', specifically 'Amendment proposed by 52020PC0314'. This is a proposal for a Council Directive to make various amendments to EU DAC. Under this proposal a reference to the GDPR is to be substituted in Art 25, instead of the reference to the EU Data Protection Directive 95/46/EC. See https://eur-lex.europa.eu/legal-content/EN/TXT/?uri=CELEX%3A52020PC0314.

Article 25 also says that each Member State shall ensure that each reporting financial institution under its jurisdiction informs each individual reportable person concerned that the information relating to him referred to in EU DAC will be collected and transferred.

Article 25 specifies that information processed in accordance with EU DAC shall be retained for no longer than necessary to achieve the purposes of the

DAC, and in any case in accordance with each data controller's domestic rules on statute of limitations.

As regards the phrase 'Member State', all references in EU law to Member States is treated as including the UK during the Brexit transition period (see **2.8** and **2.9**).

HMRC explicitly say that they have undertaken relevant data protection and privacy assessments and that they do not consider that individuals' privacy rights are disproportionately interfered with by AEOI. They say that their exchanges of information are also consistent with GDPR.

Accordingly, HMRC will not therefore redact any information that they exchange with another jurisdiction on a data protection basis alone. See HMRC's International Exchange of Information Manual IEIM406040.

See also **7.2** regarding the wider approach to AEOI due diligence as regards compliance with data protection legislation.

WHAT DO HMRC CONSIDER CAN BE EXCHANGED?

20.4   HMRC say that taxpayer specific information is confidential and cannot be disclosed except where there is a specific legal enactment allowing for it. See the Commissioners for Revenue and Customs Act 2005 ('CRCA'), s 18.

In their guidance, HMRC warn their officers that CRCA restricts their ability to disclose HMRC information to anyone. Sharing information with anyone in a way that is not covered by CRCA means an HMRC officer may personally be liable to a criminal sanction – see HMRC's Information Disclosure Guide IDG40100.

HMRC say that only by acting in accordance with the provisions of CRCA is an officer using HMRC information in a lawful way.

Disclosing information to persons outside HMRC is permitted in certain limited circumstances detailed. HMRC say that one of these is where their duty of confidentiality is specifically overridden by legislation that permits the disclosure of information to a particular third party. These are often known as 'legal' or 'information' 'gateways'.

Focus

CRCA, s 18(3) states that HMRC's duty of confidentiality is 'subject to any other enactment permitting disclosure'.

HMRC say they have three kinds of legal gateway through the restrictions in CRCA, s 18, enabling them to exchange information with another jurisdiction:

- a bilateral double taxation agreement;

- a bilateral tax information exchange agreement; and

- multilateral exchange agreements (eg the Common Reporting Standard ('CRS') and EU DAC).

The UK is party to two multilateral exchange agreements:

- the EU Directive on Administrative Cooperation 2011/16/EU ('EU DAC'), for exchanges with EU Member States; and

- the OECD/Council of Europe Convention on Mutual Administrative Assistance in Tax Matters.

See HMRC's Information Disclosure Guide Manual IDG40120 and IDG40320. See also HMRC's International Information Exchange Manual IEIM200010 and IEIM210010.

20.5   HMRC list three recognised methods of exchanging tax information:

- exchange on request;

- spontaneous exchange; and

- automatic exchange.

HMRC say that all double taxation agreements and other exchange instruments allow exchange on request.

The OECD has set a minimum standard for exchange on request: broadly, this requires that the tax authority must be able to provide the information from its own records, or, if necessary, obtain it using information powers.

Spontaneous exchange happens when an officer in one tax authority spots something that they believe to be foreseeably relevant to another tax authority, and gives it to their competent authority to send on. Most double tax treaties permit spontaneous exchange, but some older tax information exchange agreements do not.

Automatic exchange is where the competent authorities of two or more jurisdictions make agreement to systematically exchange large quantities of data on a given subject. Some existing examples include property data regarding one another's tax residents, financial accounts data, and employment income.

Most double tax treaties permit automatic exchange, but some older tax information exchange agreements do not.

See HMRC's International Exchange of Information Manual IEIM102000.

HUMAN RIGHTS AND AEOI

20.6

> **Focus**
>
> HMRC say: 'The information reported under the AEOI agreements has the potential to impact on the human rights of account holders in some circumstances.'
>
> However, HMRC also warn that reporting information about some individuals to some jurisdictions, could put those individuals at risk.
>
> HMRC therefore ask any individual or financial institution who is concerned about that kind of risk arising from information which is required to be reported under AEOI, to discuss the situation with them.

HMRC say that they:

'will continue to monitor the policies and practices of other jurisdictions with which it shares customer information, and will not share any data where its use may be contra to UK public policy.'

'Each jurisdiction on [the list of AEOI reportable jurisdictions] has been reviewed by the UK and a decision has been taken that they have the correct safeguards in place.'

See the list of AEOI jurisdictions in **Appendix II** in relation to this.

In most cases, jurisdictions which have committed to exchange information under AEOI, have also signed the OECD's and the Council of Europe's Convention on Mutual Administrative Assistance in Tax Matters ('the Convention'). See https://www.oecd.org/tax/exchange-of-tax-information/convention-on-mutual-administrative-assistance-in-tax-matters.htm.

Article 21 of the Convention sets out the limits in place to protect the persons whose information is exchanged. For example, this includes that Article stating explicitly that the Convention does not override a person's rights under UK law (where the UK is the 'requested State').

In cases where exchange is under EU DAC, that EU Directive contains similar limits on what may be exchanged. See Art 17 of EU DAC.

A financial institution is legally required to report to HMRC any information that is required under AEOI. However, where HMRC agrees that the exchange of such information may result in a threat to someone's human rights, HMRC will redact that information from the information that is exchanged.

Where HMRC agree to redact data in this way, they will redact all data relating to the particular person or persons concerned. They will not send partial information as this could lead to unintended identification of individuals.

Where HMRC do not agree that redaction is appropriate, the exchange of information will proceed without redaction. HMRC will explain why they considered that redaction was inappropriate. Either the financial institution or the individual can ask for the matter to be reconsidered at any time if there is a change of circumstances or if they consider that HMRC has not taken everything relevant into account. HMRC will not exchange data while the matter is under review or appeal.

Those who wish to apply for HMRC to redact data for that reason will need to use HMRC's application form, available at http://www.hmrc.gov.uk/gds/ieim/attachments/IEIM406120_application.pdf.

The application will need to include:

(1)   a statement of the grounds for redaction including which rights may be under threat if the information is transmitted to the recipient jurisdiction;

(2)   whether the application relates to specific individuals or to a class of individuals (for example, a class of individuals to whom a charity makes grants);

(3)   evidence of the threat, which might include:

- police reports, documentary evidence of threats, other evidence of threats involving the jurisdiction in question;

- testimony from individuals who have suffered human rights abuses in related and relevant circumstances.

Applications should be made by 30 April following the first year the financial Institution or individual becomes aware of the threat to allow HMRC time to review before the reporting deadline.

If a financial institution or individual becomes aware of a threat after this date, they should get in contact with HMRC as soon as possible to allow the case to be reviewed before any data is exchanged. Failure to meet the 30 April deadline, will not be treated as grounds for HMRC refusing the application to redact data.

HMRC advise those who are considering whether to raise a potential human rights concern to look at the Foreign and Commonwealth office guidance on human rights internationally, at https://www.gov.uk/government/policies/human-rights-internationally.

HMRC officers will use a checklist when assessing an application to redact on human rights grounds, available at http://www.hmrc.gov.uk/gds/ieim/attachments/IEIM406100_checklist.pdf.

HMRC ask that applications for redactions on human rights grounds and related queries should be sent to enquiries.aeoi@hmrc.gsi.gov.uk.

See HMRC's International Exchange of Information Manual IEIM406010 to IEIM406120.

A POSSIBLE LEGAL CHALLENGE FOR THE TAX AUTHORITIES?

20.7

> **Focus**
>
> The law firm Mischcon de Reya is reported to have taken on the UK case for a US expat individual who alleges HMRC is breaching her data protection and privacy rights by transferring, without her permission, her financial and personal information to the US government under AEOI, including FATCA.

On 24 June 2020, the firm published in relation to this issue more generally, a press release on its website stating that an appeal has been filed before the Austrian Federal Administrative Court in respect of a case concerning an Austrian individual who owns a bank account with a German bank holding €40.

The press release stated: 'Separately, we hope that we will be able to bring a judicial review before the English High Court in [another individual's] case concerning FATCA.'

See also, for example, Kalyeena Makortoff, 'HMRC faces legal fight for handing Britons' data to US tax officials', The Guardian, 12 September 2019.

Appendix I

List of countries with a FATCA agreement with the USA*

* As at 27 May 2020, see https://home.treasury.gov/about/offices/tax-policy/foreign-account-tax-compliance-act.

Jurisdiction	Status	Date jurisdiction is treated as having an intergovernmental agreement in effect
Algeria	In Force	30 June 2014
Angola	In Force	30 November 2014
Anguilla	In Force	30 June 2014
Antigua and Barbuda	In Force	30 June 2014
Armenia	In Force	30 June 2014
Australia	In Force	30 June 2014
Austria	In Force	30 June 2014
Azerbaijan	In Force	30 June 2014
Bahamas	In Force	30 June 2014
Bahrain	In Force	30 June 2014
Barbados	In Force	30 June 2014
Belarus	In Force	30 June 2014
Belgium	In Force	30 June 2014
Bermuda	In Force	30 June 2014
Brazil	In Force	30 June 2014
British Virgin Islands	In Force	30 June 2014
Bulgaria	In Force	30 June 2014
Cabo Verde	Agreement in substance	30 June 2014
Cambodia	In Force	30 November 2014
Canada	In Force	30 June 2014
Cayman Islands	In Force	30 June 2014

App I *List of countries with a FATCA agreement with the USA*

Chile	Signed	30 June 2014
China	Agreement in substance	30 June 2014
Colombia	In Force	30 June 2014
Costa Rica	Signed	30 June 2014
Croatia	In Force	30 June 2014
Curaçao	In Force	30 June 2014
Cyprus	In Force	30 June 2014
Denmark	In Force	30 June 2014
Dominica	In Force	30 June 2014
Dominican Republic	In Force	30 June 2014
Estonia	In Force	30 June 2014
Czech Republic	In Force	30 June 2014
Finland	In Force	30 June 2014
France	In Force	30 June 2014
Georgia	In Force	30 June 2014
Germany	In Force	30 June 2014
Gibraltar	In Force	30 June 2014
Greece	In Force	30 November 2014
Greenland	In Force	30 June 2014
Grenada	In Force	30 June 2014
Guernsey	In Force	30 June 2014
Guyana	In Force	30 June 2014
Haiti	Agreement in substance	30 June 2014
Holy See (Vatican City)	In Force	30 November 2014
Honduras	In Force	30 June 2014
Hong Kong	In Force	30 June 2014
Hungary	In Force	30 June 2014
Iceland	In Force	30 June 2014
India	In Force	30 June 2014
Indonesia	Agreement in substance	30 June 2014
Iraq	Agreement in substance	30 June 2014
Ireland	In Force	30 June 2014
Isle of Man	In Force	30 June 2014
Israel	In Force	30 June 2014
Italy	In Force	30 June 2014

Jamaica	In Force	30 June 2014
Japan	In Effect	30 June 2014
Jersey	In Force	30 June 2014
Kazakhstan	Signed	30 November 2014
Kosovo	In Force	30 June 2014
Kuwait	In Force	30 June 2014
Latvia	In Force	30 June 2014
Liechtenstein	In Force	30 June 2014
Lithuania	In Force	30 June 2014
Luxembourg	In Force	30 June 2014
Macao	Signed	30 November 2014
Malaysia	Agreement in substance	30 June 2014
Malta	In Force	30 June 2014
Mauritius	In Force	30 June 2014
Mexico	In Force	30 June 2014
Moldova	In Force	30 June 2014
Montenegro	In Force	30 June 2014
Montserrat	In Force	30 November 2014
Netherlands	In Force	30 June 2014
New Zealand	In Force	30 June 2014
Nicaragua	Agreement in substance	30 June 2014
Norway	In Force	30 June 2014
Panama	In Force	30 June 2014
Paraguay	Agreement in substance	30 June 2014
Peru	Agreement in substance	30 June 2014
Philippines	Signed	30 November 2014
Poland	In Force	30 June 2014
Portugal	In Force	30 June 2014
Qatar	In Force	30 June 2014
Romania	In Force	30 June 2014
San Marino	In Force	30 June 2014
Saudi Arabia	In Force	30 June 2014
Serbia	In Force	30 June 2014
Seychelles	Signed	30 June 2014
Singapore	In Force	30 June 2014

App I *List of countries with a FATCA agreement with the USA*

Slovenia	In Force	30 June 2014
South Africa	In Force	30 June 2014
South Korea	In Force	30 June 2014
Spain	In Force	30 June 2014
St Kitts and Nevis	In Force	30 June 2014
St Lucia	In Force	30 June 2014
St Vincent and the Grenadines	In Force	30 June 2014
Sweden	In Force	30 June 2014
Switzerland	In Force	30 June 2014
Taiwan[1]	Signed	30 June 2014
Thailand	Signed	30 June 2014
Trinidad and Tobago	In Force	30 November 2014
Tunisia	In Force	30 November 2014
Turkey	Signed	30 June 2014
Turkmenistan	In Force	30 June 2014
Turks and Caicos Islands	In Force	30 June 2014
Ukraine	In Force	30 June 2014
United Arab Emirates	In Force	30 June 2014
United Kingdom	In Force	30 June 2014
Uzbekistan	In Force	30 June 2014
Vietnam	In Force	7 July 2016

[1] Consistent with the Taiwan Relations Act, the parties to the agreement are the American Institute in Taiwan and the Taipei Economic and Cultural Representative Office in the United States.

Appendix II

OECD Common Reporting Standard ('CRS') participant countries[*]

* As at 27 May 2020, see https://www.oecd.org/tax/automatic-exchange/crs-implementation-and-assistance/crs-by-jurisdiction/#d.en.345489.

Jurisdiction	Committed to first exchange in	Participant in the Convention on Mutual Administrative Assistance in Tax Matters[1,2]
Anguilla	2017	Yes
Argentina	2017	Yes
Belgium	2017	Yes
Bermuda	2017	Yes
British Virgin Islands	2017	Yes
Bulgaria	2017	Yes
Cayman Islands	2017	Yes
Colombia	2017	Yes
Croatia	2017	Yes
Cyprus	2017	Yes
Czech Republic	2017	Yes
Denmark	2017	Yes
Estonia	2017	Yes
Faroe Islands	2017	Yes
Finland	2017	Yes
France	2017	Yes
Germany	2017	Yes
Gibraltar	2017	Yes
Greece	2017	Yes
Guernsey	2017	Yes
Hungary	2017	Yes

Iceland	2017	Yes
India	2017	Yes
Ireland	2017	Yes
Isle of Man	2017	Yes
Italy	2017	Yes
Jersey	2017	Yes
Korea	2017	Yes
Latvia	2017	Yes
Liechtenstein	2017	Yes
Lithuania	2017	Yes
Luxembourg	2017	Yes
Malta	2017	Yes
Mexico	2017	Yes
Montserrat	2017	Yes
Netherlands	2017	Yes
Norway	2017	Yes
Poland	2017	Yes
Portugal	2017	Yes
Romania	2017	Yes
San Marino	2017	Yes
Seychelles	2017	Yes
Slovak Republic	2017	Yes
Slovenia	2017	Yes
South Africa	2017	Yes
Spain	2017	Yes
Sweden	2017	Yes
Turks and Caicos Islands	2017	Yes
United Kingdom	2017	Yes
Andorra	2018	Yes
Antigua y Barbuda	2018	Yes
Aruba	2018	Yes
Australia	2018	Yes
Austria	2018	Yes
Azerbaijan	2018	Yes

Bahamas	2018	Yes
Bahrain	2018	Yes
Barbados	2018	Yes
Belize	2018	Yes
Brazil	2018	Yes
Brunei Darussalam	2018	Yes
Canada	2018	Yes
Chile	2018	Yes
China	2018	Yes
Cook Islands	2018	Yes
Costa Rica	2018	Yes
Curacao	2018	Yes
Dominica	2018	Yes
Grenada	2018	Yes
Hong Kong (China)	2018	Yes
Indonesia	2018	Yes
Israel	2018	Yes
Japan	2018	Yes
Lebanon	2018	Yes
Marshall Islands	2018	Yes
Macao (China)	2018	Yes
Malaysia	2018	Yes
Mauritius	2018	Yes
Monaco	2018	Yes
Nauru	2018	Yes
New Zealand	2018	Yes
Niue	2018	Yes
Pakistan	2018	Yes
Panama	2018	Yes
Qatar	2018	Yes
Russian Federation	2018	Yes
Saint Kitts and Nevis	2018	Yes
Samoa	2018	Yes
Saint Lucia	2018	Yes
Saint Vincent and the Grenadines	2018	Yes

Saudi Arabia	2018	Yes
Singapore	2018	Yes
Sint Maarten	2018	Yes
Switzerland	2018	Yes
Trinidad and Tobago	2018	
Turkey	2018	Yes
United Arab Emirates	2018	Yes
Uruguay	2018	Yes
Vanuatu	2018	Yes
Ghana	2019	Yes
Kuwait	2019	Yes
Albania	2020	Yes
Ecuador	2020	Yes
Kazakhstan	2020	Yes
Maldives	2020	
Nigeria	2020	Yes
Oman	2020	Yes
Peru	2020	Yes

[1]   In addition, Armenia, Burkina Faso, Cameroon, Cape Verde, Dominican Republic, El Salvador, Guatemala, Jamaica, Kenya, Liberia, Mauritania, Moldova, Morocco, Mongolia, Montenegro, North Macedonia, Paraguay, Philippines, Senegal, Serbia, Thailand, Togo, Tunisia, Uganda, Ukraine, USA are participants in the Convention, but are not in the OECD's list of countries that have committed to an exchange under CRS.

As regards Greenland, it is not listed by the OECD as having committed to an exchange under CRS, but the OECD's website refers to its participation in the Convention as 'Extension by the Kingdom of Denmark'.

[2]   For a list as at 9 December 2020 of participants in the Convention on Mutual Administrative Assistance in Tax Matters, see http://www.oecd.org/tax/exchange-of-tax-information/Status_of_convention.pdf.

Flowchart 1 – Is this a financial institution?

App III *Flowchart 1 – Is this a financial institution?*

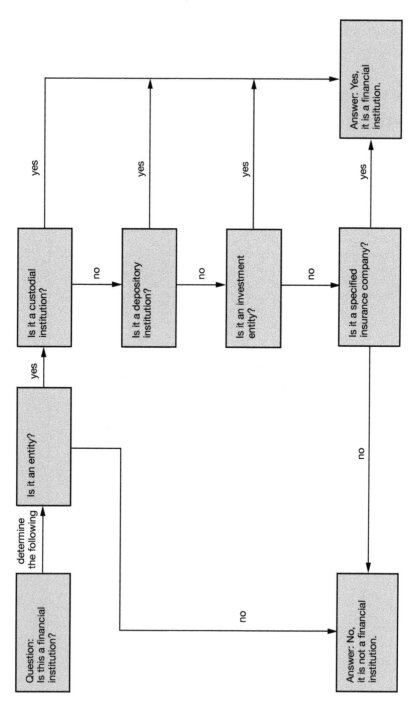

Flowchart 2 – Is this a UK reporting financial institution?

App IV *Flowchart 2 – Is this a UK reporting financial institution?*

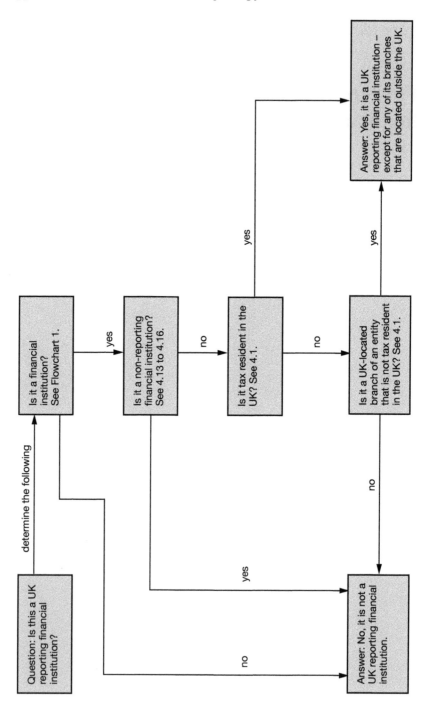

Flowchart 3 – What FATCA and CRS due diligence must a reporting financial institution carry out?

App V *Flowchart 3 – What FATCA/CRS due diligence must an RFI carry out?*

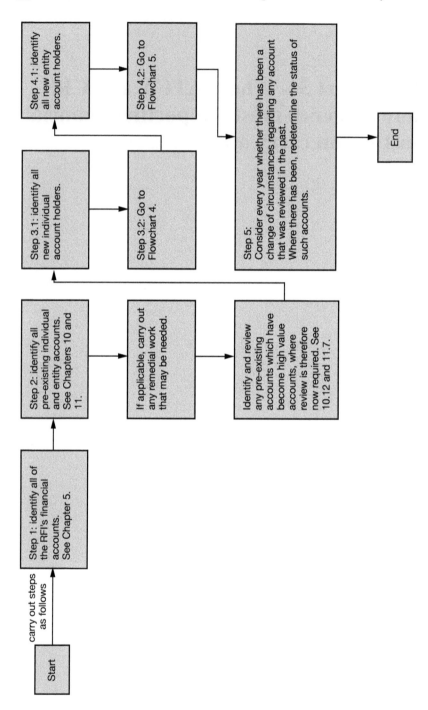

Flowchart 4 – FATCA and CRS due diligence in relation to new individual accounts

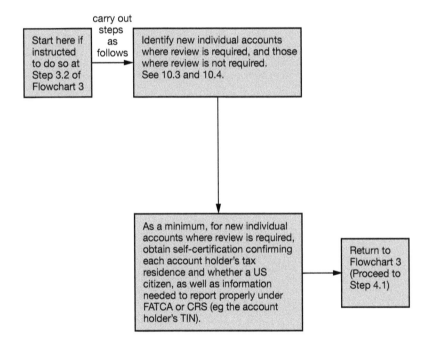

Flowchart 5 – FATCA and CRS due diligence for a reporting financial institution in relation to new entity accounts

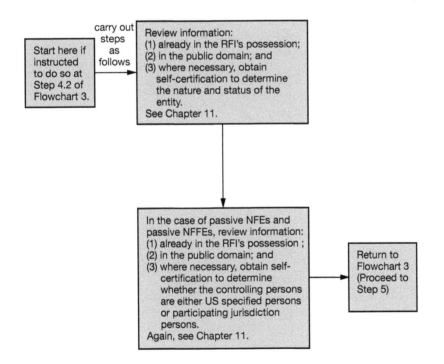

Start here if instructed to do so at Step 4.2 of Flowchart 3.

carry out steps as follows

Review information:
(1) already in the RFI's possession;
(2) in the public domain; and
(3) where necessary, obtain self-certification to determine the nature and status of the entity.
See Chapter 11.

In the case of passive NFEs and passive NFFEs, review information:
(1) already in the RFI's possession ;
(2) in the public domain; and
(3) where necessary, obtain self-certification to determine whether the controlling persons are either US specified persons or participating jurisdiction persons.
Again, see Chapter 11.

Return to Flowchart 3 (Proceed to Step 5)

Flowchart 6 – Must a UK reporting financial institution treat this as a CRS or FATCA reportable account?

App VIII *Flowchart 6 – Is this a reportable account?*

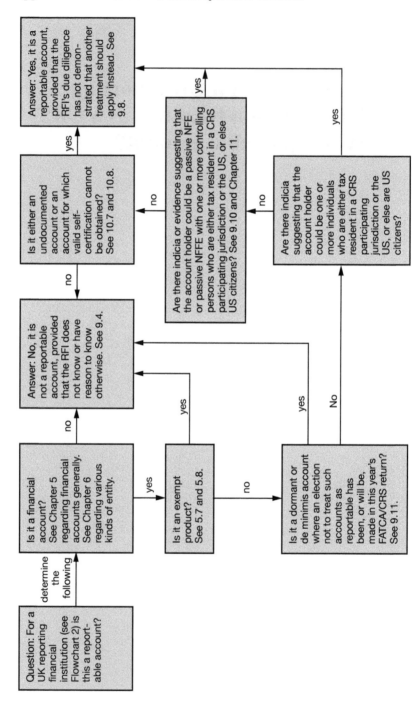

Flowchart 7 – Must a DAC 6 return be made?

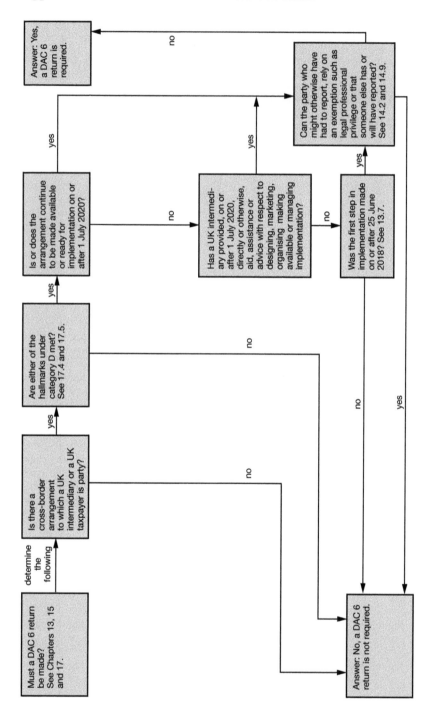

Index